All Signs
Point to Paris

All Signs
Point
to Paris

*A Memoir of Love, Loss,
and Destiny*

Natasha Sizlo

HarperCollins*Publishers*

HarperCollins*Publishers*
1 London Bridge Street
London SE1 9GF

www.harpercollins.co.uk

HarperCollins*Publishers*
1st Floor, Watermarque Building, Ringsend Road
Dublin 4, Ireland

First published in the US by Mariner Books, an imprint of HarperCollins*Publishers* 2022
This US edition published by HarperCollins*Publishers* 2022

1 3 5 7 9 10 8 6 4 2

A catalogue record of this book is
available from the British Library

ISBN 978-0-00-850842-5

Designed by Emily Snyder

Printed and bound in the UK using 100% renewable
electricity at CPI Group (UK) Ltd

For my sister, Tara
For my mother, Edna
And for my father, the Great Bob Sizlo

The wind beneath my wings

Contents

Author's Note

This book is the true story of my quest for love. As such, a person's truth is subjective and I recognize that some people's memories of the events described in this book may be different from my own. To protect privacy, certain names, locations, and identifying characteristics have been changed. Dialogue and events have been re-created from memory and, in some cases, have been compressed to convey the essence of what was said or what occurred. Due to the confidential nature of the real estate industry, the houses, sellers, and buyers mentioned in this book are a composite of the many transactions I have been privy to throughout my career in Los Angeles real estate. This book is not intended as a substitute for the medical advice of physicians, real estate advice, or the guidance of an astrologer. The voices in my head are all real.

Each chapter opens with a short passage about one of the twelve houses of the zodiac. These passages are meant to spark both curiosity and introspection. The renowned astrologer Stephanie Jourdan, PhD, advised me in writing them, but any errors are mine.

Prologue

Tuesday, October 22, 2019
12:37 a.m.
Paris

What the hell was that?" Tara said as we rounded the corner. She stopped cold on the sidewalk and turned to me, eyes wide.

We stood in the soft glow of a streetlight. My pulse pounded. *Was that real? Did I just meet . . .* "I don't know," I replied, catching my breath. "He just appeared. Out of nowhere. Like in a dream. He said he's a writer. Working on something about love and destiny. And he's only in Paris for tonight. I don't understand what just happened. It all felt so familiar."

"Oh my God, could he be The One? Holy shit, Tasha, you have to go back. Right now. Before he *dis*appears."

"But is that weird? I mean, he's probably gone inside the hotel by now. How would I find him? He could be in the bar or on his way to his room. What am I going to do, knock on every door? I don't even know his name."

"Yes. That is exactly what you should do. After what we've been through in Paris, not to mention this past year, you running through the streets after the hottest guy in all of Europe is literally the most *not* weird thing. He said it himself—you just had a brush with destiny. Does a crystal ball have to fall from the sky and hit you on the head? It's meant to be. This guy might be your soulmate."

This wasn't how I'd pictured it. I was supposed to be dressed in my midnight-blue velvet gown, with strappy heels, a smoky eye, and the sexiest lingerie in my suitcase. My hair was supposed to be a cascade of effortless waves, damn it. I glanced down at my chipped nails, at my jeans and boots, then back to the Hôtel Costes, its grand outline just barely visible in the dark.

Tara sighed. "Isn't this what you came here for?"

She was right. I was supposed to be running toward instant sparks and undeniable magic, not walking coolly away. Taking a deep breath, I forced myself to focus on where I was and why: A cobblestone sidewalk on rue Saint-Honoré in the first arrondissement, the windows of Saint Laurent, Balenciaga, and Louis Vuitton dim around us. The heart of Paris. *Love.* The Eiffel Tower glittered in the distance, a spire made of stars bright against the vast black sky.

Stars. I'd followed them halfway across the globe, all the way to Paris, in search of love. No joke. "I'm not dreaming, am I?"

"It's late, but you're not dreaming. I was there too. There's something about him. He's different from the others."

Shit. Was I really going to do this? Break the one promise I had made in Paris, forget about my crack-of-dawn wake-up call, and run back to a hotel that we weren't even staying at in search of a possibly destined-for-me man I'd only just sort of met? I couldn't believe it, but my sensible, look-before-you-leap big sister was ordering me to do exactly that.

Maybe it was a sign?

If only the stars could truly tell me what to do.

First House

Enchanté

The starting point of an astrological chart, the First House, is also the starting point of a person's life. The chart, a circle, is divided into twelve portions called houses. Each house represents a field of potential power and growth, such as relationships, health, money, or purpose. When you were born, each of the planets, along with the sun and the moon, were in one of the twelve houses. Sometimes more than one planet occupies a house, and sometimes a house is empty. A birth chart (also called a natal chart) reflects where the planets and luminaries were positioned on the date, minute, and location of a person's birth. The chart changes roughly every four minutes, which is why having your time and place of birth is important.

The First House is about how you define yourself. Appearances. Beginnings. It invites us to ask, *Do I like this? Does this feel good? What do I want? How do I get what I want?* The First House also reflects your first seven years and how those formative years created both your personality and alter ego that later becomes your other side, your partner in life. The alter ego consists of aspects that are discarded from the whole of a person's identity, but they are not lost. The aspects reside as the alter ego in the Seventh House and are a gold mine of hidden wisdom, talents, and desires.

> Pisces, ruled by the planet Neptune, is in my First House. Pisces is about letting go and surrendering to the unknown.

I HAD GIVEN UP.

I was forty-three years old, soon to turn forty-four, a single working mother renting a tiny yellow bungalow and barely scraping by in the Pacific Palisades, a quiet but expensive neighborhood in the west side of Los Angeles. After my divorce, I put almost my entire budget toward renting this house so I could be around the corner from my older sister, Tara. She helped with the childcare I could no longer afford. Money—when and how I'd make enough to keep my little family of three afloat—was a constant source of worry, one I had to hide from the glittering industry in which I now worked: selling high-end residential real estate to celebrities and other VIPs for a company called the Agency. (Yes, the luxury brokerage founded by Mauricio Umansky and Billy Rose, as seen on *The Real Housewives of Beverly Hills* and *Million Dollar Listing Los Angeles*.) Appearances mattered.

Which is why, after my first big sale, I used most of the commission to buy a few "essential items" for my new career: one fancy purse, one trendy pair of overpriced sneakers, a leased Audi, and a weekly car wash. I had no choice back then. I needed many more sales than just the one, and fast. My son, Dashiell, was only eight and my daughter, Margot, just eleven when I started selling real estate out of necessity. They depended on me. Blending in as best I could with the sleek agents at my office was critical. As my friend Katie reminded me, "Who in their right mind would list a ten-million-dollar home with an agent driving a mom-mobile and carrying a bag from Forever Twenty-One?" Katie knew all about the paycheck-to-paycheck hustle herself and she had a point. But even a few years and several houses sold later, my workday ruse still exhausted me. It's not easy to pretend to be someone you aren't, even just part-time and for a good reason.

Then there was the problem of my smashed-to-shit heart. Some days I thought heartbreak might, well, break me. That's how much I missed a man named Philippe. And how scared I was about what my near future held. But Philippe first. He was always easier to talk about. Endlessly. To anyone who would still listen. Philippe and I had recently broken up. Again. We'd tried and tried to turn our passionate-but-batshit-crazy love affair into a practical relationship. We were both divorced, both *parents*. With responsibilities. We knew what this was supposed to look like. And yet.

I thought of him every single day.

But the worst heartbreak of all, far more horrible than my divorce or financial woes or even Philippe, was my beloved father's prognosis. Two years earlier, he'd been diagnosed with a terminal disease, one that steadily ravaged his lungs. His doctors now said he had three months at most to live. My father was the one person in my life who never failed to listen to even my smallest problems and who somehow still believed his daughter could do anything. I didn't allow myself to think about saying goodbye or about how devastating it was that Dash and Margot, now twelve and fifteen, would lose him too. I couldn't. I'd sooner stick my hand into an open flame and hold it there. Instead, I obsessed over how I had failed myself yet again. How I'd wasted years with Mr. Not-So-Right-After-All. How my second chance at the happy ending I'd always dreamed of—the one with my father proudly watching while I walked myself down the aisle and into the arms of my loving partner, who would cherish me and my kids forever—was definitely not happening. I didn't find The One while my dad still had time. I thought he had all the time in the world and always would. Now I needed to let my dream go and make other plans for my little family's future. But I didn't know where to begin. My heart had gone numb.

So when my totally out-there but true-blue best friend Nicole gifted me a reading with a sought-after astrologer for my birthday that October, I thought, *Why the fuck not?* Whatever else had been guiding me thus far clearly wasn't working. As if I needed any more cosmic proof that I'd better do *something* differently, earlier that week while I was walking an outrageously luxe property in preparation for its open house that afternoon, the seller asked me to scoop her toddler's poop from their infinity pool. She'd noticed the little brown log drifting by as we discussed the merits of pricing a home based on "Zestimates" versus looking at actual comps. Would I mind just taking care of that? Except it wasn't a question. Was it because I'd worn sneakers (cute, I swear!) with my dress instead of the vertigo-inducing, don't-mess-with-me five-inch heels some of my colleagues favored? Did I look like someone who would smile and say "Absolutely!" no matter what the universe threw at her—even toddler poop? In case you're wondering, I did scoop the poop out of the pool. And the next afternoon, I dropped off a potty-training gift basket complete with a copy of the book *Everyone Poops,* by Taro Gomi. Because sometimes we all need a reminder that shit happens. It's okay. But also? Whatever signal I was sending out, it needed to stop, and if the stars could somehow help, then sign me up. Never mind that I wasn't the cosmic-proof-finding, signal-sending type. And I definitely did not believe in astrology.

Raised by parents who revered the trinity of education, logic, and hard work, I'd been conditioned to think about astrology much as I did about Impossible Meat and Burning Man: fine for my New Agey LA friends, but *so* not for me. My understanding of astrologers was limited to the headscarf-wearing, crystal-ball-gazing, blinking-neon-light variety on Hollywood Boulevard. And you didn't want to get me started on readings of any kind. Why would anyone want to waste good money on a flattery-and-lies sandwich with a side of total BS? Simply put, I had *never* been the kind of person who saw an astrologer.

But now, without Philippe and, unimaginably, soon to be without my father, I no longer knew for sure what kind of person I was. Or who I would become.

I met Philippe on the heels of my disastrous divorce. I imagine most divorces are disastrous, but mine was the kind where your husband moves out, you lose your house, your dog dies, your business falls apart, your money disappears, you're forced to file for bankruptcy, and you find yourself, shell-shocked, unpacking boxes in a shoebox apartment, all within a matter of months—this while trying to raise two young kids in Los Angeles. Life got real hard, real fast. My door was wide open for the devil to walk in.

Enter Philippe. He was handsome, French, tan, and, most of all, *fun*. He came bounding into my house of cards full of a kind of reckless *joie de vivre* that I'd forgotten all about as a busy wife and mother. A welcome distraction from my newly up-in-flames world, gorgeous Philippe chain-smoked cigarettes, guzzled endless bottles of rosé, and rudely yelled things like *"Merde!"* and *"Putain!"* from his white Porsche convertible as he sped down Abbot Kinney Boulevard to his bachelor pad in Venice. He flirted with the boho-chic neighbors, squeezed the baguettes at Gjusta's artisanal bakery with a self-assured grin, and knew his way around the kitchen almost as well as he did around the bedroom. Philippe was loud and offensive, sexy and intoxicating. Everything about the man felt wrong. Except for his heart. Which is perhaps why I fell so hard for him.

In the beginning, my relationship with Philippe was a divorcée's dream. Happy to abandon reality and embrace as much freedom as I could when my ex had the kids, I picked up smoking, drank more bottles of wine than I ever thought possible, and discovered the true definition of *the best sex of my life*. To my surprise, our fever-pitch affair grew into a full-blown love story. We might have been on American soil, but Philippe was all French, and it was just what I needed. We went to wine tastings, rode bikes, and had picnics in the park. We enjoyed salad niçoise and rosé for lunch, cocktails on the roof at sunset, steak frites with a few bottles of Bordeaux or côtes du Rhône for dinner, and frozen vodka and caviar as a midnight snack. I felt like a different person. The old me knew nothing about fancy French wine or how seriously some people take their omelets.

Philippe and I danced in the kitchen until dawn, chain-smoking Marlboro Lights and losing ourselves in the music of Al Green, Van Morrison, and Nina Simone, especially her rendition of Jacques Brel's "Ne Me Quitte Pas." We held hands in the street, dunked croissants into our Blue Bottle lattes as the sun rose over the Venice canals. I rubbed lotion on his back at the beach, and he read French poetry to me in bed. We had mad, passionate sex at every hour of the day in every room of his beach loft. I even invited him to my high-school reunion so I could impress my old classmates with my perfect French boyfriend. We had undeniable chemistry. Before I knew it, we were a thing. One night turned into one month, one month turned into one year, and one year turned into half a decade.

But Philippe and I weren't only about our whirlwind lovescapade. We synced schedules with our exes so his three teenagers, Josephine, Theo, and Charlie, and my two kids could all spend time together. Philippe taught Dash about the Monaco Grand Prix and helped Margot with math homework. Charlie and Margot became confidantes, as close as sisters. Dash and Theo, despite the difference in their ages, bonded over video games and golf. Philippe would take all five kids to the grocery store and tell them to choose the craziest-looking food they could find—lychee fruit, Spam, horned melon, and bone marrow—and then bring it all home for a *Chopped*-style mystery-basket challenge. Philippe somehow made a delicious meal out of nonsense every time. We had a ball. A beautiful, messy ball. I liked to think of it as a practice run. *Wouldn't it be great if this was our always?*

I thought I'd found the love of my life. Philippe never failed to walk me to my car, to open a door. He made sure I had quiet time to study for my real estate exams. He often put a sweater over my shoulders moments before I felt cold. But most important, he lifted me up when I did not have the strength to rise after my marriage and business collapsed. He encouraged me not only to stand up for myself and my future but to stand tall. He refused to call me "Tash" or "Tasha" like almost everyone else did. "Natasha," he would whisper in my ear with his romantic French accent, urging me to step into the strong name my parents had bestowed on me in homage to my dad's Slavic roots, a name that had intimidated me my whole life. "Own your name," he would tell me. "You are Natasha. You've lost a lot, but you can never lose that." Philippe saw my insecurities and my well-intentioned mistakes but opened his arms without judgment. He was recently divorced himself, and we spent hours discussing loss, heartache, and pain. Well, mostly I talked and Philippe curated our post-divorce playlist and danced around the kitchen, cigarette in one hand, glass of wine in the other. *"Chérie,"* he would say, tipping my chin up and kissing me on the lips, "what we have is perfect. I don't ever want things to change."

And it kind of was perfect. Until it wasn't.

Though I loved Philippe madly, I was silently drowning in a sea of increasing disappointment and frustration, knowing that I craved a tame, more conventional future that Philippe didn't seem interested in providing.

"I just don't see it yet," Philippe would tell me when I asked him about blending our families and moving in together. "What's the rush, anyway? We've both done the marriage thing, and how did *that* work out?"

Perhaps he was right. Was I craving something just because society told me it was the ultimate goal of a relationship?

But with a life to rebuild and my children to raise, I couldn't help questioning the *perfection* of it all. When we both had our kids, I had to pack up my family of three and lug mountains of stuff to Philippe's just-big-enough loft (my tiny apartment was a nonstarter) and then back again. The shuffle drained us all. When Philippe and I were alone, the long nights of cigarettes, booze, and wild sex began to wear on me. The casual smoking turned into an awful addiction that I had to hide from my family and friends. The fun nights of drinking meant I was too hungover too much of the time to keep up with my demanding new career in real estate (not to mention the demands of motherhood). The best sex of my life resulted in a recurring UTI that I chased with antibiotics and then an unexpected pregnancy that neither of us was remotely prepared for. That news shattered me and, later, us, in a way. And my high-school reunion? We got caught having sex in the bathroom while waiting for AAA to tow his car, which had somehow managed to dangle itself precariously off a cliff. We were out of control.

I found myself at a crossroads, deeply in love with *un beau gosse*—that's French for "the hottest guy I ever knew"—but daydreaming about a happy home and a stable future where I wasn't constantly smelling like an ashtray, fighting a hangover, and living part-time out of a suitcase on the floor. As wonderful as our affair was when it began, given Philippe's carefree, *joie de vivre* lifestyle, it simply wasn't sustainable. After one too many disagreements about where our relationship was heading, I packed my bag and said goodbye. It was one of the hardest things I'd ever done.

I hoped that Philippe would come after me, but he didn't. Not in any meaningful way, that is.

I thought it would be easy to move on, but I was wrong. Months passed, and still my heart belonged to Philippe. I scoured the city for the next love of my life, getting Botox for the first time and jumping into the LA dating scene. I hung out with my girlfriends at all the singles' watering holes—with the Hollywood types at Chateau, the wannabes at Bungalow, the writers at Alfred, the foodies at the farmers' market, the manscaped hotties at Hot 8 Yoga, and all the clean-eating hipsters prowling the Whole Foods in Venice on Friday night. I downloaded Tinder, Hinge, and the League. I deleted more than a few unsolicited dick pics and gave each promising match the old college try. I looked past my general height requirement and made out with Short Belgian Billionaire while waiting for my Uber outside Catch LA. I had a fling with a sexy surfer whom my friends and I called Awesome Sauce but ended it after I grew tired of hearing about "gnarly waves" and "bitchin' barrels"—not to mention his cringeworthy nickname for me, "the N-Meister." I watched in horror as a man I called the Russian Surgeon flexed his knife skills by dissecting an innocent bee right before my eyes in the middle of our picnic at the Hollywood Bowl. I hooked up with Hot Millennial at SHOREbar and then Hotter Millennial during a sexy live concert at the Peppermint Club. I even dated a man who made his own kimchi. Fair warning to all: too much kimchi gives a person horrible gas.

I tried. I really tried.

But no matter how hard I attempted to find my next true love, my heart always went back to Philippe. I was stuck. I asked my friends for help, but no one could tell me how to get over him. My sister, Tara, had given up. No hairstylist could solve this. Even my favorite bartender at Tasting Kitchen—the cute one who looked like Ryan Gosling—eventually seemed annoyed at my inability to move on.

"Just so you know, I don't believe in astrology," I told the astrologer when she phoned a few days after my birthday.

"I understand," she said in a calm, all-knowing voice. "You don't have to."

The astrologer, Stephanie Jourdan, was well known in certain circles and had amassed a cultish but discreet following of top celebrities and politicians all over the world. She'd been in the field for thirty-plus years, and her full-time practice was more exclusive than the terrace at Little Beach House (Soho House's members-only club on Billionaires Beach in Malibu). She accepted new clients by referral only and the waiting list ran six months to a year. Stephanie began the reading by explaining how she works. "I'm sorry to make you learn astrology in, like, two minutes," she said, laughing, "but I want to make sure you understand what I'm talking about."

I'd already e-mailed Stephanie my birth date, birth time, and birthplace weeks before. She described how she'd used these elements to calculate my natal chart, or the map of my reading. "Your natal chart is a representation of where the sun, moon, and planets were in relationship to the Earth specific to your city of birth at the exact time that you were born," she said. "I believe in reincarnation and read astrological charts from that perspective. Some charts appear to be barely influenced by past lifetimes, while others are saturated with past-life issues, relationships, losses, and achievements. Your reading is rooted in your birth chart, which depicts the life you planned for yourself prior to your physical incarnation."

Wait, wait . . . what?

"Humans are delightfully creative and often exercise free will by choosing a different course than the one they chose prior to birth. The astrological chart reflects what is possible according to your original chart. Looking at your chart, I see that you're pretty psychic and you have a lot of dead people hanging around you, always. You're in constant communication with spirits, to the point where you may not even be aware that this is unusual. You may just think these are the voices in your head or thoughts that you have, but they're not. There are a lot of people in your living room," she said with a laugh, "they just don't have bodies."

OMG, this woman is legit crazy, I thought, looking nervously around my living room.

"Okay. So, you likely know your sun sign, the most famous zodiac sign, even if you don't believe in astrology," Stephanie continued. "You are a Libra. But the placement of the moon and each of the other planets at the time and location of your birth adds additional shades to the picture of you. Like a clock, the zodiac is divided into twelve segments, or houses, each one ruled by a different sign. The zodiac begins at nine o'clock with the First House and goes counterclockwise around. Do you follow?"

"Yes. I think so," I said, wondering how on earth I'd committed to wasting an hour of my life with some trendy LA astrologer talking about past lives and sun signs.

"Now, let's take a look at your chart," she continued. "When you were born, the Earth, sun, and Pluto were all lined up. This is called a Pluto alien, or a Pluto power alien, in astrology. Pluto rules things like birth, death, sex, and taxes. It rules transformation and mysteries, people who see things that others don't see. It rules shamanism, and it rules power. On your chart, it's in the Eighth House. People who are born with it here mostly die at birth," she said matter-of-factly. "Or at seven and a half, fifteen, twenty-one, or thirty. It's not an easy beginning. But it's a fantastic life once you make it to forty-four. That's when it starts to activate. That's when you get strong and start to reap the benefits of that power. You just turned forty-four, right?"

"Two days ago," I replied, dumbfounded, flashing back to four of the most pivotal moments in my life: almost drowning in a pool at age seven, being expelled from boarding school at fifteen, battling panic attacks and an awful drug addiction at twenty-one, and having an unexpected fight with severe postpartum depression at thirty. Floaty-scarved wingnut astrology lady or not, Stephanie Jourdan suddenly had my full attention.

"Okay, great!" she exclaimed. "So you are in your superpower time now. Fun! Essentially, this is saying that the hard part of your life is over and now your job is not to care what anybody thinks anymore. We call a person with this kind of chart an alien, because you're not like anyone else. You're a Libra, so it's difficult for you to stop comparing yourself to other people, but it's time to stop. You are going to be different from most people. That's just the way it is."

As Stephanie went on to explain the other characteristics of my chart, I found myself hanging on her every word. "You were born when Pluto and Venus were at six degrees," she said. "Venus rules attachment and Pluto rules detachment. This gives you an interesting dynamic of being intensely passionate and all in, then immediately saying, 'This is it, I'm done,' if something doesn't feel right. Does that make sense to you? Do you identify with this?"

"I do," I said. It was the story of all my relationships. I had even earned myself the nickname "Cut-and-Run" from a girlfriend who was shocked to see how quickly I took flight at the first sign of trouble, never sticking around to deal with my emotions in a healthy way. This was a big source of tension in my relationship with my compulsively responsible sister, Tara, who was terrified I would disappear as our father's illness quickly progressed.

As Stephanie continued with her reading, I became mesmerized by her almost scientific explanation of the position of the planets and how they seemed to directly describe my life story. Stephanie knew details about my life that simply defied explanation.

Some of these details were simple: "You dress too young for your age" (*Hello? I'm single and dating in LA!*). Some were more serious: "Your father doesn't have a lot of time. This illness has been long and difficult, but as soon as he passes to the other side, he will feel immediate relief and will remain by your side. He's actually a very helpful, funny spirit!"

Stephanie also spoke about my former career as a journalist— something I gave up long ago—and saw me returning to writing within the year. "You have Mercury, the planet of the writer, in the Ninth House of your chart, the house of publishing," she said. "Real estate will always be there; you're good at it. But it is not the thing to bring your soul satisfaction. You need to start thinking of yourself as a writer again. Your point of destiny is to tell a story."

"Point of destiny? What's that?" I asked.

"The point of destiny is the highest expression of your being where you receive the most support from your own higher self and the universe. It is not something easily attained in the way we usually think of destiny as a given; it's more like a precious journey that, if undertaken, provides the most sublime results," Stephanie replied.

Honestly, I couldn't remember the last time I'd even thought about the word *destiny*. It seemed so old-fashioned, like something that had been canceled long ago. But maybe it wasn't?

"Now, at age forty-four, you will start to understand the definition of a life partner," Stephanie continued. "How you are meant to go into a relationship as whole and complete, not really *needing* a partner, but open to sharing your life. To having fun. Now you need to just be out there, making an entrance. You've got a weird chart, and it's great. This is a big, wonderful year for you. There's an adventure on the horizon!"

For sixty minutes I listened in silence as Stephanie gave me great insight into my childhood, my family, my career, my life path. Not all of it made sense—"It sounds dramatic, but people with charts like yours are rare. You're a triple alien, for God's sake!"—but the majority of it resonated beyond coincidence. I was blown away.

"Is there anything specific you would like to know before we end the session?" she asked.

"Yes," I said sheepishly. "There's a man in my life, someone I just can't get over. Could you maybe look at that?"

"Sure," Stephanie said. "Do you happen to know his birth date and birthplace?"

"Yes, um, let me think . . ." I racked my brain. I've never been one to remember dates. I traumatized my kids when they were little by repeatedly showing up for parties on the wrong day. Once, very memorably, I was mistaken for a stalker outside Kiss guitarist Paul Stanley's Mulholland estate two weeks before his son's actual birthday.

"November fourth, 1968," I spat out, worried we were running out of time. "Paris, France."

"What's his first name?"

"Philippe."

"Philippe, great. I'm going to assume you don't know his time of birth, so I'll just put in twelve noon." Stephanie went quiet for a few moments, and I could hear her typing away and mumbling a bit to herself. I held my breath, waiting.

"I don't know that this person wants to grow with you," she said reluctantly, giving me details of how our birth charts and planets were not in alignment. Then, finally: "This isn't your guy."

It's hard to describe the tidal wave of emotion that washed over me at that moment. It wasn't relief so much as a mixture of love, sadness, grief, and an immediate sense of letting go. Philippe was not my destiny. Our love story was not written in the stars. It was time to move on.

And that's exactly what I tried to do. My four best girlfriends—Nicole, Katie, KC, and Heather—plus my sister, Tara, surprised me with a belated birthday celebration, showering me with presents for my superpower year ahead: rose quartz crystals for attracting love, flying wish papers for manifesting The One, pineapple vagina spray to prep my hoo-ha for brighter days ahead (if you do nothing else today, Google *pineapple for your vagina*), poppy-red Chanel lipstick, and a black lace bralette with a matching thong. I said a final, silent goodbye to Philippe, made a wish to find true love, and blew out the candle on my birthday cake.

With my father's condition deteriorating, I knew the next few months would be some of the hardest of my life. And yet, my newfound release from obsessive thinking about what might have been with my ex gave me a sense of hope that I had not felt in years. I bragged about my all-knowing astrologer all around town and walked with a fresh skip in my step.

That is, until Facebook sent me a birthday notification one morning.

Philippe has a birthday today blinked on my phone on my bedside table. I sat for a moment in quiet contemplation, the golden autumn sun filling my room. For the first time in years, seeing Philippe's name did not come with the shock-to-the-system adrenaline rush that I had grown so accustomed to. I tapped on his profile, saw a photo of him drinking margaritas with a cute brunette, and felt nothing. It was official. I was over him.

I turned on the TV and put the kettle on the stove. *This is amazing,* I thought. *I'm finally free.* I grabbed my French press and poured in some ground coffee. Savannah Guthrie smiled brightly from my television. "Live from Studio One A in Rockefeller Plaza, this is *Today.*"

That's when I saw FRIDAY, NOVEMBER 2, staring back at me in brightly televised orange.

Philippe's birthday. It was November 2, not November 4.

November. Fucking. Second.

I rushed to my computer and opened a new e-mail, the kettle screaming in the background.

Hi, Stephanie,

I just learned—after our reading—that the man I was asking you about (my ex-boyfriend, Philippe) was born on Nov. 2 in Paris (not Nov. 4 in Paris). Does this change what you would have told me about him? I hope I didn't make a big mistake!

—Natasha

Stephanie's assistant (*Astrologers have assistants?* I thought) e-mailed me back immediately.

Hi, Natasha,

I'm afraid Stephanie is booked solid for the next six months, but if you have a specific question, I can call you with the answer in about three weeks. She charges seven dollars a minute.

—Sheri

Seven dollars a minute? That's more than my divorce attorney! I thought, recognizing the absurdity of it all. And yet:

Amazing, thank you, Sheri. Five minutes would be great.

I was stuck in rush-hour traffic on the 405 freeway when I got the call from Stephanie's assistant three weeks later. Malibu had just been evacuated due to the Woolsey fire, and I was on my way to meet a girlfriend for drinks at Shutters, a hotel on the beach in Santa Monica. After all, I thought, what better place to find true love than at a five-star hotel filled with hot, displaced Malibu dads?

"Hi, Natasha, it's Stephanie Jourdan's assistant, Sheri. Do you have five minutes to chat?"

"Sure," I said, looking at the endless sea of cars in front of me. I could taste the smoke in the air.

"Okay, great. Starting the clock now," she began. She took a deep breath and rustled some papers. "November second, 1968, Paris . . . ready for this? He's perfect for you!" she exclaimed, her voice bubbling with the pleasure of delivering good celestial news.

"I'm sorry, wh—"

"The time could make a difference," Sheri continued, "but Mars is in the Seventh House, which is your *husband*. Venus is sixty degrees from the sun—that's a long-term relationship or marriage. And, most important, he's aligned with your point of destiny! This is so exciting! *He's perfect for you!*"

As Sheri went over the details, I stared ahead at the gridlock, unable to speak.

Shutters was surprisingly devoid of any hot Malibu dads, as was Casa del Mar next door. But that didn't stop me from finding a spot at the bar and ordering the stiffest drink I could stomach.

"Casamigos Blanco, plenty of lime," I told the bartender as I texted Nicole.

Stephanie said Philippe is PERFECT for me. She said he's The One!!!

I threw back the tequila and sucked on a lime. I added: He can't be The One!!!

Nicole texted me back immediately: An astrologer once told me, "Only a fool follows the stars, a wise man heeds them."

Me: WTF does that even mean?!

Nicole: Meaning these readings are guidelines—not absolutes—and meant to be kept on the back burner. Only when you are at your center do you find your true north.

Me: Well, according to YOUR ASTROLOGER, my true north is currently fucking the cute brunette from Facebook.

It was a long night. Four tequila shots, three glasses of chardonnay, and one very blurry Uber ride later, I found myself alone in my little yellow house with my heart aching once again for a man I couldn't have.

I woke up the next morning to a splitting headache and a missed call from my sister.

"Hey, sis. Dad took a turn last night, and it's not good," Tara said on my voice mail. "He's asked for a family meeting today to discuss his end-of-life options. He's looking into something he calls assisted suicide. And he's obsessing over finding the perfect song to listen to when he pulls the plug. Yeah . . . I . . . need help. Call me when you wake up."

I stepped into the shower and let the warm water run over my face, trying my best to push past my hangover and process my sister's words.

End of life.

Assisted suicide.

Up until that moment, I had done a pretty good job of remaining stoic in the face of my dad's battle with pulmonary fibrosis, a disease that slowly hardens the lung tissue and makes it progressively difficult to breathe until one day, you simply can't. Even after being shown dozens of grim X-rays, consulting with countless doctors, untangling an endless spiderweb of oxygen tubes, and interviewing nearly every hospice nurse in Santa Barbara County,

I was in relative denial that my dad was dying. People like my father didn't get sick, and people like my father most certainly didn't die.

A Detroit native and a graduate of MIT (the first person in his family to go to college), my dad was a man of values and drive, science and logic. He possessed an indefatigable intellect and could solve almost any problem. From teaching me long division and parallel parking to helping me put the pieces of my life back together after my divorce, my father was always lovingly present. He was my true north; he'd selflessly guided me from the day I was born. I still needed my dad. It would have been great if I'd woken up at forty with everything figured out, no fucks given, but that didn't happen to me. Or anyone else I knew.

I wanted to believe that pulmonary fibrosis was just one more of the many seemingly intractable dilemmas my father had overcome in his lifetime. I wanted nothing less than the impossible: my father by my side forever.

But there would be no forever. This was it.

End of life.

Assisted suicide.

I sank to the shower floor, gasping for breath, unable to escape the reality of my crumbling world. I curled into a ball and hugged my knees to my chest as water pelted my skin and tears ran down my cheeks. This time, I cried for the loss of not just my father, my rock, but for Philippe, who was apparently my one shot at true love but who was also uninterested in building an adult future. My destiny, as it turned out, was for me to live life alone. I cried and I cried and I cried. The water turned cold, and I felt like someone had carved out my insides. I cried till I had nothing left. And then I lay there in silence, cheek pressed to the tile, watching water slip down the drain.

I finally pulled myself up, stepped out of the shower, and took a hard look in the mirror. I no longer recognized the woman looking back at me. My eyes were swollen and red, devoid of light and life; my face was gaunt and exhausted. I was gone.

Then, just past my reflection, something caught my attention: a photo of me as a child, tucked behind an endless supply of anti-aging creams and tonics. I picked the photo up and studied it. Age six. Floral dress. Blond pigtails. Bright blue eyes. Tiny Natasha, full of hope. Six was an age when I believed in love, magic, and the infinite possibilities of the universe. An age when my heart was open, and my imagination soared.

I turned the photo over. In my dad's handwriting, faded but still legible:

> Anything can happen, child, anything can be
> —Shel Silverstein

That's when it hit me. I texted Nicole.

I just had the most brilliant epiphany! I need to find as many men as possible born in Paris on Nov. 2, 1968. Philippe's not the only one, is he?

Nicole immediately wrote back. Ha-ha-ha-ha Ha-ha-ha-ha! Perfect! Let's take out an ad.

Me: OMG that's BRILLIANT!!!! YES!!!

Nicole: And then you can write about it, like Stephanie said.

Me: Yeah, sure. I'll call it MY PATHETIC LIFE.

Nicole: No. THE AMAZING AND INCREDIBLE TALE OF HOW NATASHA FOUND HER SOULMATE.

Me: I like the soulmate part

Nicole: We'll have to go to Paris, of course.

Me: YES!!!

Nicole: I love you, Tash.

Second House

Paris Is Always a Good Idea

The Second House represents what's important to you, what you value. It's passive in nature. The First House starts something and the Second House receives the compensation. It's a little bit like a tree that knows that it is enough to just grow and be its most wonderful self. This house fully expects that all the resources it requires will present themselves when needed.

I have the sign of Aries occupying my Second House. Aries is about knowing what you want, going after it, and claiming your reward for a job well done. It is a very different energy from allowing yourself to receive what you deserve just for being you.

Aries also rules men, and the Second House rules receiving love. Somehow, my soul had to put these two together in a way that made sense to a tree.

WHEN I ARRIVED AT MY PARENTS' HOME IN SUMMERLAND, A small seaside town ninety miles north of Los Angeles, Tara's car was already in the driveway. I'd left Dash and Margot with their dad that afternoon. The family decisions that needed to happen were too grown-up, too upsetting. Only a couple of weeks earlier

Dash had been here, snuggled next to his grandpa Bob, both of them totally absorbed in a black-and-white World War II movie. I smiled at the memory. In more recent days, we FaceTimed when Bob was too weak for visits, propping a phone up on our kitchen counter while Dash made his famous steak and Margot told stories about school. Bob loved these "family dinners" and always requested his favorite—chicken wings—for next time. Never mind that he was well past being able to eat chicken wings. Or much of anything else.

I grabbed the mini–white orchid I'd picked up at one of the farms on the way, took a deep breath, and went inside. My sister sat at the foot of our father's rented hospital bed with a yellow legal pad in her hands.

"Hey, Tasha. Glad you're here!" Tara said. "I'm helping Dad with an end-of-life pros-and-cons list to explore 'Dignity in Dying.' By the way, Dad, I looked it up this morning and that's what this option is properly called." She shot me a look and raised one eyebrow in her best *Welcome to crazy!* secret sign we had perfected over the years. "You know how Dad loves to make lists."

It's true. The inside of my parents' ocean-view house was cloaked in a layer of neon sticky notes and never-ending to-do lists. There was one, appropriately directed toward my forgetful mother, on my father's lifesaving oxygen tank that read DO NOT TURN OFF and ✓ KEEP BOB ALIVE! in bold Sharpie.

My eighty-two-year-old father smiled at me from his bed and wiggled his toes under the blanket with delight.

"I made the same kind of list for Colin when he couldn't decide what kind of piñata to get for his eighth birthday," Tara said confidently. "This will help."

Well, it looks like the train has left the station, so I'd better get on board, I thought to myself, stepping across the trail of tubes and leaning over my father's bedrail to give him a kiss on the head. "Hi, Dad. How are you feeling?"

My dad gave me a thumbs-up. "Cool," he managed over the

loud drone of the tank. The problem was, my dad looked anything but cool. His body was brittle and thin, his once-rosy cheeks a pale shade of gray. His nose was red and chapped from constant exposure to the high-flow oxygen from the plastic tubes of a nasal cannula. His hair was long, and he needed a shave. His large gold MIT class ring and shiny wedding band slipped loosely around his skeletal fingers. "But I would much rather have a piñata." He smiled.

Humor was big in our family. Lost on a mountain? Emergency trip to the ER? That's when the Sizlo family shone. We were the life of the party in moments of despair. Most people would panic while rushing to the fire department on Christmas morning with their child's finger stuck in the serrated jaws of an angel-shaped tree topper. Our family? *Check out the fire pole! Let's take a ride!* Bob was our leader, teaching us from day one that when things don't go as planned, it's *how* you handle the situation that matters most. He was the master of making lemons out of lemonade and turning disaster into adventure. Monty Python's "Always Look on the Bright Side of Life" was the theme song of our accident-prone, laughter-filled childhood.

"Dad is very worried about the end," my sister explained as I settled in. A hospital-issue whiteboard hung on the wall with an exhaustive list of my dad's daily medications. ATIVAN, MORPHINE, HALDOL, TIKOSYN, SENNA, MIRTAZAPINE were printed neatly in cherry-red dry-erase ink, followed by *Remember to fill water in oxygen compressor* in blue and *Success is not final; failure is not fatal: it is the courage to continue that counts—Winston Churchill* in green.

"He isn't crazy about the idea of suffocating, as his lungs will be giving out fairly soon," Tara continued. "He wants to die on his own terms and has qualified for an end-of-life medication. Mom picked it up this morning." Tara's eyes started to well with tears, her humor fading as she pointed to a prescription bag from the pharmacy on the table. "His doctor told him last night that he only has a few weeks left, and we're trying to decide if the medication truly is the right way to go and, if not, what the other options are. Sound right, Dad?"

"And I want to listen to 'The Wind Beneath My Wings' when I drink it with everyone here by my side," Dad added. "Preferably on a Tuesday."

"Oh, balls. Bette Midler's going in the minus column," my sister said, scratching on her notepad. "How about 'My Way'? Or 'Midnight Train to Georgia'?" Tara raised her eyebrow again. "We're still working on Dad's death playlist."

I never knew it could be like this. I thought death was a flat line in the hospital while the family was downstairs grabbing a club sandwich (my dad's favorite) in the cafeteria. Or perhaps something that happened suddenly—a car swerving out of control, an unexpected heart attack, a headfirst dive into the shallow end. I had no idea that death could be so slow and painful and confusing and drawn out; that there were decisions to make, doctors to consult, nurses to hire, family to call, mortuaries to interview, and cemeteries to tour. That letting go of life was as complicated a process as coming into life. And I most certainly didn't know I would ever be called into a family meeting to discuss if it was better for my father, my one true rock, to throw back a big cup of life-ending medicine or slowly suffocate to death. And why Tuesday, exactly?

"It's okay, Dad," my sister said. "You've got your girls here now. We're going to help you and we will support whatever decision you make."

"Where's Mom?" I wondered out loud.

My mom, or Edna, as we often called her, alternated between shock and denial at the thought of losing her husband of fifty-six years. For the past few months, she'd gone inexplicably missing from all our important family meetings. I'm washing my car, she'd texted Tara when the doctor presented us with a bright pink Do Not Resuscitate form in the hospital three months ago. "I'm getting my teeth whitened," she called to say when I stopped by the

Carpinteria-Summerland Fire Department to ask the chief if his team could help carry Dad up the stairs into their home. "I'm walking the neighbor's dog," she announced before sprinting out the front door the morning my sister and I sat down to interview a bevy of strange caregivers whom we'd found using Google after one of the hospice nurses wisely recommended hiring additional help for when we needed to rest. Caring for someone as sick as Bob was a 24/7 job. But I couldn't fault Mom for skipping out on the interviews. After the Crier (a professional caretaker who literally could not stop bawling after seeing my father's end-of-life state) and the Diva (a self-described "overly qualified candy striper" who refused to grant us a full interview due to her celebrity status), I hadn't wanted to be there either.

"Who does the Diva think she is, Cher?" I'd asked, slamming the door before collapsing in exhaustion. "Let's just hire Celeste. She may not know how to use a microwave or be able to give Dad his meds, but she asked me to take her Match profile photo before the interview ended, and, I don't know, I can relate to someone who's looking for love and knows good lighting." We'd seen Celeste first and liked her sweet personality, but we were worried that she had never taken care of so much as a houseplant. But compared to the Diva, the Crier, and other such outstanding candidates? Especially when we'd need more than one caretaker? Done.

My mother, Edna, is a tough-as-nails Scotswoman who was born in 1936 in the slums of Edinburgh. She remembers cowering at midnight in the neighborhood's bomb shelter during air raids, the fear of capture and then torture by the Nazis constantly on her mind. Growing up with two brothers in a one-bedroom tenement with no hot water and no heat meant life was rough. Her mother? Crippled by polio. And her father? An asthmatic determined to serve his country. When my mom was three, the Royal Air Force finally accepted her father as a ground gunner. She wouldn't see him again until World War II ended. By then, she was ten. My mother grew up malnourished, surviving on sparse government rations, with only one dress and a pair of shoes to her name.

As a girl, Edna looked up to the Hollywood movie stars on the screen at the neighborhood cinema and the heroic American soldiers strutting outside the castle down Princess Street, passing out clothing and candy while protecting the locals from the threat of invasion. "Got any gum, chum?" children would call out, and the soldiers would give them their first taste of chewing gum and hope for a better future. By twelve, Edna decided that the path out of poverty was to move to America and marry an American. School ended at age fourteen for working-class children like my mother. Edna pulled double shifts delivering newspapers, worked as a waitress and then as a secretary, and somehow managed to scrape together enough money to buy a one-way ticket to the United States at the age of twenty-one. She arrived with only forty dollars in her pocket.

My parents met in Los Angeles in a building on Wilshire Boulevard. Edna lived upstairs; Bob lived downstairs. Neither of them had much to begin with. My dad had just graduated from MIT and moved to LA to start a new life under sunny skies and palm trees. Though my father barely understood my mother's thick Scottish accent, it was love at first sight. An engineer by day and a law student by night, my dad wooed my mom by expressing his love in mathematical terms, telling her, "I love you to the nth degree, the highest power," and drawing sideways figure eights— the symbol for infinity—on cocktail napkins. Educated and kind, my father was my mother's Prince Charming and better than any Hollywood star or man in uniform. He introduced her to a life she'd never dreamed possible; he spent any money he had (and, thanks to credit cards, sometimes money he didn't) on delighting his Edna. They painted Los Angeles red, with Bob surprising Edna with dresses from Bullock's and fancy rum drinks in tiki mugs at the Luau in Beverly Hills. He spontaneously proposed when her parents were visiting from Scotland and married her just days later so her father could walk her down the aisle the way she'd always dreamed he would. Dad vowed to provide a good life for Mom, one where she would always feel safe and never be afraid or hungry again. He was committed to her beyond words; he dedicated his whole life to her happiness and, consequently, ours.

"Mom's at an open house for work,"Tara said, cracking her gum and nervously clicking her pen. (Did I mention that my mother worked in real estate? That's how I got my own foot in the door after a series of false starts elsewhere.) "Now, back to the list. The pluses and minuses of taking the medicine versus dying naturally."

My sister tried to sound strong, like a camp counselor, but beneath her sugar-sweet words, I could hear raw grief and utter exhaustion. "Plus: I spoke with the pharmacist today and he said he mixed the end-of-life drink with a lemon flavor to cut the bitter taste you were worried about," she said. "So that's a good thing! But minus: Unfortunately, now that I see it, this is a big bottle of medicine. You have to drink the *whole thing,* Dad. *In just two minutes.* I'm worried that, as weak as you are and as hard as it is for you to swallow, you might not be able to do that. And I'm not sure what happens if you only swallow half of the final-curtain cocktail."

Oh my God. Are we seriously doing this? I thought, envisioning my father struggling for life to the *Beaches* soundtrack.

"Plus: You could do it on Tuesday!"

Tara is my big sister by three years. An A+ happily married mom of two boys, she's the kind of person who never misses a parent-teacher conference, who volunteers for every fundraiser, and who sends her kids to school with labeled pencils and Pinterest-worthy lunch boxes even though the boys are well into their teenage years. To the outside world, we are complete opposites. She's short; I'm tall. She's curvy; I'm straight. She's blond; I'm a dark brunette. She plans and schedules down to the last detail; I leave it all to the last minute. She follows the rules; I go out of my way to break them. We drive each other bananas. I'm frustrated by her structured parenting ways and overly cautious approach to life; she's annoyed by my impulsive decision-making and inability to think potentially dangerous situations through before diving in headfirst. For as long as I can remember, I've pushed boundaries. Like the time I climbed out of my bedroom window in the middle of the night when I was barely sixteen and tried to steal my parents' car to join friends at Don Q's, the local pool hall, only to be ambushed by my rule-following big sister who dramatically sprawled herself across the hood in protest. We laugh about it now. "On your way to Don Q's?" she asks whenever she thinks I'm getting a little too close to the edge. It's her way of watching out for me, gently positioning herself between me and the big bad world. It's also her way of being in control, a dynamic I've struggled with my whole life.

"Dad, if you decide *not* to take the end-of-life medication, we will stay here, right by your side, to the end," Tara said. "The doctors are ready to increase your regular dose of morphine so you're comfortable. That should help with your breathing and any anxiety. The hospice nurses have instructed me on how to administer the meds when they're not here. So I'll be giving you the prescribed dose myself when you need it. You won't be alone," she said, her voice unsure of the words tumbling out.

"We promise to take care of you," I chimed in, sensing my cue, "and we'll make sure you're not in any pain or discomfort when you, uh . . ."

No one prepared me for how hard it would be to say the word *die*. Over the past year, my family had sidestepped all mention of it, replacing it with euphemisms like *kick the bucket, cash in your chips, meet the Big Kahuna in the sky,* and, my father's favorite, *expire.* But there were no buckets to kick. No chips to cash in. And people didn't expire. Milk expired. Coupons expired. People *died.* There was no way around it. My dad was *dying.*

A tear ran down my father's cheek.

"Are you okay, Dad?" Tara asked. "Are you in pain? Should we call the nurse?"

Despite suffering from a difficult and frightening disease that caused a tremendous amount of discomfort, my father had never complained. In the months leading up to this day—as my dad slowly lost the ability to drive, walk, stand, eat, drink, speak, and, ultimately, breathe—he'd never once said, *Why me?* He never once told the family, *I'm in pain.* Never once uttered the words *I'm scared.* Dad just smiled at us with bright blue eyes and told my sister, my mother, and me that everything was "cool."

"I don't want to leave your mom," he finally responded, embarrassed and struggling to find his voice. "I promised I would love her to infinity. I promised I would take care of her forever. But I can't."

It was heartbreaking to watch my once invincible father—now bedridden, tubes everywhere, with the loud hum of his oxygen tank playing in the background—weep inconsolably. I had never seen my father cry before.

"It's okay, Dad," Tara lied. "It's going to be okay."

After telling my father what an incredible man he had been, a spectacular father and husband, promising him that she and I would take care of my mother no matter what, and crying with him, my sister turned to me, exhausted.

"I can't do this anymore," Tara said when Martin—the hot twenty-something hospice caretaker who had been patiently waiting outside the bedroom during our meeting—came in to check my dad's vitals. "You have to lighten the mood. Change the subject. My heart is breaking. Do or say something—anything!"

"Okay," I said, trying to process both the severity of the situation and the weight of her request. After all, my big sister had just, in effect, offered to be responsible for monitoring his pain as he slowly suffocated, slipped into a coma, and died. "Let me think."

So I told my father about my reading with the astrologer. "I have a plan, Dad. And I think you'll like it."

My father and sister listened intently as I told the story of Nicole's wacky birthday gift. About me being grouchy and skeptical at first but a full-on believer after just a few minutes. About giving the astrologer the wrong birthday, then talking to her assistant— "Can you believe it, Dad? Astrologers have assistants!"—then discovering my thoroughly unsuitable ex-boyfriend's birth chart was perfectly in sync with my point of destiny. "What are the chances of that?" About me breaking down and then ultimately coming up with the possibly brilliant idea of meeting every man I could find who was born in Paris on November 2, 1968—"Because, come on, Dad, he's not the only one, is he?"

I wasn't sure how my dad would respond. He wasn't a spiritual man, and he most certainly didn't believe in astrology. He'd refused to meet with the hospice chaplain and had made us promise there would be no mention of religion at his funeral because his religion was "facts and logic." He didn't even want a funeral. But Bob had also been, for him, unusually interested in a crystal that a girlfriend had given me for my birthday. So much so that he'd asked me to buy some for his bedside table. Surprised, I'd called Nicole for advice. I didn't know a thing about crystals. "That's easy—amethyst, carnelian, and kunzite. Those will be helpful during your dad's sacred passage," she'd said.

"I believe in energy," Bob often told Tara and me as he held the glimmering crystals in his hands. He'd start talking about how the old radios used crystals to transmit sound waves, a type of energy, and *boom!*—MIT Bob was back. I'd thought on those occasions that my dad simply couldn't resist one last science lecture, but now, as I spoke to him about fate and stars, I wondered if he'd been leading us toward something different, something far less quantifiable. But as soon as I had that thought, I dismissed it. This was *Bob.* Mr. Facts and Logic. I suddenly worried that news of me chasing down an imaginary person based on some woo-woo prophecy might send him into cardiac arrest. I shuddered at the thought of him leaving this earth thinking his baby girl had completely lost her mind. The last thing I wanted to do was upset my father on his deathbed.

My sister and I stared at him for a good fifteen minutes while he thought my story through with his scientist brain. Then he said haltingly, "Sounds like you're going to Paris. Just make sure you check ID! You want the right guy."

Wait a minute. My dad thought that my harebrained idea was *cool*.

"Go get 'em!" he managed. "I'll meet you there."

Dad's response was unexpected, light, and happy. His whole body relaxed, and the twinkle returned to his bright blue eyes. This was the Bob I knew and loved so much. It was as though we had just solved a math problem that had stumped experts for the past fifty years. Before I knew it, his tears were replaced with stories about the outrageous things he had done for love too. "I once drove nonstop from Detroit to Los Angeles just to take your mother to dinner," he said. "Two days with no sleep, and I almost got thrown in jail for pushing a hundred miles per hour, but let me tell you, it was worth it. Promise me you will always believe in magic and never give up on love."

What? Bob Sizlo believed in magic? Was this the morphine talking?

"Promise me," he said again, very clearly.

"Okay, Dad. I promise I will always believe in magic and never give up on love."

"Yes! To magic and love! Enough with the sadness. Fuck you, life, telling us how to live!" my sister said. She laughed, gave the sky the bird, and went to get a bottle of tequila from the kitchen.

"Grab me a Modelo," my dad said, shocking us both by asking for his favorite Mexican beer.

"Will you meet me in Paris, Dad?" I asked. "Would your ghost fly all the way to France to help me find my soulmate?"

My father raised his thumb in the air. I could see he was growing tired.

"This is amazing! We're going to Paris!" I exclaimed. I reached through the tubes and rubbed my father's feet. He was wearing a pair of yellow, hospice-issued no-slip socks; the soles were un-touched, a sucker-punch reminder that he would never stand again. "I love you, Dad."

My dad nodded back, too tired to say the words.

"Tara, you should come too," I said. "This is going to be fun!" I could see my sister, in her typical way, already making a pros-and-cons list in her head. "Come on! Dad's going to be there. Who doesn't want to take a trip to the City of Love with Bob?"

"Uh, okay, I'll go," she said grudgingly, passing me a shot of tequila and pouring my father a short glass of beer. "But your ghost better not scare me, Dad. You know how jumpy I am."

My dad went silent, closing his eyes and struggling to breathe. Tara and I watched him intently, not knowing if he had fallen asleep or if he was just too weak to carry on. We sat there for a few minutes, wondering if we should call Martin.

When Dad's eyes eventually fluttered open again, he seemed poised to speak, but no words came out. His doctor had warned us about him inevitably losing his voice. We both leaned in, straining to hear over the loud hum of the oxygen. I shot Tara a look. *Have we taken this too far? Is talking frankly about Dad's ghost while throwing back shots of tequila on his deathbed too much? Is this the way most people say goodbye? Is that what's happening? Are we, in fact, saying goodbye?*

Then, suddenly, my dad broke the silence.

"Boo!" he howled as loud as he could in his friendliest ghost voice. *"Booooooo!"*

My sister jumped like I'd never seen her jump in my life, and I laughed so loud that Martin came rushing in. It was the funniest thing I had ever seen. My father giggled with delight. My sister let out a roaring laugh. Before I knew it, we were all snorting and howling, tears once again flowing, but this time from joy. Even Martin was laughing. Nothing could stop us. We laughed and we laughed until there was nothing left.

Tara eventually finished her pros-and-cons list, and it was de-cided that Bob would die naturally with his three girls by his side.

My father bravely faced his destiny on his own terms, the perfect balance of fate and free will. We completed his deathbed playlist, granting Dad his Bette Midler but sprinkling in a healthy dose of Motown and Sinatra, and rounded out the day with a bedside dance-off to the Nappy Roots song "Good Day." Even Martin joined in. Who could possibly stand still as the kids in the chorus sang the bubbly, upbeat refrain?

It was a good day. One of the best.

"I'll see you in Paris," my father said, a smile fixed on his face, before he drifted off to sleep that night.

He died two weeks later. It was a Tuesday. At least, I think it was. I've never been very good with dates.

Third House

Dancing with the Frenchman

Thinking, talking, writing, and walking—welcome to the Third House. This house also includes the people you learn with and move with throughout life, such as siblings, neighbors, classmates, and fellow travelers.

The sign you have in your Third House determines how you express yourself. And the planet that rules that sign shows how you go about fulfilling your expression.

I have the grounded earth sign of Taurus in the Third House. Sounds nice, right? "Gracefully and elegantly" is how I express myself, according to a quick glance at my chart. But look closely. Taurus is ruled by Venus, which is in the Eighth House on my chart, and that placement affects what happens in my Third House. The Eighth House is intense. Sometimes it attracts characters from the underworld. Stephanie would say that's not always a bad thing; it just is.

REMEMBERED FOREVER CREMATION CARE, THE SIGN IN THE window read. COMPLETE DIRECT CREMATION $1,450. The mortuary, a small storefront, sat between a gym and a holistic therapy center in a strip mall. I was there to get Bob. And pick out an urn.

But there were so many urns. Polished walnut urns and utilitarian metal urns, chinoiserie urns and marble urns. An urn made entirely of salt so that it would melt seamlessly into the sea. There were Christian urns and Jewish urns, military urns and sports urns. One, shaped like a golf ball but the size of a basketball, read FAIRWAY TO HEAVEN across its dimpled white surface. Display cases held heart-shaped pendants, angel-wing brooches, and samples of the blown-glass art that could be custom-made using the ashes of your loved one. A small sign decorated with images of Christmas ornaments and greenery suggested that memorial jewelry would make a thoughtful gift, a tasteful nod to the holiday season. The space was both prosaically retail, with its acrylic shelves and laminated price tags (I could imagine those shelves filled with dog treats and leashes or orthopedic shoes), and extremely weird. *Did* people truly want to turn their beloved aunt Deedee into a diamond?

Despite the atomic-level weirdness, it felt kind of good to be shopping. Aside from the twenty black dresses I'd had shipped to my house to try on in preparation for the funeral (all but one would be sent back when it was over, of course), this was the first shopping I'd done in months. Back when I could afford it, shopping was my therapy, because nothing bad happened in stores. On the contrary, stores were happy places full of possibility. No matter that this particular store sold containers to house the remains of dead people. I wasn't going to think about that. I could just as well be in Elyse Walker sampling perfumes or at Zara hoping my credit card would work.

I told myself to keep moving. The mortuary was but one of many post-death practicalities that needed to be dealt with. The rented hospital bed had been removed, along with the whiteboard, now wiped clean of Winston Churchill's wisdom and the demented poetry slam of Dad's med list. We'd returned the oxygen tank, and the end-of-life medication had been properly disposed of. The only thing left in my dad's room was the bright pink sticky note that had been attached to his end-of-life medication: *For Bob only. Do not take!! YOU WILL DIE!!* Next up, the urn. Which just required shopping. *I got this,* I thought.

"How can I help you?" The mortician appeared from behind a curtain, snapping me back to reality.

My mind immediately ran wild with thoughts of what might be behind the curtain of a crematorium. Were there, like, bodies back there? Piles and piles of bodies? An oven? Mountains of ash? *Focus, Natasha.* As I met the undertaker's warm blue eyes (so like my dad's), I felt my cheeks color and tears gather. *Breathe. It's just shopping.*

"Hi, um, yes. I'm Natasha Sizlo. I'm here to get my dad. Bob. Robert Sizlo. He's . . ." I paused, tapping my finger nervously on a biodegradable urn sold with a living tree. *Wait, you can bury ashes and plant a tree at the same time? That's kind of cool.*

"Ready, Natasha," the undertaker said gently. "Your father is ready. You just need to select an urn. Take your time. My name is Ken and I'll be right here."

"Right." I swallowed hard. And realized I wasn't sure how to do this kind of shopping. How had going to the mortuary become *my* job? How come I wasn't home ordering death certificates over the internet, like my sister? Or getting my teeth cleaned, like my mother? My head hurt; my heart hurt. Ken busied himself behind the counter and I walked anxiously around the shop.

We could scatter Dad with wildflower seeds and he could transform into a field of poppies like The Wizard of Oz! I texted Tara as I picked up a wildflower-seeds scattering tube. Wildflowers are so much better than an urn in a cemetery.

Dad doesn't want to be a flower, Tara texted back. Stick to the plan. He picked his grave site years ago. It's all paid for. He loved that damn cemetery. Remember when he took Mom there to see the tombstone he designed as a surprise on Valentine's Day?! Nothing says "I love you" like an eternal plot with ocean views. Ha-ha.

OMG, Dad was so weird. How did we survive our childhood?

I don't know. Did we?

But he may have made a different choice if he knew he could become a sunflower . . .

No.

Can he please be a tree?

He didn't want to be a tree.

If he was a tree, I could hug him again. I just hate putting him in a box. It's so . . .

Tasha. You're the best sister. Thank you for doing this. Pick out an urn. Now.

"This one," I finally said to Ken, pointing to the simplest, most modest-looking vessel I could find: a softly burnished gold box with no adornment whatsoever. Bob hadn't liked to draw attention to himself. "When I die, I'm gonna be an oak tree," I mumbled awkwardly.

Ken smiled. "It will be a few minutes."

The thought of my dad and all his greatness reduced to something that fit neatly into a small square container that would be covered with dirt for all eternity was more than I could handle. Just a few days ago my dad had told me he loved me. And now his body, the same one that had whispered to me, was ash. Ash that would momentarily be in a box. This box. And then in the ground. Forever. I couldn't remember why anyone had thought this was a good idea. It wasn't.

"Wait," I called just as Ken disappeared into the back room. "I just . . . I mean . . . can you . . . uh . . . separate part of my dad from my dad, and, I mean, can I take a small pinch of ashes? Just for me?"

"You want to reserve some of the ashes in another vessel? A small scattering wand, perhaps?"

"Yes! That." I forced a smile, relieved he understood. But Tara would not understand. In fact, she would probably be furious when she found out. But I could wait for exactly the right time to tell her. Maybe it would be fine. A tear slid down my cheek. I was shaking. I knew I was doing the wrong thing, but I couldn't stop myself. "Perfect. Thank you."

He returned with two packages: one urn for the cemetery and then the most beautiful little gold wand, my dad, just for me.

"You know," Ken said in the soothing voice he must have perfected over the years, "I'm glad to see you here today. I apologize if I'm overstepping, but I was worried about you. You made quite an impression on me the other night."

Damn it. I'd been half hoping that by some miracle, this kind and competent man had forgotten all about that. *Just another day, er, night on the job! It's all a blur.* Or not.

Ken and I had met for the first time a few days earlier, at three in the morning. In the hours after Bob died, after all the calls had been made, Tara had gone to help our mom into bed, and I was left alone to meet the mortician, Ken. I had already called and then canceled Ken three times that night, and now it was nearing dawn. He probably thought I was completely insane. Maybe I was. I didn't want Bob to leave his room, his house, forever. But I knew my mother couldn't handle waking up with his body still there, so Ken was on his way at last. I waited with my dad. His nurse and caretaker had cleaned and dressed him in fresh clothing and then covered him with a stark white sheet. Dad's soft crimson blanket lay folded neatly on a chair alongside the LOVE YOU MORE pillow I'd given him and a stuffed puppy from Tara. I touched his hand.

"Dad," I whispered. "They're coming to take your body somewhere but you have to stay here with us. Because we are super-fun. Don't forget that."

I don't remember them coming into the house. So many strangers had been in and out of the front door in the days leading up to my dad's death, we finally just put a lockbox outside and gave the hospice staff the code. Ken and his assistant—a tall, quiet guy who, with his moon-pale face, disheveled hair, and flannel shirt, looked like central casting had selected him for the part—asked me to step out of the room so they could prepare my dad for transport. Not knowing what that meant, I waited nervously in the hall, the same hall Bob used to greet me in whenever I visited.

"My babe!" he would shout, giving me a giant hug. "How ya doin'?" His voice sang. My dad had been so full of life. I looked around at the house he'd built, my eyes resting on a framed poster of Joe Montana he'd proudly hung on the wall. I used to think it was obnoxious having a poster of a football player in the living room. But I saw Joe differently that night. Dressed in a red-and-gold uniform, he stood on a football field, his arms raised triumphantly in the air. The poster was autographed by Joe himself: *To Bob, Anything is Possible!—Joe Cool,* it read. That's what my father used to tell me. *Anything can happen, child.* When life got rough, he would smile, give me a thumbs-up, and urge me to "be Joe Cool!" My dad saying that to one of his beloved girls meant he'd arrived, and we could put down our worries. It's why we named his death-bed playlist Joe Cool. Bob *was* Joe Cool.

But there were no more big hugs that night. No "My babe!" It was quiet. I was alone.

When the mortician and his assistant finally emerged from the bedroom, my father was strapped to a gurney. A navy sheet swaddled his entire body, from head to toe. *Like a fucking mummy.*

I couldn't see his face. I wanted to see his face. But now he was a mummy about to be interred in the catacombs. I didn't know what to do. No one told me about the shrouding of the body, how it changed the person you loved into an object that wasn't him.

I wept and followed the two men as they carefully made their way out of the house. Though *wept* might be too dainty a word. You find out after a loved one's death that your body makes sounds you never knew possible. And that no one, ever, can prepare you for how it will feel as you follow two strangers carrying your dead father out of your childhood home on a gurney.

The stars overhead were extraordinarily bright and I stopped, transfixed. We didn't get stars in LA. Not the kind in the sky that night, at least. We have too much light pollution and smog. These stars seemed to pull me right up to them. For a strange minute I floated in a dreamlike state and watched the world and my life from high above. *Is this what happens when grief and exhaustion mix and you lose whatever grip on reality you had left?* Warm Santa Ana winds swept around me, the same winds that had carried the fires through Ventura and Santa Barbara Counties, causing heavy layers of smoke that further damaged my father's frail lungs. That had tipped him over the edge. The universe is powerful. *She's in charge,* I thought. *Not me.*

"Stop," I cried suddenly as Ken and his assistant moved to load my father into their van. "I need a minute. Please! Stop!"

The men backed away and I approached my father. I tore at the tightly wound sheets until I got to his face. He was frozen. Cold. Gray. I looked at him one last time, another part of me still high above my own self, gazing down at the two of us, a father and daughter below a skyful of the most beautiful stars. I remembered him teaching me how to throw a baseball in the cul-de-sac at our old house in Oregon. Him proudly watching me ride a horse in boarding school. Him wrapping his arms around me when I returned home after being expelled from that same school. Him walking me down the aisle at my wedding, bagpipes playing, a white flower in his lapel. Him promising me it would be okay before I stepped into the final mediation for my divorce. Him helping me pack up after selling the house. Him meeting with my accountant to dissolve my company. Him standing beside me in the courtroom downtown when I formally filed Chapter 7. Smiling, telling me to "be Joe Cool."

I kissed his forehead, his cheeks, his nose, his whole face over and over. "I love you, I love you, I love you, I love you," I repeated louder and louder as tears poured down my face onto his. I needed to make sure he would hear me. *"I-love-you-I-love-you-I-love-you!"* I sobbed. "Don't go with the van," I told him. "That's not you anymore. You are not your body. Stay here with us. Stay with Mom. You have to stay with us, Dad."

That's when I felt it. For the first time. That's when I first felt my dad's spirit. And it didn't get into the van.

"Me? I'm fine. Good, even. Real good now that I have this lovely urn, thank you," I assured Ken as he handed me both the understated box and the glinting gold wand full of Bob's ashes. I tucked the wand deep into my purse. The same bright red Celine purse that I'd bought with Katie at Barneys New York after I sold my first big house. The purse that had helped me maneuver my way out of dumpster-fire-divorce-land and back into the working world. But despite the best fake-it-till-you-make-it bag money could buy, I wasn't good that day at Remembered Forever Cremation Care. Or even remotely fine.

Pulling into my driveway an hour later, I felt a bone-deep relief at the sight of my front door. Not many people realize this about me because my circle of friends is large and I talk a lot, especially when I'm nervous, but I'm an introvert at heart. My home is where I retreat and recharge. But that afternoon I wasn't mentally prepared to face the twenty black "maybe" dresses hanging throughout my tiny yellow house, tags still on, reminders of the upcoming funeral—yet another impossibly sad task—and of the way that death can ruin everything good. When I got inside, I sank onto the couch, wrapped myself in a blanket, and tried not to lose it yet again. My bright, quaint yellow house with its miniature garden full of flowers and butterflies looked so perfect from the outside. But inside, it was black. That was me. I was a yellow house filled with funeral dresses.

Bob died in the thick of the holiday season, a time of year my family normally loved. But that December, while other people rushed about buying presents and baking cookies, I could not get off the couch. Or get dressed or cook or think. I felt heavy and

yet empty at the same time. When the neighbors hung their sparkling holiday lights, I pulled all my blinds so I wouldn't have to see
them. Friends called; I didn't pick up. I didn't go to work. I wanted
the world to stop, for Christmas to be canceled. But also, I desperately wanted this Christmas to be magical for Dash and Margot.
Over-the-top holiday cheer was once my specialty, the thing I
could do better than anyone. Looking back, I think my Christmas
spectaculars were a way of making up for the fact that our traditional family structure was slowly imploding. This year would be
the first Christmas in the little yellow house for my kids and me.
We'd bounced from the big house with their dad to the shoebox
apartment to a minuscule condo where I shared a bedroom with
Dash to, finally, the yellow bungalow. A place where I could make
holiday magic for my kids once again, albeit on a different scale.
And for a different reason—to celebrate the three of us finally
finding a place to make a home together. But grief made even the
simplest of tasks seem entirely out of reach.

Dash and Margot had been traveling with their dad for a couple
of weeks and would return home soon. I felt their absence keenly.
The house was too quiet without Dash yelling joyfully along to
his video games and Margot telling me I could either start com-
posting immediately or submit to making a TikTok about it with
her. I needed to laugh with them, to hug them. I told myself I
still had lots of time to drag the ornaments out of storage and fill
stockings. But two days before my kids were due to arrive, I had
nothing ready. No holiday dinner planned, no hot cocoa supplies.
No candles lit. Just a small, bare tree I'd left lying on its side on the
living-room floor. I could easily imagine what Bob would have
said: *Good grief! This poor tree, Natasha. You can't celebrate like this.
Don't worry. I'll have it set up straight in no time.* Except my father
would never help me with a Christmas tree or anything else again.
I stared numbly at the tree from my nest on the couch. Who was
I kidding? Christmas this year was going to be a fucking disaster.

"Oh, honey."

I blinked and looked up. Sunlight flooded the dim interior of my house. The Agency's mother hen, my dear friend Monique, stood in my doorway with an armful of flowers. I must have left the door unlocked. Monique set the flowers down and rushed over to hug me.

"So it's pretty bad here, isn't it?" she asked, glancing around at the dark, the disarray, the black dresses in plastic, the tree on the floor.

I nodded, not trusting myself to speak.

"That's why I'm checking on you. And I'm glad I did."

I didn't like to talk about my personal life with anyone, especially colleagues, but Monique was a single mother too. And she'd lost both of her parents. She would never judge me. "How am I going to do this? Poor Margot and Dash. It's Christmas. But I don't have the decorations out or anything to wrap, let alone wrapping paper. Bob was dying and . . ." I was sobbing at this point and gesturing wildly around my tiny living room.

"Let it all out." Monique rubbed my back. "Here's what's going to happen. I want you to listen to me. Christmas will be okay. Better than that, even. I'll be back tomorrow and you'll see. You focus on resting. And, honey? All black dresses look the same at a funeral. Just pick one that's comfortable."

The next day, Monique returned with another colleague and friend from my office, Alejandra. They must have had ten bags from Target between them. I was still on the couch.

"You don't have to move, honey. We are decorating your tree, your house, and the kids' rooms, wrapping presents. You don't even have to cook. The Agency has arranged for Gelson's to deliver Christmas dinner for your whole family."

I couldn't stop crying. I couldn't even get a coherent "Thank you" out. But Monique and Alejandra understood. I just lay there on my side while Christmas went up all around me, a widening pinprick of light in the suffocating darkness of grief.

Christmas was different without Bob, but it was also a good day. For the first time since my divorce, I invited Tara's family and Edna over to celebrate the holiday. In a normal year I would have considered my little yellow house far too small, too humble to hold us all. Besides, we'd gotten into the habit of going to Bob and Edna's on Christmas. But this year, thanks to my colleagues, I had all the food and twinkling decorations. My family squeezed in around the table, grateful for the comfort of a beautiful meal and the kindness of friends. Monique had even thought to get Margot and Dash cozy Christmas onesie pajamas. It's impossible to cry in a reindeer onesie. Holiday magic had indeed come to our little yellow house.

We made it, I thought after dinner was over and our guests had gone home. *We survived the first Christmas without the Great Bob Sizlo.* I flopped back onto the couch, glass of wine in hand. I closed my eyes and listened to Dash and Margot as they sweetly picked up bits of wrapping paper and stray plates. They were good kids.

"Mom!" Dash said excitedly. "There's one more thing under the tree! We missed a present!"

Oh . . . um . . . what?

"Oh my God, Dash," Margot said. "Remember Mom and Dad used to do that when we were little? Hide one last present until bedtime on Christmas? One last surprise before the best day of the year ended? Awww . . ."

"It's . . . a big envelope. Full of lots of paper," Dash said, confused.

"Lottery tickets?" asked Margot hopefully.

"Bring it to me," I said from the couch. Dash handed me a sheaf of official-looking papers and the large manila envelope they had come in. STATE OF CALIFORNIA. DEPARTMENT OF PUBLIC HEALTH. An elaborate blue state seal. And then, in smaller but still bold caps: CERTIFICATE OF DEATH. Below that, my father's name. My mom must have brought these papers and then left them under the Christmas tree. As one does. Not that she'd said a word about receiving them to anyone, of course. We hadn't seen much of my mom until today. The frenetic schedule of back-to-back open houses, Apple Store appointments, CVS runs, and any other busywork she could think of as my dad's condition worsened had only intensified since his death. *Thanks, Edna.* I immediately texted my sister.

You'll never guess what Santa brought me. I attached a photo. Ho-Ho-Ho.

OMG! The death certificates! I wondered when those would arrive. You must have been a good girl this year. BA-HA-HA-HA, that's so funny! It's Dad! His spirit! He wants us to laugh!

And then I started to chuckle, slowly at first, but soon I was snorting and laughing with abandon. I hadn't laughed that hard since my dad scared Tara on his deathbed with the loud, otherworldly howl after I told him about my insane Paris idea and he'd promised his ghost would meet me there. That moment, like this one, was dark and absurd and hilarious. *Hi, Dad.*

Just put them somewhere safe, please, Tara texted. DO NOT lose Dad's death certificates.

I went to my desk in the kitchen and opened the drawer where I stored keepsakes I didn't know where else to put. An elegant card caught my attention, nestled among the many treasures jumbled there. Philippe's personal stationery; his embossed name at the top slashed out with a firm pen stroke. Written on it was a poem in French that he had given me for my birthday last year before we broke up. I had no idea what it said or how to pronounce any of the words, but I knew I missed Philippe. I studied his handwriting. His name. I put the card in my purse next to Bob's ashes. *I haven't forgotten about Paris, Dad. Merry Christmas.* And then I went to bed.

As my father had wished, his funeral was small. Just seven people graveside at the Santa Barbara Cemetery overlooking the ocean on a sunny January day. I wore comfortable black pants with a black top and jacket I already owned. And sneakers. Monique was right: at a funeral, black is black is black. All twenty of my "maybe" dresses went back to Nordstrom, Shopbop, and Revolve. There was just one thing left to do: celebrate. We'd promised my dad's extended family that although the burial would be private, an unforgettable, amazing celebration of the Great Bob Sizlo's life would be held and *soon*.

It had been my responsibility to send out the Paperless Post invitations. But I didn't want to celebrate. Neither did Tara or my mother. At a party celebrating Bob, we would have to spend hours talking about him and his death to other people, and that would make it real. We kept putting it off until my dad's brother called us wondering if he had somehow missed the invitation. He needed closure.

And I needed another shot of tequila if I was going to start planning this party. I went into the kitchen, sliced some lime, and opened my laptop.

We really have to do this, I texted my sister. Don't worry, you focus on the food, flowers, and video. I'll handle the invites and give a big fabulous speech.

You're the best, Tasha, Tara replied.

I agonized over the invitation's font. And the color of the font. Who knew there were so many fucking fonts? And the photo. The invitation obviously needed a photo of Bob. But how could I pick just one photo to represent the man who had given me so much? One photo that summed him up? Should I use a recent one of him? One with Tara and me as kids? There were too many photos to choose from. And so, after drinking myself into a stupor and drafting revision after revision of the invitation, I went with a picture my sister had sent me of my parents when they were first dating. Black-and-white, likely once part of a strip of four images. Edna must have been sitting on his lap; the two of them were like sardines in the photo booth, both of them smiling from ear to ear, newly in love, in their early twenties in Los Angeles. My dad never lost that smile around Edna.

I chose a red font. Cardinal red, one of MIT's school colors.

Would anyone ever love me as much as my dad loved my mom?

As much as my dad loved me? *To the nth degree, Natasha. I love you to infinity.*

There. I did it. I hit Save and started adding guests. First, family: Bob's little brother Tom. The cousins. Edna's younger brother Murdoch and the whole Scottish clan. I e-mailed my mom and asked her for a list of all their local friends. I e-mailed Tara for hers. And then I opened my contacts folder. All the phenomenal women in my life: Nicole, my spiritual-pioneer bestie. Katie, my keeping-it-real girl. Kira, my fashion muse. Sonia, full of earned wisdom. KC, funny enough for stand-up. Heather, always up for one more dance. And Penelope, a die-hard romantic who'd moved across the world, from LA to Ibiza, for love. The list kept growing and growing. And I kept drinking and drinking.

I'm doing this, I texted Tara, hours later. It was the middle of the night. This is HAPPENING, sister. We're throwing a party for Dad. A big, mind-blowing party. No going back now.

I didn't stop there. I invited my colleagues from the Agency, anyone who had been in my sphere the past year. Billy Rose, Mauricio Umansky, Michel Grady, Keri White, and, of course, Monique and Alejandra.

I kept throwing the tequila back. Fuck. Fuck, fuck, fuck.

This is going to be the most incredible party ever! I texted Tara again, sucking on a lime.

I'm scared, what exactly is happening? Tara finally replied.

I couldn't stop. I invited childhood friends. Hospice nurses. Martin. Friends overseas. Friends who had never even met Bob. My ex-husband. My ex-in-laws. I even invited a couple of Bumble dates.

And then I invited Philippe.

The day of the Great Bob Sizlo's Celebration of Life dawned stormy and cool. Dark clouds gathered overhead and the wind blew. I arrived at my parents' house to find Tara setting up rows of chairs outside in the garden, oblivious to the weather. I saw a microphone. And a lectern. *Oh no.* I knew I'd somehow invited seventy-five people to this party, but I hadn't thought about what that meant in terms of *giving a speech* in front of all of them. I did *not* belong on a microphone. I did *not* belong in front of people. Sure, I'd smoothly delivered the eulogy at my dad's funeral. But that was attended by just seven relatives, not every ex within a fifty-mile radius plus my colleagues. I'm the kind of person whose mind goes blank in front of a crowd. I always have been. When I was in kindergarten, someone thought putting me on a stage in a shiny purple leotard and top hat to dance and sing to Frank Sinatra's "New York, New York" was a cute idea. My dad sat beaming in the front row, holding a clunky black camera to his eye. The music started. But I froze like an animal caught in headlights. I forgot my lines, my steps, all of it. I was petrified. Because do you know what usually happens to those animals frozen in the street? *They die!*

"Tara? Tara! Listen to me. It's going to rain. Look. Bad for the microphone. We should move this inside. Where we don't need a microphone."

Tara glared. "It's *not* going to rain. I forbid it. Dad loved to show off his garden and share it with friends, and that's what we're doing today. It's what Dad *wants.* Now get the wine out of your car. And see if you can find Mom. She's here somewhere."

Tara had lost her mind. Bob would not have wanted us sitting in freezing rain. But she was unfolding even more chairs, muttering about the flowers, and somehow tracking the caterer's every move. I had no idea then that she'd been up the whole night before, sorting through photos and prepping the house to her standards or that she'd felt my dad's friendly spirit when she'd gone to tidy his old room. (Of course Bob had come to help with the party.) I only knew I'd better get the wine and get out of her way for now. I walked back to my car and saw a tall man carrying the very cases I had been about to unload.

"Wine delivery." *That French accent. Philippe.* He'd come.

"Hi . . . I . . . um, thank you for coming today. It's still a little early and—"

"I wouldn't miss Bob's party. I loved your dad. I'm so sorry, Natasha. How's my girl?"

Why does he always have to look so fucking good? "Scared. Terrified. I don't know if I can do this. Tara is setting up *chairs.*"

"Ah." He winked. "Chairs. I see. Natasha, you will be great. I know it."

My heart was racing. It wasn't just the speech; on an already intense day, Philippe's presence only unmoored me further. But I was the one who'd invited him.

"I got this part, Natasha. Go be with your family." Philippe smiled at me as he carried the wine into the house.

The house and garden began to fill. My girlfriends. Relatives. Strangers. My boss. I greeted people, asked them to sign the guest book, accepted flowers. All while crumpling my speech nervously in my hands as I moved about. Tara had been right earlier when she advised me not to wear the rainbow sequin skirt and bright graphic tee I'd been planning on as a giant middle finger to death. "Yeah, Tash, I'm just not sure anyone's gonna get that one." Everyone was dressed tastefully in black, just as she'd said they'd be. Well, except for Philippe. He knew I would not want him in black. And he knew damn well how much I liked him in a crisp white button-down shirt. Somehow that guy pulled off sexy in a white shirt like nobody's business. Even at a memorial party.

I glanced fearfully over at the chairs, screen, and projector Tara had set up. She knelt on the ground, checking the many wires leading to . . . giant speakers. *Good God.* I had to try again. Especially since the clouds overhead looked even more threatening. Not only would I be humiliated; I'd be electrocuted.

"Tara. Let's just move the damn thing inside! Look at the sky!" I *might* have raised my voice.

Tara stood and turned to me, her eyes full of tears and fiery determination.

"*No.* Tasha, I'm tired of you just going off the rails whenever you feel like it in this family. Like the vial of Dad's ashes you took without asking Mom. Or me. Bob was my dad too. Don't think I've forgotten about that for one second—"

Tara had discovered Bob's ashes in my purse at the funeral. *After* we'd buried the main urn and said our goodbyes. As it turns out, bright golden scattering wands aren't exactly discreet. She was as angry with me as I had worried she'd be. More, even. But it was too late to do anything about it. When I asked the cemetery worker if we could somehow join the wand with the urn, just rewind things a little bit, he looked at me like I was nuts. "Lady, we're not exactly in the business of digging things up around here, if you know what I mean."

Now I'd poked the hornet's nest at exactly the wrong time.

But just as Tara was about to go off on me, the dark clouds overhead parted dramatically, like curtains in a theater, and the sun burst through. The edges of the clouds were lit from within, otherworldly mauve cotton candy against a Tiffany-blue satin sky. The kind of rare sky that made people stop their cars, pull over, and take a picture. The day Bob died, the sky had been exactly the same. Tara and I were struck silent in the garden. *Dad?* He always hated it when we fought. He'd often intervene, trying to make us make up, even long past our childhood. Tara and I stared up at the stupendous sky, each thinking the same thing: It was time.

If there is one event in life where you don't covet the front row, it's a memorial. I wanted to give my seat to someone else. And hide. Instead, I stood and took the mic. I saw a sea of faces before me, expectant and quiet. For a moment, I lost the ability to speak. I froze like the poor animal in the headlights, just like I'd known I would.

And then my eyes met his. Philippe's. He sat in the last row of chairs with his daughter Charlie. I'd seen her and Margot earlier, huddled close as they talked. The girls were forever conspiring to get us back together. Philippe was farther away than everyone, but he felt closer than anyone else there in that dreadful moment. His soft expression said he knew the bottomless despair in my heart and also how scared I felt. I could feel the ghost of his touch on my body, hear the echo of his smooth whisper in my head: *Your name is Natasha.*

And so I began. I spoke of my father's legendary love for his family, for banana and onion sandwiches, for Frank Sinatra, MIT, trips to Costco, and long conversations. About the outrageous things he did in the name of enjoying life to the nth degree, like the time he bought an old van that had belonged to the Utah Jazz for us to use as the *family car.* Tara learned to drive in this extra-long 1980s curiosity, which was essentially a bus complete with a minibar, TV, and foldout bed. The boys in town called it "the party van," forever branding the Sizlo sisters as some kind of mythical unicorns. I spoke about how much he loved Edna.

"I've never seen someone love another person as much as Dad loved you, Mom."

We cried in the garden. And laughed. I felt wrung out and relieved. We moved inside to where Tara had arranged elaborate displays of mementos from our father's life. The Scottish side of my family began singing loudly, as Scots do at a funeral party. Imagine "Auld Lang Syne" on repeat. Someone attempted to lighten the mood with 1950s music and people started dancing. Tara and I danced and danced and burned away some of our sadness. A Sizlo sisters' dance-off, something we'd done since we were small. Tara, a trained ballerina with a sixth sense for her own body in relation to any physical space, can *really* dance. Me? I'm all spastic elbows and knees, no matter what. Eventually, my sister, doubled over with laughter at me, crowned herself the victor yet again. She went to the kitchen to catch her breath and drink a glass of water.

Philippe appeared at my side.

"You did great," he said, wrapping his arms around me, kissing me on the cheek. A kiss that lasted a little too long, but I didn't stop him. "I'm proud of you, Natasha. Bob would be proud." I sank my head onto his shoulder. That was my spot. It felt like home. He smelled so familiar. So *alive*. I breathed him in. Brown eyes. Sun-kissed skin. The white button-down shirt. I still loved him. It felt good to have his strong arms around me. I heard the first notes of "La Vie en Rose" and then Philippe and I were dancing. Slowly. *Is this what Stephanie meant when she said Philippe was perfect for me?* Maybe I didn't have to go to Paris in search of every other man born there on his birthday after all. Maybe Philippe *was* my point of destiny.

Tara later said some of the people who'd been dancing stopped to watch us because we looked so perfectly in love, but I didn't notice that. She also said KC, who knew my history with Philippe and also knew that Tara wasn't his biggest fan, elbowed her and whispered, "Oh no! Your sister's dancing with the Frenchman!" But I didn't hear KC. All of my attention was on Philippe.

Reader, I got back together with him.

It is said that when you lose a parent, you become part of a club no one wants to be a member of. I didn't find that to be true. I didn't have a club. I didn't have anyone. Not anyone I would let in, that is. Not even Tara or Nicole (because they might have had something to say about Philippe and me, something I didn't want to hear). There was only Philippe, who felt safe. Familiar. I didn't have to explain anything to him. We were a club of two and I didn't want to let him go. Ever. Which is why I asked him to marry me soon after my dad's celebration of life. We were away for the weekend at a friend's ranch, picnicking under an old oak tree with a bottle of rosé. I was just about to tell him about Stephanie, his birthday, and the rather unconventional plan I'd almost put into action when he stopped me.

"I have a question I have been meaning to ask you," Philippe said, brushing my forehead with his lips.

"What is it?"

"Would you like to go to Paris with me? We never went, and I'm not sure why. It's my home. And I want to show it to you. I have been thinking about it a lot. I've been thinking about us a lot."

"Yes, I want to go to Paris!" *It's a sign! The stars are aligning!*

I grabbed Philippe and kissed him. I never did get around to telling him about my soulmate search that afternoon.

"I love you, Philippe. I love you more than anyone, ever. Let's be together. Forever. Let's get married. Here. Under this tree. And we can figure the rest out later. Marry me."

Philippe answered me with a long kiss. He never did say the word *yes*. But I didn't notice that then.

When I was at home in LA, far from the magic of Bob's memorial and the romance of a ranch picnic, my old concerns about our relationship started to creep back in. Somehow our whirlwind weekends *à deux* always involved the perfect sunset cocktails, bottles of French wine, and forbidden cigarettes smoked late into the velvety night. Just like old times, except I was older and less able to bounce back the next day. I was also busier with real estate and needed my wits about me. The dreaded suitcase shuffle with the kids was as disruptive as I remembered. And we still had no solid plans for the future. Worried that Philippe and I would end up in the same untenable place as before, I decided to get expert help from a miracle worker of a couples therapist a friend had recommended and who had also been featured prominently on Goop. If anyone knew complicated relationships, it was Gwyneth Paltrow. Sold! Well, I was, anyway. Philippe, not so much.

"*Goop?* You found us a couples therapist on Goop? You've got to be kidding, Natasha. Are you serious? It feels like you are looking for someone else, another version of me. But I am who I am. No Goop therapist can change that. This feels like a mountain to climb."

Like that, we were over again. And this time, it was mutual. Now there was no engagement. No Philippe. And my father was still dead. Most evenings, exhausted from work and heartbreak, I sat in my kitchen and nursed a glass of wine before bed. I didn't go out much.

On one of those nights, I decided to clean out my treasured bag. As Katie would say, "Who in their right mind would list their pristine Brentwood spec home with a custom movie theater, pickleball court, and an actual Botox salon with an agent carrying an entire week's worth of Starbucks trash around in her bag?" Near the bottom of my purse, I found the card with the poem from Philippe. I studied the poem, wishing again that I could read it. His handwriting, so French. His name, tattooed on my heart. A tattoo I very much wanted to remove. I put the card back into my purse. It didn't belong in the garbage with a bunch of lipstick-blotted napkins, but I wasn't sure what to do with it. Next came the little gold wand of Bob's ashes. I felt a *frisson* of energy and sadness as I held it in my hands.

I set Bob on a small shelf near my desk where I kept little talismans of hope. He went right next to the photo of me as a child, the one he'd scrawled the line from the Shel Silverstein poem on the back of. That photo was propped against my natal chart from Stephanie. I smiled. The shelf was getting crowded. It also held some of the birthday presents my ride-or-die friends had given me last fall: The rose quartz crystal. The red Chanel lipstick far too bold for me to wear. The pineapple vagina spray. And the flying wish papers.

The wishes. I forgot about the wishes!

I plucked the small packet off the shelf. The Love Letters Mini–Flying Wish Kit. My friends had given them to me specifically for manifesting The One.

A whimsical kit to make your dreams come true, the packaging read. *Write it, light it, and watch it fly! Float your wish off into the sky with this whimsical kit. Simply write your special wish on the flying wish paper,*

*shape your paper into a tube, and place it on the wish platform. Light the
top edge of the tube and watch it burn down in a small beautiful flame. At
the last moment, your wish magically lifts off the platform and rises right
into the air. Includes 15 sheets of Flying Wish Paper, 5 wish platforms,
pencil, and instructions.*

I pulled out a wish paper and the accompanying pencil and
closed my eyes hard. The last time I had made any kind of wish,
it was for my father's peaceful passing right before he died. But it
was time to look to the future. To my point of destiny, like Stephanie had said. I thought for a minute. And then I knew exactly
what to write.

Someone who will fight for me

But I didn't light the wish paper on fire. Nobody sane lit random pieces of paper on fire in a house in LA and tossed them into
the air. Instead, I tucked the wish into a blue glass mason jar and
put that on the shelf too.

Fourth House

Zumba

Primal and changing, the Fourth House is like the moon that rules it. It's about pausing, observing, instinctual knowing, feeling the vibration of Mother Earth and our relationship to our human mother as well as our own mothering abilities.

At the same time, the Fourth House is about absorption. All of the information taken in through the Third House is assimilated through the planets in or ruling the Fourth House. It keeps records of what's meaningful. It rules history and your relationship to the history of your family, which includes behavior patterns and habits. It's also about food, digestion, nurturing, emotional support, pregnancy, and home.

I have Gemini in the Fourth House. Mercury, which rules Gemini, is in Scorpio in my Ninth House of foreign countries. Scorpio rules the soulmate. My Mercury line runs through Germany, eastern France, and northwest Italy.

"IS IT WEIRD THAT I DON'T MISS HIM?" DASH ASKED ME ON the way to school. We were in the right-hand lane, waiting to turn off Sunset Boulevard onto Allenford Avenue, a few blocks from the drop-off line at Paul Revere Middle School. "Grandpa Bob never seems gone to me."

Nope, no weirder than our new normal, I thought.

I'd picked Dash up at his dad's house that morning. The kids had spent a lot of time there over the past few months. I suppose now is as good a time as any to mention it wasn't only my ex's house. His girlfriend, the supremely talented, stunningly gorgeous, totally-has-her-shit-together actress Anna Faris, lived there too. Yes, my ex-husband, Michael, a cinematographer, had moved blissfully in with the hot House Bunny. And yes, a long time ago my own life had been much more Hollywood-adjacent than it was now. Michael had worked on some big movies and TV shows and I sometimes got to attend glamorous red-carpet events as his plus-one. But those days were gone. The only carpet I walked on now was the stained shag one at the listing I was currently (desperately) trying to sell. While Michael, on the other hand . . .

Anna was standing outside the house when I pulled up. I rolled my window down and called out, "I can't thank you enough for all your help with the kids." Anna had been wonderful to Dash and Margot during a sad and unpredictable time for our family, never failing to welcome them at a moment's notice if needed. I was grateful to finally have a chance to thank her in person. Even though the kids were back and forth between households often, I hadn't seen Anna since right before Bob died. Real estate hours are all over the place, and that's even more true of an actor's schedule.

Anna plunked a bag into the recycling bin and approached my car. "Oh, Natasha, I am *so* sorry about your dad. I can't imagine what you've been through. If there is anything more we can do . . ."

I smiled, willing the lump in my throat away. "I don't know what I would have done without you. You saved me and I'm thankful for that."

Even at seven a.m., before coffee, Anna brimmed with a sunny kindness and a radiant, stop-you-in-your-tracks natural beauty. A crew could have pulled up and started filming her immediately.

There's a reason she's a movie star and I'm . . . I glanced in the rear-view mirror at my gaunt face, straggly hair, and tired, puffy eyes. *Don't finish that thought, Natasha.*

"Well, I'm glad to see you this morning," she said. "Promise me you'll take care of yourself."

"Okay, I will." I gave Anna a thumbs-up as I drove away, know-ing I didn't mean it. I had other priorities. Like finding a buyer for that listing. And listening to my sweet, tenderhearted son, who filled me in on his fun night with his dad before turning to the subject of Grandpa Bob's whereabouts.

Soon, we reached the head of the drop-off line. Dash unbuck-led his seat belt, grabbed his backpack, and opened the car door. I put my hand on his shoulder.

"It's not weird at all, Dash. Sometimes I feel Bob nearby too. I just wish it was an always kind of feeling, like you have. You're lucky. Have a good day at school. Remember, dinner tonight at Auntie Tara's for you and Margot. Love you."

I carefully inched my way toward the school's exit, and when I stopped at the red light, I tapped the large screen in my car's dashboard. My phone and the car's stereo system were meant to effortlessly sync. Right. It worked maybe once a week, and to-day was not that lucky day. I tried again because the relentlessly caffeinated "morning drive" 97.1 FM top-forty music currently playing was Dash's wake-up routine, not mine. I wanted to trans-port myself back in time to age six, when Lionel Richie ruled the airwaves and an "Endless Love" felt guaranteed. I fiddled with my phone. Nothing. More pointless jabbing on the dashboard touch-pad. I flicked the windshield wipers on and off, because why not? Abruptly, 97.1 FM stopped and a woman's strong, soothing voice blasted at top volume from the car's speakers.

"At age forty-four, you will start to understand the definition of a life partner," the voice called. "How you are meant to go into a relationship as whole and complete, not really *needing* a partner, but open to sharing your life. To having fun."

What the actual fuck?

The light went green. Heart pounding and now thoroughly awake, I turned sharply into traffic and quickly found a place to pull over.

"Now you need to just be out there, making an entrance. You've got a weird chart, and it's great. This is a big, wonderful year for you."

Stephanie. I'd totally forgotten that she'd sent me a recording of my astrology reading and I'd saved it on my phone. I hadn't listened to it in months. I cut the engine—and Stephanie's voice—and sat in silence. Making an entrance? Fun? A wonderful year ahead? Not really needing a partner? Ha. *Zero for four, Natasha.* I closed my eyes. Cars whizzed past and some honked, loudly. I couldn't stay illegally parked on the shoulder of Sunset Boulevard on the verge of a mini-meltdown forever. Not only was it ridiculous, but if an officer happened to stop by, with my luck, it definitely wouldn't be a hot single man in uniform. I had to get home to do laundry. And work. I'd been so focused on trying to keep my dad alive that I'd let my business slow to a frightening degree over the past year. I had to get back in the game. Right away. I pressed the car's ignition, expecting 97.1 FM to blare as usual. But Stephanie's melodious voice picked right back up from an earlier part of the reading.

"Your father doesn't have a lot of time. This illness has been long and difficult, but as soon as he passes to the other side, he will feel immediate relief and will remain by your side . . . You need to start thinking of yourself as a writer again."

Giving in, I turned the volume down to a reasonable level and listened to Stephanie as I drove. I felt sadness as she talked about the death of my father. But the words *fun* and *entrance* and *wonderful year* also echoed in my car. And *writer.* A tiny sliver of something that wasn't despair but not exactly hope cracked open inside me. "You don't drown by falling in the water, you drown by staying there," one of my friends had told me recently. At the time, I thought this was bullshit. I would stay in the fucking water as long as I damn well pleased. But what if she was right? What if *Stephanie* was right? Suddenly, I knew exactly where I needed to go next.

The hairstylist stared at my head, her eyes wide.

"Whoa," she said, lightly running her fingers through my hair. "I can remove what's left of the extensions and trim it up a bit, but there's absolutely no way you can go blond. Your hair can't handle it. It would be a disaster."

"I understand, thanks," I said politely, paying for the trim and tipping 20 percent but deflating a bit on the inside. My hair already *was* a disaster. That was the whole point. I didn't want to put a colorist in a no-win position, but there had to be a fabulous fix that wasn't a wig or a hat. A second opinion seemed in order. I jumped back into my car and texted friends with great highlights: What's the name of your colorist? I have an emergency. Thirty minutes later, thanks to a cancellation, I found myself in master colorist Sarah Conner's chair at a trendy Beverly Hills salon. I tried not to think about how I'd pay for it.

Sarah studied my hair for a moment. "What's been happening here?"

Over the past several months, I'd watched in horror as my glossy dark brown hair turned brittle and dull. It broke when I brushed it and fell out in the shower. Stress, Dr. Google said. Needing a quick fix as I rushed from my father's bedside to Agency meetings to Margot's lacrosse games to failed Bumble dates, I made a Hail Mary investment in hair extensions. Which only damaged my poor real hair (and my bank account) further. Now the extensions— what was left of them, anyway—were ragged and slipping out in places. Not exactly a "making an entrance" look. But maybe I could change that. And a lot of other things. I took a deep breath and looked Sarah in the eye.

"Here's the truth. Ready? My dad just died a wrenching death, my real estate career needs an urgent reboot, I'm a single mother, and I just ended things for the millionth and truly final time with the man I'd hoped to marry. My heart is trashed. Then there's my tequila, red wine, and Xanax diet. *But* . . . my astrologer told me I'm supposed to be having *fun*. So, and I'm not kidding, I'm going to find every man I can who was born in Paris on November second, 1968, because . . . *fuck that guy!* And I would like to do it as a blonde."

"Fuck *which* guy?" Sarah asked with a laugh, confused.

I explained about Philippe and his birthday, my point of destiny. I figured I might as well.

Sarah's eyes lit up. She was all in. As she applied the bleach and foils to my hair, she told me her own improbable story of love and fate, one that stretched over almost two decades and went from Los Angeles to Greece to Palm Springs.

"And after all that," Sarah said, "I totally believe in destiny. You have to go to Paris. You *and* your hair can handle it."

Four hours later, I sat in complete shock in front of Sarah's mirror. More often than I liked to admit, when I made impulsive decisions like this one, the results surprised me—in a bad way. But that day, I had no regrets; I saw a (literal) lightness that felt instantly right. It was liberating in the way that only a big change can be. I went straight from the salon to Walgreens and bought the brightest red lipstick I could find and applied it immediately. Firetruck-red lipstick! Me!

Next, I headed to Bel Air for an Agency twilight open-house event already on my calendar. It's one of the more glamorous parts of the job. Tour a stunning thirty-million-dollar property while sipping (free!) champagne and sampling caviar with fellow home-obsessed people? Yes, please. I was also looking forward to seeing a few women from work there. We jokingly called ourselves the Agency Boss Babes and met periodically to talk shop. On that night, we'd promised one another to raise a glass—to ourselves. Real estate is a commission-based, feast-or-famine industry. A hustle, one I surprised myself by loving and that I'd been, little by little, succeeding at. Before my dad got sick and things with Philippe went to total shit, my colleague Keri and I had both been named to a prestigious list of America's best real estate professionals. Almost a full year later, we were finally toasting. True, I still lived from one erratic paycheck to the next, but I hoped the list said something about what I could and would do with a little luck in this industry as I tried to revive my business.

"Wow! You're blond! Like, *blond*-blond," Keri said when she saw me.

"Holy shit, mama," Gloria exclaimed. "You're fucking hot!"

"Get it, gurl!" Marci raised her glass.

I could get used to this. Typically (and understandably), my friends had been greeting me of late with "I'm *so* sorry about your dad" and "How are you *doing*?" *You're blond* felt amazing by comparison. Maybe I *was* ready for the wonderful times my stars supposedly had in store for me.

The kids were still over at Tara's, so after the event, back at home, I took a quick selfie and posted it on Instagram before I could talk myself out of it. I didn't use Instagram much. Or any social media. Outside of what I needed to post for work (social media is a key tool for selling luxury homes), I didn't see the point. Who but a small circle of friends I already saw in real life would care what a forty-something harried mom was up to? But that night, I thought maybe Instagram could be a way to hold myself accountable. If I announced publicly that I was having fun, then I'd have to get out there and do it. *Already having more fun,* my caption read. I added a cartwheel emoji. It was my first Instagram post since the tribute I'd written for my father.

The comments and emojis poured in: Hearts! Flames! 100 percent! Not a single comment came from a place of condolence or pity. Except, perhaps, for Margot's deadpan observation:

oh she's blond

I tapped my fingers impatiently on my kitchen counter. I wanted to be on a roll. Music! That's what needed to be next. Loud, joyful music had been my church, my medicine, my love language ever since I was a small child. It still was. Music had come flooding back into my life post-divorce. When Michael and I were married, he had often worked long nights on set, which meant his days were understandably reserved for sleep and solitude. "Daddy's nocturnal," Margot whispered at an early age. "Be quiet." Wanting to be a supportive wife, I respected the need for a hushed and peaceful home. And so I mostly gave up music back then. Our old house was as quiet as I could make it. But to do that, I had to pack away an essential part of me.

Philippe adored music as much as I did. But I wasn't going to think about that tonight.

"Alexa. Create a new playlist."

"Sure. What's the new playlist name?"

"Get Up."

"Creating your new playlist, Get Up."

"Alexa, add the song 'Good Day' by Nappy Roots to the playlist Get Up." I sat at my counter shouting out song titles. Loudly. Music would save me. Along with the red lipstick and blond hair, music would lift me back up. "Survivor" by Destiny's Child. "Confident" by Demi Lovato. "Break Free" by Ariana Grande. "Let's Go Crazy" by Prince. "Flawless" by Beyoncé. "Dancing on the Ceiling" by Lionel Richie. I quickly texted friends, my sister, and Margot asking them for their own favorite songs of empowerment. The replies came instantly.

"Superwoman" by Alicia Keys

Nicki Minaj!!! "Feeling Myself"!!

Gloria Gaynor!!! "I Will Survive"!!

Anything Cardi B!!!

Taylor Swift!

"Brave Honest Beautiful," Meghan Trainor!

Kelly Clarkson! "Stronger"!!!

And then Margot weighed in:

LMAO, how about "One Less Lonely Girl," Justin Bieber 😵

This IS fun! I AM fierce! My new playlist filled my little yellow house with a rousing beat as I poured myself a glass of wine and found my laptop. *Now, then. I said I'd find my Parisian soulmate and I'm doing it! Tonight.* I clicked open a new window in Safari. *How hard can this be? I'll be done by ten.* I typed *Born in Paris on November 2, 1968* into the search bar. Aside from a short list of celebrities born on that day—none of them in Paris—my search revealed little else. *Hmph.* I tried Facebook next. I figured I could do a reverse search by birth date. Wrong. Ancestry.com was the same. *Your search returned zero good matches,* my computer told me. What could I be doing wrong? Wasn't the media forever warning us all about how privacy was dead and everything about everyone was out there for the taking? But it was *much* harder than I expected to come up with a list of people with just a birth date and place to go on.

Hours later, after the kids were home and settled in their bedrooms, I found myself down a rabbit hole and on the France Civil Registration website. By this time, it was morning in Paris. I learned the civil authorities in France had been recording births since 1792. The archives included the child's name, sex, date, place of birth, and parents' names. Brilliant! If I collected the names of males born in Paris on 2 Novembre 1968, I could then do a cross search on Facebook, DM these guys, see who was single (and straight, and alive), and, one by one, track them down! Okay, so I was *not* going to be done by ten tonight or even tomorrow night, but at least I was onto something.

Paris, I discovered, is divided into twenty arrondissements, or boroughs, each with its own *mairie,* or town hall, where the births, marriages, and deaths are registered. I would need to contact each *mairie* separately. Fine. I sent a few test queries to *mairies* using Google Translate. So exciting! Finally, I found a search engine for birth certificates. Was this it? I plugged *2 Novembre 1968* into the *Si la date de naissance est connue* prompt and hit Return. A big red *Identité de la personne dont vous demandez l'acte*—NOM ET PRÉNOM flashed on my screen. Back over to Google Translate to see what that meant. "Identity of the person whose act you are requesting— LAST NAME AND FIRST NAME."

FUCK! If I knew his last and first name, I would already be on a plane to Paris, potential wedding dresses packed! I slammed my laptop closed, frustrated. I needed a break. Or, better yet, to go to bed, seeing as I had a showing in a few short hours. But I didn't want to end the night on a note of defeat. That didn't feel right after such a banner blond day. I thought back over the past several hours about what had felt so good to me. Action. *Intention.* I grabbed my phone. If I was going to do this, it was time to call in help.

PARIS OR BUST, I typed. If you're on this group text it's because you believe in True Love. I added a red heart emoji. And so, the adventure begins . . .

My best friends would be full of brilliant ideas, I knew.

Katie texted back immediately: Natasha, go to bed!

"What was that group text about last night?" Tara asked me the following day after she'd brought Margot home from practice. "You okay? And OMG, your hair!"

"I'm doing it. I'm going to track down every man I can find who was born in Paris on November second, 1968."

"Wait. I thought this was a joke."

"I'm dead serious. We promised Dad. My soulmate is out there."

"This is a *bad* idea. There are also a lot of weird people out there, Tasha."

"I like weird people," I said. "Weird people are my people."

"Can you just promise me you'll think this through? That you won't go running off without a plan?"

"I'm not fifteen, sis. I'm forty-four. I got this."

"That's what I'm afraid of."

✳ ✳ ✳

Later, I saw Nicole. We met at Crossroads, a vegan restaurant she and her new boyfriend, Justin (who was not there that day), loved, for Sunday brunch. With her wavy blond hair and cut-glass cheekbones, she was always easy to spot across a crowded restaurant. I'd met Nicole, an actress turned writer/producer, years ago; we'd been introduced by our husbands, who'd worked together on set. We grew exceptionally close after we both divorced around the same time and discovered that we had more in common than we knew: our need for solitude *and* deep friendships, our appreciation for trees and nature, the way our children were the joyful center of our emotional lives. We could be ourselves with each other. I'd do anything for her, even eat a plate of vegan chicken and waffles. (Which turned out to be delicious.)

"So, how are things with Justin?" I said playfully. I loved asking Nicole about him. He was gorgeous. And funny. And kind. Plus in totally amazing shape—they'd met at a yoga retreat. But he was also twenty-six.

Nicole smiled and blushed. "It was supposed to be casual, you know that. I thought we'd end up just friends."

"Uh-huh," I replied. I didn't know any woman who could be just friends with a single man as handsome as Justin and who liked her back.

"I can't believe it, but we're pretty much dating-dating. Like, exclusively. But where is this even going?"

"Straight to the bedroom?" I laughed. Then, more seriously: "Do you know where you want it to go yet?"

Nicole sipped her fresh celery juice. "No, but I like him. A lot. Anyway, enough about my new romance. Let's talk about you."

"I have news. The search for my soulmate is a go!" I said, raising my farm-to-glass virgin bloody mary in the air.

"Yesssssss!" Nicole practically jumped out of her chair, shrieking with excitement. "Paris, here we come! I *love* this plan!"

"But I'm gonna need your help, Nicole. It's not as easy as I thought it would be to find potential soulmate candidates." I told her about my frustrating midnight attempt at searching French birth records.

"Hello? Tinder!" Nicole pulled up the app on her phone. "Tinder has a Passport thing so you can be here in LA but search for guys in Paris. Just swipe right on every fifty-year-old Parisian, then narrow it down from there. You have something like a one-in-three-sixty-five shot after that! But you'll need new photos now that you're a hot blonde. Ooooh! Let's do a photo sesh at my house. I'll do hair and makeup. Rohina can take the pics; I'm texting her right now. This is so fun! Get some clothes and meet me at my house."

Fun. There was that word again. The grief over my dad and Philippe still stung, but I was undeniably having *fun.* And it felt good.

When I got home, I rummaged through Margot's closet and pulled out the sexiest outfit I could find, a little black-lace corset dress that I'd gotten for her from the last-chance bin at a sample sale downtown. It still had the tags on it. Maybe the dress wasn't Insta-perfect in Margot's opinion (*And thank goodness for that,* I thought when I got a closer look at the almost transparent fabric), but it seemed like promising Tinder Paris bait for me. In other words, it was something the old Natasha would never, *ever* have worn.

The pictures our friend Rohina took that afternoon at Nicole's house were a revelation. I'd half expected to look exactly how I'd felt the past few years—oldish, knocked around by life, depleted. Like someone who was faking it. *Who are you kidding, thinking some lipstick and a dye job can hide your problems?* But the radiant woman I saw was beautiful. Open. She looked happy. Something shifted deep within my heart when I saw myself as my dear friends saw me. I'd never considered I might be beautiful on the outside until that moment. *I'm single and over forty! I was divorced and then effectively dumped!* That's what usually ran through my head. But Rohina and Nicole's Natasha told the beginning of an entirely different story.

Natasha, 44
Point of Destiny

Our love was written in the stars . . . Only if you were born in Paris on 2 Novembre 1968. All other birthdays need not respond.

"We are all of us in the gutter, but some of us are looking at the stars."—Oscar Wilde

Just like that, I started swiping. Age fifty, swipe right. No matter what the profile looked like. Any other age, left. Well, except for when I saw a Philippe. Then my heart would lurch. And so I swiped right on them too for a while. I just couldn't let go of *a* Philippe, even if it wasn't *my* Philippe. But eventually I did. It was like therapy, learning to swipe left on Philippe.

Coucou, Natasha. Do you speak french?
No, I do not, sorry. Were you born on 2 Nov. 1968? Could we be soulmates?
Sorry my birthday is May 17. Pity I will not be your soulmate.
I couldn't agree more. You're quite handsome!

On to the next.

Hello there.
Bonjour, Jeff. What is your birthday, S'il Vous Plait?
Bonjour. In November but not the 2nd. ☺
This is terrible news! 💔 But I've got to follow the stars.
Best of luck, my lady! I hope that you find your gentleman.
Merci, dear Frenchman with the wrong birthday! ✨🎏

I had hundreds of matches.

Hello. My proposal is to make love to you intensively and creatively now or this evening, in Paris or close, I drive my superb brand-new BMW 530e Hybrid and come to your place with an exceptional bottle of champagne or wine bottle. All yours.

What is your birthday, s'il vous plait?

4 Fevrier

As suspected, we are not soulmates.

Are you very sure?

This was going to take a while.

Hi, Natasha, nice to meet you! I was born in 1968, close to Paris, some days from November. Is this enough to reach the stars?:)

Hi, Franck. I was told by an astrologer my soulmate was born on November 2, 1968, in Paris. Do you think I'm crazy?

Yes, I think you are a bit crazy . . . but a bit of craziness is charming:) if you don't find the Nov. 2, 1968, ask your astrologer for June 26, 1968. I'm quite sure it should fit:)

One more before bed.

Bonjour! Enchante par ce match!

Hi, Didier. Hope you speak English. Is your birthday Nov. 2, 1968?

Hello! No I was born in July . . . and you?

Ah, sad news. I'm looking for my soulmate. He was born in November. I know it sounds strange. Wishing you love and light and passion and happiness ✦ 💋 🕯 ✩ 💕

Faith is faith! Enjoy your journey!

Love this. You too.

I need your help. You around? I texted Tara the following morning.

What is it? Are you okay?

I need to hang something. And there are just some things I never learned how to do after my divorce. Like anything involving a hammer. Michael did that stuff. Dad did that stuff. Philippe did that stuff. And—I glanced at a big silver meat tenderizer and the nail I'd been trying to bang into my now-tenderized wall—I don't even have a toolbox.

I'll be right over.

"Yipes! Now what did you do?" My sister spun slowly around my cramped kitchen, which had been turned upside down. Maps of Paris, crystals, palo santo, and sage bundles lay scattered on the countertops and table. "Is that a new desk?" She gestured to the elegant walnut desk I'd crammed into the corner where a schoolkid-size one had been, next to my shelf of treasures.

"A client gave it to me after I sold his bungalow in Venice in record time and he needed to clear things out fast," I told her. "Can you believe it? A bigger desk is *exactly* what I need right now. Command central for finding my soulmate. Next step is a vision board, obviously. Well, *boards.* I bought three."

"Uh . . . right. Yes. Well, I brought my Makita." Tara waved a power drill at me. "Let's Go Crazy" by Prince was playing. "Love this song. You know, Dad got you a toolbox too."

"No clue where that is." I held one of the large corkboards up against the wall. "How's this? Crooked?" Tara stepped back and squinted one eye.

"Have you talked to Mom today?" I asked. We took turns calling Edna and visited her on weekends. We were worried. But Edna always brushed off our concerns and then handed us each a little paper bag from Rite Aid—mascara or hand cream. Just in case we'd run out.

"Yeah, she's all wound up. She's discovered Zumba, and now she's taking a class every day. Sometimes twice a day." Tara made a mark on the wall with a pencil. "Are you sure you want to install

all . . . *this* . . . in your kitchen, where people can see it? Please don't be the unhinged mom with the psycho wall. You're creeping me out, Clarice."

"Just drill." I grabbed a box of thumbtacks and started adding things to the vision board: My astrology chart. The photo of me as a child. The map of Paris. "I'm serious, Tara."

"I can see that."

"I have a new Instagram account now too. One just for my search. You should follow it. I mean, you *are* going with me to Paris. You promised Dad you would." I tacked up photos of my girlfriends taken at my birthday, the notes I took when Stephanie's assistant told me my soulmate was born on November 2, 1968. A couple of fortune-cookie messages. My passport.

"I don't exactly *do* Instagram. I mean, I have, like, five followers on a private account," my sister said. "And that's counting you!"

"And Mom."

"Yeah, no. Mom's not on there. Are you seriously going to post all of this *online?*"

"Yes. I also joined Tinder Paris. It's shockingly fun. And I was thinking about trying some kind of targeted advertising in Paris on Instagram or Facebook, but I need to figure out how to do that. And obviously totally on the down-low. Can't let my clients see this. Or Michael. Or Philippe! Can you imagine?"

My sister stopped drilling and looked at me, horrified. "You lost me at Tinder. Have you thought this through?"

"Quit worrying," I said, lighting a small bundle of sage and waving it gently around the kitchen.

"What the hell is that? You're going to trigger my asthma! I'll need my inhaler!"

"It's sage. An energy-cleansing expert came to the Agency last week and taught us all how to use it in our listings. I'm clearing your negative energy."

Tara opened a window and laughed, despite her misgivings. "Put that out!"

"Mom keeps asking me what I'm up to and I'm afraid to tell her. Is that bad?" I lit a stick of palo santo and wafted it around the room. "Calling all the good spirits to serve our higher purpose. Alexa! Play 'Boys' by Lizzo."

My sister sighed. "I'm not sure Mom can handle all this right now. Maybe you should wait a bit."

Soon after I started my soulmate search in earnest, I attended a lunch celebrating a friend's new clothing brand. *It's just lunch,* I thought, psyching myself up as I drove there. *Ninety minutes, tops.* Ever since filing bankruptcy six years earlier, I loathed small talk with strangers at events like these. Even the most banal conversations about travel plans or the hot new reservation that you just *had* to get felt like an emotional minefield. My vague replies almost never aligned with their expectations. Questions would inevitably follow, along with quizzical, concerned faces. *No vacation? But what will you* do *all summer?* (Um . . . work?) I became a master at spotting a "friend" across the room and dashing. Back soon! No matter what, I couldn't admit out loud to someone I'd just met that I was far from financially sound after filing Chapter Seven. Sure, I was closing deals and I was a rising agent at the Agency. I had some child support to help while I hustled to get listings. And I looked and dressed the part of a woman who was (almost!) on top of the world. But I had a long way to go. Building myself back up after my financial collapse was like making a cake out of air. I felt like a failure and I didn't want anyone to know my big, dirty secret: I had totally ruined my finances. But now that we're sharing, dear reader, here's the short version.

I'd been a full-time mother for eight years when I unexpectedly had the chance to turn a series of small, long-ago gigs in the fashion industry (which, in a roundabout way, was how I ended up at that lunch) into a real business—designing clothes for kids. I leaped at the opportunity, and every mom I knew understood why:

I'd earn my own money. And I'd finally solve the maddening back to work but how/what/where conundrum. I didn't consider the fact that most successful start-ups *can't* be founded, run, and scaled in the roughly seven hours between drop-off and pickup. Truthfully, I probably didn't even know that fact. I had no idea what I was getting myself into. In hindsight, I should have found mentors, explored online classes (Business Plans 101, perhaps?), and taken things more slowly in general. That's easy to see now. Back then, I was excited to be doing something that felt bigger than picking Pirate's Booty out of the center console of the car. And I dreamed of being able to contribute financially to our family. Though I was grateful to have the choice to stay home with the kids, I felt guilty about the long hours Michael worked to support us.

After only a few dizzying months in business, the adorable children's clothing brand that I started, curio + kind, was carried by major retailers such as Nordstrom, Fred Segal, and Garnet Hill. Sounds like a success story worthy of the cover of *Fast Company,* right? Wrong. What nobody tells you, or maybe I didn't listen long enough to hear, is that you're chasing those thrilling orders with huge sums of borrowed money and it's not a game. It's also not a paycheck. On the contrary, it's a full-on money pit and I had the maxed-out credit cards to prove it. Any profits from one order went toward fulfilling the next, and so on. The cycle resembled a ravenous, never-satisfied, always-awake beast. Forget part-time or even full-time work. This was *constant.* But I had two young kids who still needed their mother. And a disintegrating marriage. I redirected my energy homeward. I had to. The business, not surprisingly, collapsed. My marriage followed.

In the aftermath, I felt like a woman who had failed in almost every way possible: as a mother, as a wife, as an entrepreneur. Filing for bankruptcy is a maelstrom of shame, stress, grief, and fear. There's something about putting the fact that you have nothing into stark black ink on crisp white paper and then handing those horrible documents to a judge presiding over a courtroom that makes you feel like you're nothing. My self-esteem took an even harder hit than my bank account or credit score. I looked in the mirror and saw a loser who had lost it all. Except for my kids and my health, and that's what kept me going. It would take me years to understand both the far-reaching effects of the shame I carried and that the flip side of having nothing is you get a fresh start.

Chin up, I thought as I walked nervously across the urban farmhouse-chic room to my table at the event. *They don't know a thing about you. Maybe there's a great new real estate client here. Besides, if you can't do lunch in LA, how will you ever survive back-to-back dates with the dozens of potential soulmates you're destined to find in Paris?*

I forced myself to turn to the elegant woman seated beside me and say hello. When she asked me about myself, instead of my usual evasive chitchat, I impulsively told her about Philippe, Stephanie, and November 2, 1968. Which, truthfully, was awkward at first. This wasn't a heart-to-heart in a salon chair, after all. But as I spoke, her eyes sparkled and her smile grew wide. "I'm Hope," she said, extending her hand. *Hope!*

It turned out my new friend Hope's professional expertise lay in social media—getting people (lots of people) to pay attention. She laughed gently at my inept, infrequent posts on my soulmate search Instagram account and generously offered a few helpful tips. I didn't exactly turn instantly into a fearless social-media maven, but I began posting more regularly. Maybe my astrological match was a friend of a friend of a new follower? Anything was possible. I invited the universe in.

What if someone told you the birth date and birthplace of your soulmate? How far would you go to find him?
02 Novembre 1968 • Paris

Friends and strangers alike started to find my soulmate-search account. True, an objective observer might have said it was a tiny group, just a couple hundred people, but to me that was a staggering show of support. People I barely knew offered assistance and threw out ideas. Good ones. An old flame of Nicole's who happened to be French and living in Paris—François—even took a meeting with a private detective to get advice for me. A woman who would soon be visiting France offered to hang a few homemade "Wanted" signs outside the Arc de Triomphe. I loved that idea. Little things like this—Hope, private-detective tips, the gift of the command central desk, and the thoughtful stranger traveling to Paris—began to happen with regularity. People didn't laugh at me. They wanted me to succeed.

Around the time that I met Hope, a friend reached out with a referral for the kind of property I'd only dreamed of representing thus far in my career.

Hi, Natasha. I'd love to introduce you to this business manager I know. Your go-the-extra-mile reputation is just what one of his artists looking to sell a house in the Hollywood Hills needs right now. LMK.

My pulse quickened as I read my friend's message. Because this business manager wasn't just any manager. His clients were huge—pop stars who topped charts and hosted reality-TV shows. The house in question had to be spectacular.

Absolutely, I replied. I'm available whenever he is.

Now, these were signals I liked sending. And receiving. But I also took to heart the Agency's ethos, which was to leave our egos at the door and collaborate whenever possible. Because I knew this referral was likely for a major celebrity, and I hadn't handled such a listing on my own yet, I called my boss, the Agency's cofounder Billy Rose, right away to fill him in and see if he'd want to partner with me if the lead went anywhere. But Billy didn't partner with just anyone. Though his and Mauricio's office doors were always open to any agent seeking guidance, Billy's commanding, no bullshit core combined with his fierce intellect and exacting standards meant he could be intimidating at times. He also worked his ass off and had both the sparkling client list and the impressive sales to show for it. Somehow, he even managed to make it all look easy. Billy Rose is a rock star in our world, plain and simple. And if there was one thing this rock star who happened to be my boss did not ever waste, it was time. Still, I had to ask.

"Whatever you need, Natasha," Billy said immediately. "I'd love to do a deal with you. It would be fun. Keep me posted."

Could my cosmic energy be changing for the better? Finding my soulmate. The reboot of my real estate career. The vibes were *good*. I didn't want to count my chickens or anything like that, but for the first time in a long time, I felt hopeful. Lighter. Centered. I wanted more of those good feelings. So I finally did what Nicole had often suggested over the years as we weathered our divorces, my dad's illness, her own dating disasters, and my Philippe problem: I embraced spirituality and healing practices that once would have sent me fleeing in the opposite direction. After all, an astrology reading had set me on this path in the first place.

Nicole was something of a master at many of the alternative practices I usually scoffed at. In an effort to address a childhood marked by abandonment and abuse, she'd gone on a pilgrimage to Mount Kailash in India with her guru, done the Hoffman Process, and had recently completed a ten-month university program in spiritual psychology called Soul-Centered Living. Even though Nicole found solace and strength in her studies and various retreats, I couldn't help but think that maybe they were also part of the mystical trend that the whole of LA seemed increasingly to be into. But now I wondered if I'd been unfair. Too defensive. Deep down, I knew I had been. The truth was, I didn't like looking too closely at myself. And I'd been afraid some of those healers really did have special powers to "see" things in me, things I was ashamed of facing. My dismissive attitude was more about that than anything else.

The next time Nicole offered me a Reiki session (of course she's a certified practitioner), I accepted. I downloaded the guided-meditation apps she recommended and used them. When she texted me the name of her favorite psychic "just for fun," I didn't reply with the eye-roll emoji. I also consulted a numerologist and a tarot-card reader. I signed up for the Class by Taryn Toomey and took workshops at the Den, a personal-growth center with offerings like How to Work with the Universe and Cosmic Embodiment. I even went to a New Moon Sound Bath in the hills of Malibu with a group of women dressed in flowing white maxi-dresses and toting ikat throws to zhuzh up the dusty yoga mats we'd be lying on while letting go of all that did not serve us. I have to say, it was awesome. Why hadn't I ever signed up for an afternoon of acoustic healing with planetarily tuned gongs before?

"What's this?" Margot asked, waving her phone at me as she emerged from her room. "What's two Novembre 1968? You spelled *November* wrong." At just fifteen years old, Margot had somehow mastered the art of social media. She had over ten thousand followers on Instagram and had even been asked by Snapchat to speak on a panel. Most of the time, Margot and her friends exuded the sweetest cool-girl vibes, a mashup of agency and innocence. Even with me, her mom. Except when I did something she deemed uncool.

"You found my Instagram! It's the French spelling. It's *Novembre*," I said with my best French accent, pleased.

Margot scrolled. "Oh God. Oh God. Is this your weird astrology-soulmate thing? You made an Instagram? Oh God."

"How did you find it? Did someone send it to you?"

"Mom. Are you kidding me? Instagram suggested I follow you. Do you have any clue how to make a Finsta?"

"What's a Finsta?"

"You didn't use the same e-mail for your Agency account, did you?" Scrolling more "Oh God. You're so weird. *Is that my dress?* I'm so embarrassed. Do *not* tell my friends about this. Do *not* tag me in anything. Why can't you just bake cookies, like Josie's mom?"

"Oh, come on! Don't you believe in fate and destiny?"

"I believe you're having a nervous breakdown."

The twenty-one-mile stretch up the Pacific Coast Highway through Malibu is one of the most magnificent drives in the entire United States, if not the world. The winding road, the deep blue ocean, multimillion-dollar mansions, the big sky, mountains, and cliffs. The drive was my meditation. As I sped up the highway, I watched as longboarders waited patiently for waves at Surfrider Beach, fishermen sat on the iconic Malibu pier, lifeguards scanned the sea from their blue towers along the sands of Zuma Beach, and motorcycles lined up outside Neptune's Net. Sometimes there were even dolphins. And the most spectacular sunsets. I had done the ninety-minute drive from LA to my parents' house in Summerland countless times over the years, and often twice a day in the weeks leading up to Bob's death. The Pacific Coast Highway part of the trip was like an old friend calling me home, the ocean-meets-mountain scenery never failing to lift me. The highway was my own private twenty-one-mile journey between motherhood and daughterhood. In the middle, my cell service would drop and for a brief moment, only I existed. It was never long enough. And it felt like the merest blink of an eye on the morning I drove to meet my sister in Summerland after we'd gotten a call from our mom. Edna had been on a tear, indiscriminately emptying out Bob's closets and giving God knows what away by the bagful to anyone who happened by the house. She'd told us that if we wanted anything, we'd better come get it—fast.

After I arrived, Tara and I got straight to work and carefully sorted through our father's clothes and cherished belongings, making sure we didn't overlook any mementos, important credit card receipts, or winning lottery tickets (Bob always bought lottery tickets), before packing what could be donated into boxes. It's nearly impossible to explain the feeling of reaching into the pocket of the suit your beloved father last wore to your wedding and finding a crumpled tissue. Had the day moved him to tears? Was he holding tissues for one of his girls? I would never know.

"Look," Tara said, handing me a crinkled scrap of lined yellow paper she'd found in the pocket of one of his shirts.

My dad's handwriting: *I will love you to the end of time! For ∞!* *Love, Bob*

"I found a few more notes by his bedside before he passed," she said. "All of them to Mom. About how he would love and take care of her forever."

"Bob was a legend. Come on. Let's take Mom to dinner."

The Honor Bar hummed with conversation and laughter, a busy night. My sister and I sat on one side of a booth, Mom on the other. The lights were low. Edna didn't have much of an appetite, but Tara and I insisted she eat. She looked thin, and we were worried about her. Without Bob, Edna seemed lost. She still kept busy with her maniacal schedule of more appointments than you'd think any one person could possibly have—plus Zumba, of course—but the light was gone from her eyes. We ordered salads, fries, a juicy steak, hoping to tempt her. Oh, and margaritas. Lots of margaritas.

My phone, which I'd set on the table in case the kids needed me, buzzed furiously. I peeked. Tinder! I pulled the phone under the table and opened the app.

Hello, I am Louis! Curious of my dick?

I flashed the message to my sister under the table. I loved seeing her scandalized reaction.

Not curious, no, I typed back. Are you born on Nov. 2, '68?

No . . . '67.

I think that's probably for the best. Good luck to you!

I opened the next one.

So many matches! I widened my eyes at Tara, who looked scared now.

> Bonjour.
> Hello. Do you speak English? Is your birthday 2 November 1968?
> Almost . . . 1st May 1968.
> Thanks. But it's sadly not a match.
> I am angry with my mother . . . she could have wait a little!

"He's funny," Tara whispered. I opened the next one.

"You don't think I'm crazy?" I asked.

"Maybe not. This is kind of fun! We need that."

"What's that you said? We need to believe in fate and destiny and true love?" I winked at Tara.

"Oh, for sure."

"Awwww. Well, the French believe in love!" I whispered.

And another.

> Hello. Do you speak English? Is your birth date November 2, 1968?
> Hi. I do speak English. 11.2.68. Why? Do you have such beautiful feet?
> This is 2 Nov. 1968? In Paris? My feet are incredible if this is your birth date
> Yes, it is.
> Time to get a pedicure!

"OMG, I found one!"

"You're bonkers." Tara laughed.

"What are you girls doing over there?" Edna snapped, annoyed. We were acting like a couple of phone-obsessed teenagers.

I looked up, frozen. My mom's expression was hard. I turned to my sister.

"Ugh. Just tell her already," Tara said. "Tasha wants to fly to Paris to find her true love. And it's, like, this astrology thing. There. Now it's out."

I told Edna the whole story, starting with Nicole and her birthday gift. "It's my destiny, Mom. I am following my point of destiny."

"Like when you came to America to find Dad," Tara added, sensing our mom's confusion.

"Dad knew about Paris. And the astrology reading. I told him before he died. He was supportive. He said to go get 'em! To check ID."

Our mother sat stock-still. "I'll tell you what, girls," she finally said. "You want to know what your destiny is? Your destiny is *death.*"

Had anyone but Edna said this, I would have been shocked. Maybe it was her wartime upbringing. And her Scottish outlook was a wee bit dark. The family stories she told us as children always started off harmlessly enough but generally ended with someone losing an arm or a twin. *Did I tell you about the time I went to stay at my uncle's farm during the war when I was young? They had the most beautiful chickens and land. But my auntie had to push me around in a wheelbarrow because I'd lost so much weight, the doctor said I was malnourished and shouldn't walk.* And *Your grandfather went to get his final paycheck the day before he retired. He was a braw man and worked hard sweeping the streets his whole life after he came home from the war. On the way to get his paycheck he had a heart attack and collapsed in the street. People walked past him for hours before someone finally took him to the hospital because they thought he was simply drunk and having a rest.*

Still, Edna's words that night smarted.

"I don't think that's true," I said, my cheeks growing warm. "My destiny is not death. And neither was Dad's. Or yours. I believe in so much more. And I think you do too. You believe in destiny. That you were destined to meet Dad. Think about it. You worked two jobs, clawed yourself out of poverty, saved all your money, left your entire family behind in Scotland, and got on a propeller plane with no return ticket because you *believed*. Because you had *faith* in the unknown. What if you had never gotten on that plane, Mom? And what's wrong with Paris? Do you think I'm supposed to find my soulmate here at the bar? Would that make you happy? How is this any different?" I pushed my plate away and glanced up at the crew of single women my age packed into the bar.

Mom was silent. She wasn't about to give in. And Bob was no longer here to balance things out.

Tara's voice was soft: "What if Tasha is right, Mom? Why *not* try? What if it does work? What if he is waiting for her?" she said. "Even if he does have a foot fetish," she added under her breath to me. She raised her eyebrow and grinned. "Plus," she said, "Dad said he would meet us there. Mr. MIT Logic and Reason. And I don't think we can stand him up."

So Tara *was* coming with me to Paris after all.

Oh my GOD. I think Mom's broken, I texted Tara later that night. Thank you, sis.

Before bed, more wishes in the blue jar.

Someone who believes in MAGIC.
Someone who can handle MOM.

Fifth House

My Astrologer Made Me Do It

The Fifth House rules trust, happiness, fun, creativity, love, romantic sex, vacations, children, and honoring the heart's higher wisdom. After the Fourth House has processed the knowledge assimilated in the Third House, the Fifth House wants to take that learning further through experience, because it is experience that awakens the heart beyond words.

Both the moon and Saturn are in my Fifth House. The moon rules the core for those who identify as female. The sign of Cancer fills my Fifth House, so the moon is all about love for me. My moon in Cancer is in complete harmony with my Mercury in Scorpio, which means the moon and Mercury are all in for traveling the world in search of true love.

Saturn, though, can be suspicious. It rules the father. But I had been given Saturn's blessing when Bob promised to meet me in Paris, so game on!

AS LOS ANGELES TIPPED FROM AN UNUSUALLY WET WINTER into a super-bloom spring, my dream of Paris and who I might find there became, little by little, more real. After the doomsday dinner with my mom, I wanted to hop on a plane to France the next morning with Tara. But I wasn't ready. I'd found just one potential soulmate thus far—Foot Fetish Guy—and I didn't speak a word of French. Well, except for the few swearwords Philippe had taught me and a fond farewell I'd learned years ago from the French grandmother of one of Dashiell's preschool friends: "Au revoir, *poupée*." Colette would trill those words, her melodic accent echoing down the toddler-filled halls. "*Poupée* means 'doll.' It's my nickname for *mon petit-fille,* my granddaughter," Colette explained. I nodded, mesmerized.

When Poupée and Dash moved on to different schools a few years later, Colette and I fell out of touch. But for some reason, I never forgot what she said to me one morning as we lingered by our cars after drop-off, chatting. "I tutor on the side when I'm not acting as au pair," Colette had said with a smile, handing me a business card from a slim silver case, "in case you ever want to learn French."

I still had that business card. Not only did I want to learn French, I needed to. Despite the years that had passed, Colette delightedly agreed to meet me for *un petit-déjeuner* at Starbucks in Malibu. Seeing an old friend is one of the sweetest joys in life, Natasha, she texted.

From Lady Gaga to Caitlyn Jenner, Malibu brimmed with over-the-top celebrities, and usually, just like everyone else, I enjoyed trying to spot them while strolling through the city's de facto downtown: the Malibu Country Mart. But that day the trendy boutiques, pristine playground, and outrageously expensive juice bar only made me uneasy. As I headed to Starbucks, it occurred to me that Colette was the exact same age as my mother and therefore might have the same reaction to my soulmate quest. Also, Colette would be the first actual French person I spoke to face-to-face about any of this. Our meeting could be a preview of Paris. What if it didn't go well? My chest felt tight.

"I'm on a mission to track down every man I can find born in Paris on November second, 1968," I blurted out awkwardly as we made our way to a sunny picnic table in the courtyard. Colette settled in with her coffee, eyes wide, as I hurriedly gave her the CliffsNotes version of why I'd wanted to meet her.

"It's wonderful to see you again, Natasha," Colette replied calmly as she spread jam on her croissant. "And the blond hair. *Oh là là.*"

But I should have been the one *oh là là*–ing her. Now eighty-two, Colette still turned heads. Her pale red bob perfectly framed her lovely, natural face, and she wore a gray cashmere cardigan over a cream silk blouse. There wasn't a whiff of the infirm about her. Her eyes sparkled with possibility and wit, just as I'd remembered.

"Why a Frenchman, exactly? The French are a pain in the ass. Even when I lived in Paris, I never dated Frenchmen. Why do you think I moved here?" Colette smiled.

I laughed. And then I explained in more detail about Stephanie, my father, and Philippe. And how challenging it was to find November 2, 1968, guys, even with the help of a dating app.

Colette looked at me, perplexed. Then: "Your open heart, *c'est magnifique.* And the bravery this must take. *Bravo,* Natasha! Though I don't know about the birthday part. Most French people don't believe in astrology. But as the old proverb goes, *Qui vivra verra.* Meaning 'he'—or in your case, she—'who lives shall see.'"

"I love that! Can you teach me more?" I said, encouraged. "How about how to say 'Were you born in Paris on November second, 1968?'"

"Good grief, I'm going to receive an alert on my phone with your photo on it from France! 'There's an insane American walking the streets of Paris! If you see her, call!'" We both burst out laughing. It was just like old times. "*Bon.* Repeat after me: *Êtes-vous né à Paris le deux novembre, mille neuf cent soixante-huit.*" The words rolled off Colette's tongue.

"*Êtes-vous . . . né à . . .*" I blinked, unable to repeat such a mouthful. "Uh . . . it's too much. Maybe something shorter?"

"I have just the right phrase!" Colette replied with a grin. "*As-tu déjà été arrêté?* It means 'Have you ever been arrested?'"

I couldn't help but laugh.

"*Ça alors!* Why so many rules, Natasha? Love isn't a game to be won. Not in my experience, anyway. And the idea of a soulmate, it's beautiful, but . . . sometimes *l'amour* lasts forever, and sometimes it's like a hummingbird and a flower—a perfect affair until the nectar is gone. Take my current lover. He's forty-eight, strong, and handsome. And he's Italian—not French!—so the sex, it is perfection. I adore him. And him, me. But we both know it can't last. So we're enjoying the moment. You know what, Natasha? You should do like I do. Have *fun*."

Fun. That word kept appearing like a lucky penny.

When it was time to say goodbye, I kissed Colette on each cheek and reached into my purse for my keys. My hand grazed velvety cardstock: Philippe's poem. I pulled it out reluctantly.

"Can I trouble you to translate something short for me?"

"I'd love to," Colette said, taking the card.

"May I record this? So I can remember what it says?"

"Of course," Colette replied.

I touched the red Record button on my phone. Colette cleared her voice and began.

Thousands and thousands of years
Would not be enough
To tell you about
The little second of eternity
When you kissed me
When I kissed you

She paused, briefly, and continued:

Life is long with you
I hope
   —Philippe

Colette put the card down, looked me in the eye, and smiled playfully. "*Very* romantic."

"Mmm" was all I could say, nodding a little.

"The beginning comes from a famous French poem. 'Le Jardin' by Jacques Prévert. I use it sometimes with my students to work on pronunciation. The original poem ends with *Un matin dans la lumière de l'hiver / Au parc Montsouris à Paris / À Paris / Sur la terre / La terre qui est un astre.* Which means 'One morning by the light of winter / At Montsouris Park in Paris / In Paris / On Earth / The Earth which is a star.'"

A star. Was the poem a sign?

"But Philippe doesn't end it that way. He ends with 'Life is long with you, I hope.' That's not part of the poem. That's all Philippe," Colette explained.

"Thank you, Colette," I said, tucking the card back into my bag. I had a lot to think about.

"I received a poem like this once from one of my lovers," Colette said with a sparkle in her eye. "He sent it from jail."

Normally, I would have immediately rushed off to my next appointment, returning calls as I drove. Instead, I sat in the parking lot for a moment, Colette's words reverberating in my mind. "She who lives shall see." Hummingbirds. Flowers. Philippe's poem. *Life is long with you, I hope,* he'd written. Had he meant that? He must have, at least at the time. I checked my phone and saw I'd missed a call from my mother, and then she joined the bizarre, jumbled mix in my head too. Colette, Edna, Philippe. A little shadow. A rift. There was something there. Nicole would have said that these were the connections that my subconscious wanted me to be making, that this was the path.

I wasn't good yet at piecing past experience and family history together with earned wisdom to get to something like clarity, especially not when some of those pieces hurt. I still had a long way—literally—to go on that journey. But I glimpsed a part of the much bigger whole that day in the parking lot. Colette had called me brave (God, how I wanted to be brave and not simply compulsively impulsive), but I had nothing on Edna in the bravery department.

Edna's passage from Scotland to America as a young, almost penniless woman was as hopeful and exciting as it was complicated and difficult. Her best girlfriend, Margaret, came along, easing the way. And, as was the legal requirement, the two women had found a sponsor willing to vouch for them as worthy future Americans and help them get settled. Fred Schroeder and his wife, Helen, lived near Dallas, Texas, and they welcomed Edna and Margaret with open arms. But this wasn't Edna's first attempt at escaping her impoverished upbringing. A few years earlier, still a teen, she'd tried her luck in London. Her thick Scottish brogue made it impossible for her to advance in any meaningful way, thanks to England's impenetrable class system, and she returned home even more alive to the class distinctions in Edinburgh that were just as suffocating. She had to get out.

Before they emigrated, Margaret and Edna worked as secretaries at the Scottish Home Department during the day and at a fish-and-chips joint on the docks at the end of Leith Street at night, saving every penny for America. On rare evenings off, they went to dance halls. Edna met a man at one of the dances, an affable young American soldier stationed at the base. They were just friends until two nights before Edna and Margaret left for Texas. Parting has a way of making people do funny things sometimes. All that emotion over leaving.

Soon after the women arrived in Dallas in the summer of 1958,

Edna discovered that she was pregnant. She wrote to the soldier, frantic. But he refused to marry her, breaking her heart. Kindly Fred Schroeder suggested the only way out he knew—a home for unwed mothers in rural Texas. Its staff would provide care for Edna and arrange for an adoption after the birth of her child. It was the last thing Edna wanted, a path she'd mourn the rest of her life. But with little more than forty dollars to her name and five thousand miles away from family, she could see no other option that would be good for her child. Unwed mothers in 1958 were told in no uncertain terms that they had committed a sin, that they were an affront to polite society.

Nobody except the Schroeders and Margaret knew about Edna's pregnancy. The Schroeders counseled her not to tell anyone. They didn't want her life to be harder than it already was. When she went to the home, all of her new Texan friends and colleagues thought she'd returned to Scotland to visit family. Several lonely months passed and then Edna gave birth to a healthy daughter she named Catherine even though she knew the baby's adoptive parents would change her name immediately. Afterward, she had to return to Dallas, slip back into her routine, and act as if nothing unusual had happened. The Schroeders and Margaret cared for her the best they could and Edna was grateful to them. That's just the way it was.

I found myself thinking of my mother and Baby Catherine, older than me by sixteen years, and how brave they'd both had to be. Bob helped Edna find Catherine thirty years later, and Edna drove hundreds of miles just to park outside her grown daughter's home to be near her once again and check that she had fared well; she didn't make herself known. I didn't know about Catherine's existence and my mother's abiding love for her until I was sixteen. Thinking about all my mother had given up all those years ago still caused me pain. In his final days, Bob must have been worried that the grief Edna would feel over his passing would wake up other feelings of loss in her too. Grief has a way of doing that. As I knew too well.

Philippe and the pregnancy neither of us planned on had been on my mind a lot in the months after my dad died. It happened in the last year of our relationship. Things were already rocky between us. I'd just passed my real estate exam and joined the Agency. My health insurance was shit. Maternity leave? I'd have to fund that myself. Dash, Margot, and I were still shoehorned into that far-too-small condo while I squirreled away whatever I could for a bigger place. I felt like I was crossing a wild river, hopping precariously from one slippery rock to the next, trying to stay dry, trying to make it to safety for myself and my family. Money, time, and space were beyond tight for both me and Philippe, who was also changing careers. We already had five children between us. We couldn't have added a baby to our lives. I dreamed of all the ways it might have been different in some fantastical alternative reality, but we didn't live there. I hate that I feel I have to make this list of reasons. I don't know if I will ever feel that I *don't* have to, even if only to myself.

An abortion was without question the right decision for both of us, and so, quietly, I had one, in sorrow and vivid relief. And then almost utter silence. My mother had been explicitly told to be silent about her loss; I felt I had no other choice. I couldn't imagine how to tell anyone. Would I bring it up casually while hiking the trails at TreePeople? Or confess to my girlfriends at an Alliance of Moms volunteer event? In retrospect, I wish I had tried that. But I was scared. Nobody I knew talked about abortion the way I needed to talk about it (I wanted to have a heart-to-heart, not discuss it in terms of how we'd vote or the need to support Planned Parenthood). Was that because we were in our forties and supposedly past all that? I wasn't a college kid freaking out in a dorm. Or was it because, as far as I could tell, women weren't supposed to mourn abortions out loud, especially not abortions we'd wanted, needed, and were (and still are) sure about. Nicole knew, because I'd taken the pregnancy test in her bathroom. Thank heavens for her. And Philippe, who was incredible about the whole thing when it happened. He'd been the one to lovingly hold my hand at my doctor's office before and during the procedure. He paid, because I couldn't afford it. But we didn't talk much about any of it afterward. Did Philippe think about the pregnancy, about all the ways it showed us that we weren't headed to the altar, that we weren't forming a big new family like I'd dreamed we were, that we were instead ending? I had no idea. And why was I thinking about it now? *In a parking lot?*

I didn't like these thoughts. I was supposed to be having fun. So I did what came naturally to me: I shoved the unsettling and sad feelings down deep and told myself for the thousandth time not to go there. *Ever.* What was the point?

Abruptly, I noticed the time. Dash and Margot would be home in a few hours, and I needed to meet Billy over at our new client's house. I started my car and called Edna back.

"Hi, Mom. How was Zumba today?"

My hunch that our new client would be a major celebrity was 100 percent correct. The first time Billy and I spoke to that client's manager on the phone, he immediately brought up the NDA he'd need us to sign.

"Happy to," Billy said. "Send it over right now."

Then the manager told us whose house we might be selling. Though no agent at the Agency would ever reveal personal information about a client, I could see why the manager probably made even this artist's mailman sign one. Because the artist in question was a pop star famous for two things: hits you couldn't get out of your head and stunningly immature decisions that attracted tabloid coverage like flies to, well, you know. Nevertheless, he'd secured his first movie role, a big one, and now the pop star wanted to upgrade to an even more lavish estate in Beverly Park.

Pulling up to the massive courtyard in front of the midcentury-modern estate, I had a hard time finding a spot to park. There were cars everywhere: Multiple Teslas. A neon-yellow Mercedes-Benz G-Wagon. Billy's Porsche. A shiny Range Rover. If I could have hidden my dusty little Audi behind a bush, I would have.

I didn't have to wonder who the cars belonged to; I could guess: assistants, the business manager, at least one publicist, the dog walker, and definitely a personal trainer. For starters. But I was curious about the house's interior, excited even. Because as questionable as this star's behavior in public often was, his clothes were insane. In a good way. The man had style to spare. What would his house be like? I couldn't wait to find out.

An assistant in an oversize hoodie and Crocs let me in the front door. "Hey, just so you know, we're keeping it down right now 'cause our boy needs to sleep. Like, real down. Shhh." The stench that greeted me in the foyer told me why: weed, skunked beer, vomit, a million cigarettes smoked with not a single window open. Uh-oh. Somebody had had a party.

I found Billy in the living room talking to the business manager like they weren't surrounded by taxidermied raccoons mounted on the walls and boxes of pizza in various stages of decay on every available surface. Like porn wasn't playing soundlessly on the large-screen TV. Like the famous young pop star who owned the place wasn't in his underpants and snoring softly on the shredded leather sectional, an ashtray overflowing with cigarette butts and blunts balanced on his bare chest. Like the entire interior—or what I could see of it—wasn't totally, completely trashed.

Smiling brightly, I said hello. And: "Great place!" Like I totally, completely meant it. Which I did. Or would, as soon as I got a paint crew and that energy-clearing expert who'd come to the Agency a few months ago on speed-dial. This was more than a quick tutorial and a sage bundle from House of Intuition could handle. But cleaned up, it could be an eight-figure listing.

"So," said the manager, "do you think he'll have to move *out* while you get this place ready for sale? I wanna get my mind around this."

To say I was in my own fantastical world in the spring and summer of 2019 would be an epic understatement. Yes, I'd leaped back into work in a big way, but increasingly, my 2 Novembre 1968 obsession ruled my thoughts and decisions. How could it not when so much of the feedback I'd received in those early months was intoxicatingly positive?

I began to believe I was in the middle of something beautiful and rare and not crazy at all. I started documenting each text and DM I got, and after cropping out their names and photos, I shared some of their heartfelt words on my soulmate-search Instagram. The outpouring of online support felt wonderful; life-affirming, even. I finally understood why some people—my own daughter included—loved social media. People were so kind, for the most part. So *real*. Even total strangers. I'd been missing out.

I went to bed each night adding more wishes to the blue jar. When I ran out of wish papers, I used whatever I could find— Post-its, old receipts, a scrap of notebook paper.

Someone who inspires me
Smart as fuck
Not a regular on HerpAlert.com

As time passed, my vision boards filled with items related to the search. Oracle cards representing truth and strength were tacked next to multiple maps of Paris dotted with tiny red pins noting romantic locations that seemed perfect for a first date. I even draped fairy lights to conjure the true spirit of the City of Light. The boards were immediately visible from Dash's bedroom door, and, in addition to summoning serious soulmate magic, I wanted to create an inspiring sight, because that's good parenting. *Follow your wildest dreams, kids! Anything is possible!* But both Dash and Margot just rolled their eyes. "You're *so* weird, Mom."

Weird or not, I eventually matched with several men who claimed to have been born on the right day in the right place. I gave each one a real chance. I even had a WhatsApp date with Foot Fetish Guy. Because what if Mr. Feet was Mr. Perfect? Would a foot fetish be a deal-breaker? *Let go of some of your rules, Natasha.* Yes, I got a pedicure in anticipation of our date. Yes, he confessed he was lying to me about his birthday just so he could look at my feet. And yes, it creeped Tara out, big-time. (Googling *foot-job* later, I could kind of see why.) But as I saw it, eliminating the wrong guys only got me closer to the right one.

One by one, I found men who had potential. And the right birth chart. A poet named Fabrice, who seemed normal and sane, and not only that, but I liked him. A lot. Maybe because he too believed in soulmates and fate. Then there was Maaz, a handsome single dad and architect. And Gael, a cute chef. Hopeful, I added printouts of their Tinder profiles to my vision boards. I wasn't sure how many potentials I'd need to amass before I felt comfortable buying a plane ticket, but Fabrice, Gael, and Maaz made a good case for *vive la France.*

My search didn't come without moments of frustration and exhaustion—it seemed as if I swiped my way through all of Paris looking for potential soulmates, and trolls occasionally called me stupid, insane, or worse on social media—but nothing could get me truly down. I was on a high like I'd never felt before. Heartbreak and anxiety seemed to be in the rearview mirror, and my Xanax-and-tequila habit faded. Who was that woman who could knock back four shots in one night? I barely remembered. I was taking boxing lessons. Hiking. Eating healthy. Working at a steady pace. Listening to music. Seeing friends. Having *fun.* And writing.

My @02Novembre1968 Instagram account had become a place where I could write openly. I began by describing my heartache over Philippe (never naming him—he had no idea about any of this), my father, and the improbable promise I'd made to him on his deathbed. I wrote only snippets at first, but as the months passed, a narrative grew. That's how Instagram, which I'd begun using more often because I hoped it might help me find my soulmate, became my diary, my therapy, as I searched for my destiny.

It wasn't unusual for me to wake up to a few appreciative DMs from strangers around the country or even across the globe, many of them women saying I had inspired them in some way or calling me fearless, a quality they admired. Younger women occasionally asked for advice on their own love lives. It was bizarre. Me? Give advice? What part of *divorced and single* had they missed? And I wasn't fearless at all when it came to this search. In fact, I was often straight-up terrified. What if it didn't work? What if it *did?*

Margot and I were grabbing tacos at the Gracias Señor food truck in the Palisades on a hot late-August afternoon when I got the text.

Hi. Just saw a post of yours about Nov. 2 1968. You know that's my birthday. What is that? It's weirding me out.

Oh. My. *God.*

Oh.

My.

God.

Oh my God.

I knew Philippe might eventually learn about my soulmate search. But not yet, not now! I had envisioned him stumbling on it later. Much later. Like, right after my plane touched down in Paris. My fantasy was that he'd be so moved by my passionate quest for true love that he would jump on the next flight to France. I pictured him (in first class, of course) telling the entire cabin his plans to break up all my red-hot dates, making friends with the debonair captain and some chic designer from Paris. He'd show up in the lobby of my hotel (it would be raining, and he would be wearing that sexy white shirt of his), profess his undying love, and tell me in thrilling detail exactly how much he had changed. How we belonged together. Forever. Oh, and he would get down on one knee and pull out a fabulous ring. I would happen to be wearing something devastatingly sexy. Of course it would be an excellent hair day (despite the rain). And some ridiculously handsome French guy (with the same birthday) would probably get punched out. (Sorry, Pierre!) Then someone would take a picture of our passionate embrace (a crowd would have gathered by then), and the resulting image would go viral, blowing away even Robert Doisneau's *The Kiss*. Philippe would gaze into my eyes and say with finality in that steamy accent of his, "Natasha, I am your destiny" (or something slightly less cheesy but super-romantic; I was still working on the dialogue). And then we'd have an outrageously fabulous wedding with the chic designer from the plane in charge of my dress and the captain as Philippe's best man.

I'd replayed that fantasy in my head a lot at the beginning of all this. But honestly, when I received Philippe's text that day I had almost forgotten about him. The search had become bigger than all my past romantic failures. It had become about hope, something I hadn't felt in a long time.

"You didn't think Philippe would find your Instagram? You're *so* embarrassing" was all Margot could say as I sat on the taco truck's bumper, shaking.

Hi, Philippe, I nervously wrote. It's a little too much to explain in a text. Can you meet in person?

You have an Instagram to find a man born on my birth date in my city? Why?

It's too hard to text, I typed again. *Shit. Shit. Shit.* Call u in 1 hour.

After lunch, I dropped Margot at her dad's and called Philippe as soon as I got home. I started talking, fast, the second he answered. "This doesn't have anything to do with you. You see, I promised Bob I would meet him and—"

"It doesn't have anything *to do* with me? Seriously, Natasha?" he screamed. "That's *my* birthday! Paris is *my* city! My *mother* has found your crazy Instagram and now I have to explain it to *her*! You've lost your mind. Stay away from my children, my whole family. You're fucking crazy! *Crazy!*" He couldn't stop screaming. I had never heard this side of him before. Sure, we'd had our disagreements over the years. All couples do. But he'd never once sounded like he did that day—like he was sorry he'd ever known me. The velvet voice that used to whisper in my ear now ripped me to shreds, razor-sharp with fury. I tried to explain but Philippe wouldn't let me get a word in. I finally moved the phone away from my ear and then hung up.

He's right, I decided instantly. *What am I doing?* Philippe's angry words reverberated mightily. *Crazy. Crazy. Crazy.* And then a tiny voice inside me commanded, *Give up.* The same quiet voice I'd heard in my head since my dad died but that I'd always found the strength to ignore. The voice I drowned out with *Get up.* Until now. *You are an embarrassment. You're fucking crazy. Give up.*

What was I thinking, searching the world for everyone born on my ex-boyfriend's birthday? And publicly? Holy shit. This was the most outlandish, stupidest idea I had ever had! Had I seriously promised my father I would meet his *ghost* in Paris? That I would "always believe in magic and never give up on love"? What did that even mean? And then I'd told the whole world about it? On Instagram? And Facebook? Oh my God. My father was dead! My father had been reduced to a tube of ashes sitting on a shelf in my kitchen. There was no one to meet in Paris, and most especially not Philippe. Oh, fuck. What had I done? Margot was right. The Facebook trolls were right. Edna was right. Philippe was right. Maybe I *had* lost my mind. Maybe there was no point of destiny. Maybe death was truly all there was. Thank God I'd never told my bosses about this stupid odyssey. There was still time to delete my posts and pretend it had never happened. I opened my computer, but my fingers froze on the keys.

The thing was, I would miss all the people I'd met so far. Would I just stop talking to Fabrice? And Gael? What about the incredible women who had reached out to me? Some of them were becoming my *friends*. Would I just abandon them too?

And if I decided that Stephanie was wrong, that astrology wasn't real, then all the deeply comforting things she'd said about Bob's death weren't true either. Maybe my dad *didn't* feel better after dying. Maybe he *wasn't* by my side. *No.* No, I didn't want to go back there again.

It was time for me to check in with someone who *didn't* hate me. I texted Tara. She was on a much-needed vacation with her family and was as off the grid as possible, but since Dad's illness, we had gotten in the habit of returning each other's texts immediately.

Me: BAD fallout with P today. He found my 02 account.

Tara: Shit. I was wondering when he would find it. What did he say?

Me: He's furious. Called me fucking crazy. Am I crazy? I think I might be. I'm scared.

I stared at my screen, anxiously waiting for a response. I'd had no idea how much this all meant to me until somebody I cared about told me to stop.

Tara: Noooooo. You are not crazy. Why would you think that? Don't let him take your magic. I'm 100% in for Paris. And I'm not crazy either. It's time to get plane tickets.

Me: I don't know. Was I ever really going to go to Paris? It sounds so stupid right now.

Tara: Don't let P get you down. Who cares what he thinks. You're amazing!! Paris or bust, right? YOU named the group chat.

Me: I guess we could try. People go on trips for crazier reasons, don't they? What if my soulmate is waiting for me there and I don't go?

Tara: I said PARIS OR BUST!!

Me: Okay, okay. For Dad.

Tara: For US!

Me: Even better!!

Tara: I need something to believe in. Even if it's just in us being fabulous. We will book the tickets and hotel the day I get back. You and me! Oh, and FUCK OFF, P!

Me: 💕

I put my phone down and looked around my living room. "I know this sounds strange, but to all the spirits here who are not on board with this plan, who do not believe in magic and love, who keep telling me I'm crazy and to give up, I command you to leave."

Stephanie had told me about the dead people in my living room and the voices in my head, and it finally all made some kind of sense. I could choose to listen to the doubts or I could ask them to kindly get the fuck out. "And to all the good spirits—the believers, the dreamers, the lovers—I officially need your help. Pack your bags, ghosties. We're going to Paris!" (Thank goodness the kids were at Michael and Anna's this weekend or they would have thought I'd lost it for good.)

I felt less destroyed after texting with Tara and bossing around the ghosts in my living room. But I wasn't entirely whole yet or totally sure about going to Paris. I needed my best friend. Nicole had a way of seeing the big, beautiful picture. So I wrapped up two slices of the almond cake I'd baked the night before (everything is better with cake) and drove straight to her house, a remodeled 1935 hunting lodge off Mulholland Drive in Beverly Hills. I didn't even bother texting first.

"Bonjour! Who's in for Paris?" I called out as I let myself into her backyard.

Nicole sat by her sparkling pool in a tiny bikini, meditating in the sun. A serene statue of Buddha presided over the Jacuzzi. A flock of her prize chickens (they had names like Mazey, Dazey, Coco, and Lady Dorothy) roamed around the garden, which boasted million-dollar views of the valley below. Nicole, though she too grew up middle class, now had a very different financial picture than mine.

"Me! I'm sooo in! I've never been to Paris! Let's book it *now!*" Nicole bolted up as though someone had jabbed an adrenaline shot straight into her heart.

I laughed and the last traces of the full-body stress reaction I'd had to Philippe's rage melted away. Philippe who?

"This is exactly where you need to put your energy, Tash. I can feel it. *Push* the universe in the direction of Paris with a commitment. Go all in."

Her infectious, sunny certainty was impossible to resist.

I ran upstairs and grabbed a bikini from Nicole's huge stash (if we were going to do this, we both needed a tan, obviously) while she found her laptop and a cold bottle of champagne to go with the cake. Back at the pool, we scrolled through our options. I had naively budgeted five hundred dollars for flights, thinking I could find something in that range on one of the discount travel sites. But Paris is a long way from LA. Nicole, however, wasn't about to let the fizz of our afternoon go flat.

"Tash, I have miles. And, looking at these prices, I'm pretty sure I have just enough for our two tickets. Which means fate obviously meant those miles for Paris."

I insisted she put my five hundred dollars toward the taxes and fees and she did, knowing how I felt about financial independence. We quickly found coach seats next to each other on a red-eye with a tight connection through San Francisco. It would be a long day of travel, but worth it.

Then we had to find a place to stay. We clicked through one enchanting Parisian hideaway after another while sipping champagne in the California sun and finally settled on a boutique hotel in an artsy-looking neighborhood called Le Marais. Hôtel du Petit Moulin's whimsical interiors had been created by the famous fashion designer Christian Lacroix. Our plan was to share a room with double beds, but when Nicole saw the hotel had a junior suite on the top floor with a pullout sofa, she offered to upgrade us at her expense. We could all, Tara included, stay in one room. Like a slumber party. Plus Nicole wanted to ask our dear friend Penelope, who now lived in Ibiza, if she could take a break from her toddler twin boys and meet us for a few days. Penelope's budget was tight, like mine, but we hoped she'd be unable to resist the offer of a free couch in Paris. Nicole clicked the Réserve button. Four days and four nights in Paris, October 17 through 21, 2019, were all ours. I could hardly believe that, in a little more than six weeks, we'd be in Paris. It felt like a dream. I told myself Tara wouldn't mind that we'd gone ahead and booked the trip, that she'd be home in a few days and could easily grab a seat on the same flight.

My soulmate search was *happening!*

"We're going to Paris!" Nicole and I screamed as we toasted each other and posted the announcement on both of our Instagram stories for all the world to see.

Which, of course, included Tara.

I woke up the next morning, a Saturday, to a quiet house and a text from a man named Dev that instantly set my heart racing. We'd been texting for some months now, even though he wasn't born on the right day or in the right city.

As soon as I began the search for my soulmate born on November 2, 1968, outliers popped up on Instagram and Tinder: men whose birthdays were oh so wrong but who were nonetheless oh-so-hot/intriguing/smart that it was nearly impossible *not* to swipe right or strike up a conversation with them (where had these guys been all those years I was dating in LA without my astrological marching orders?). Franz from the South of France in Ray-Bans and a scarf; Joseph, who was born on November 2 in 1966 and who spent half the year in Rome and affectionately called me "the Princess of Hollywood"; Jean-Christian, a ripped Leo who offered to be my tour guide from the minute I arrived in Paris, no matter the day or time.

And then there was Dev.

I'm not exactly sure how I matched with Dev, as he was based in Miami, although he'd lived in Paris years before. He might have been looking in LA, where he occasionally traveled for work, during one of the times I'd hopped off my Tinder Passport subscription out of guilt. Every so often in a swirl of worry about real-life things like rent, my car lease, my Agency dues, I'd have a *What am I doing, I can't possibly be spending money searching for my soulmate across the world* fit and cancel Tinder Passport. That's probably how I met Dev. And we got each other right away. Our first conversation:

Me: Hi, Dev.

Dev: Hi, Natasha. How are you? Help me procrastinate. I'm supposed to be working on book edits and my head's not in it.

Me: Do you happen to have been born in Paris on 2 Novembre 1968?

Dev: Not at all. January 20, 1970.

Me: Time and place, please.

Dev: If you ask for my Social Security number I'm out. I did live in Paris for a few years. But I don't spell November that way.

And so it began. Dev, an artist, was now working on a memoir. I'd found a writer. And a sexy one at that. What started as procrastination for Dev turned into a couple of months of constant texting, FaceTiming, sexting, and, finally, the text I woke up to that Saturday morning: Dev had gotten a plane ticket for *that same day* to come to LA. To meet me in person. That was the only reason he was coming. He didn't have work in the city or friends to catch up with. It was just . . . to see me. Only the day before, Philippe had screamed at me, called me crazy, told me to stay away from him. And Nicole and I had just bought our tickets to Paris. But despite all that, or maybe because of it, I didn't tell Dev I wouldn't see him (it was too late to tell him not to come, even if I had been inclined to do that—he was already on a plane). I liked that Dev wasn't afraid, that he was taking a leap of faith even though he knew all about my upcoming trip to Paris and who I hoped to find there.

A few hours later, as I stood in the lobby of the Avalon Hotel in Beverly Hills, where Dev had just checked in, I thought I might faint from nerves. I couldn't remember the last time I'd had a one-night stand, if that's what this even was. Online dating was so weird. And scary sometimes. But meeting Dev felt like an important trial run for Paris. Was I brave enough to just go for it with a stranger? Could I follow the advice that Colette had given me—to have fun, let go of my rules? Maybe I was also testing Stephanie and astrology. Dev wasn't born on the right date. But there was something about him.

Before I could change my mind, I texted him.

Me: Here.

Dev: Ha. Uh-oh. Game on. Coming down.

Dev, with his magnetic black-brown eyes and warm, hungry smile, put me immediately at ease but also further on edge from the second we hugged hello. It took about two minutes seated at the bar for us to kiss, a shy but electric brush of our lips. I hoped I wasn't smiling too madly afterward. And then another twenty minutes—and a quick glass of rosé—for Dev and me to head upstairs. He held my hand in the elevator, his thumb gently tracing my wrist. I stopped wondering what the hell I was doing and just did it.

It was the end of summer and the AC wasn't working in Dev's room. We were sweaty and naked, and the sex was primal and raw in a way I'd totally forgotten sex could be. If this was what Stephanie meant by getting out there and having fun, then I was game to sign up for more. Lots more.

"You're really nuts," Dev told me. "I like it." This was the blissful opposite of what Philippe had said not twenty-four hours earlier and exactly what I needed to hear.

We ordered pizza, ate it in bed, and then fell back into each other's arms like we were in our twenties and inexhaustible. But I wasn't in my twenties. And that made it delicious too, because I knew there were so many ways this—and therefore Paris—could go. I closed my eyes and tried on different versions of Dev.

First I pretended he was a complete stranger I was fucking at some random hotel. Maybe I didn't even know his name; maybe I'd left all emotions but one downstairs with the valet. A free fall into pleasure.

When Dev was on top of me, I tried on love. I wrapped my legs around his waist, my hands around his biceps, and met his eyes, and I loved him. Just like that. Just for a moment, I imagined a life together, what it would be like to fall in love again, to let someone in again, to open up all of myself to Dev. I saw us trading office war stories, me borrowing his toothbrush, him turning down my music in the car.

When Dev held me, both of us drifting between sleep and conversation, I tried on friendship. It felt good. Solid. And the most real of all. Like a place I could return to again and again.

I left the hotel well past midnight. Dev asked me to stay, but I wanted to sleep in my own bed. "Thank you for showing me it's possible," I whispered before I left.

"What's possible?"

"Anything."

The next morning, Dev texted to ask if he could visit my little yellow bungalow. Margot and Dash would be at Michael's until dinner, and the open house I was supposed to run had been canceled, so this should have been an easy yes. A morning of great sex and hot coffee. But I never had people over other than family and sometimes Nicole. I was ashamed of living in a tiny, rented place with no art on the walls and the kids' laundry piled on the dining-room table. That wasn't the self I was trying so hard to project to clients and colleagues, to my future soulmate.

And truthfully, hiding the reality of where I lived was an old family habit. My parents had done it my entire childhood, renting humble apartments but driving nice (used) cars and wearing designer clothes (bought at the deepest discount) while they tried to come up in the world. And back in Scotland, my mother had never once let anyone see even the street where she lived.

Only two men had been inside my little yellow house: Michael and Philippe. But what if I let Dev in? It could be another practice run. Dev would see where I lived, where I made my breakfast; he'd see Margot's lacrosse gear in the corner and Dash's summer reading forgotten on the sofa. He'd see me. And my vision boards. Honestly, he'd probably notice those first. They were pretty much the definition of in-your-face.

Before I could change my mind, I texted Dev, said yes, and gave him my address.

Not long after that, Dev stood in my kitchen, taking in the Tinder profiles, my birth chart, the maps of Paris, and the photos of Bob. "Wow," he said, not unkindly. "You're certainly committed."

"I am," I replied without embarrassment before pulling him into my bedroom.

We said goodbye hours later on the beach under a blazing sun while dozens of dolphins leaped in the turquoise water before us. An only-in-LA kind of fantasy backdrop. But that's what the weekend with Dev had been—a fantasy. A very sexy one.

"You know, Dev, we didn't fall in love, but we kind of did," I said, kissing his cheek.

I didn't tell anyone except for Nicole about Dev. It wasn't that I'd cheated on my soulmate search; not exactly. It was more that this version of me was so different from who I'd felt I had to be in the past. Did the perfect mom, the perfect potential partner, the has-her-shit-together woman just take a random, one-off sexy leap like that weekend had been? Yes! Yes, sometimes she absolutely did. Sometimes being impulsive is a good thing. But I was still working on owning all of that.

✳ ✴ ✳

"You booked the flights and hotel without me?" Tara asked a few days later when she got home from her trip. I could hear the uncertainty in her voice. "I looked into the Hôtel du Petit Moulin— it's gorgeous, but the carpets and heavy curtains are exactly the kind that trigger asthma attacks. And the Marais neighborhood is supercute, but I thought it would be fun to stay in the seventh arrondissement near the Eiffel Tower. I spent so much time researching Paris. I thought this was *our* adventure. Are you sure you want me to come?"

I felt terrible. I should have waited, gotten Tara's opinion on the hotel, made sure that week worked for her husband and the kids. Of course I wanted her to come. For our dad. For *us*. And Tara was used to leading on our big decisions. I'd followed her to the same boarding school, the same college, into marriage, and then motherhood. And not just because she was my older sister. I consciously *wanted* to do what she was doing when she was doing it. Except now, I was changing in a way I didn't understand. This was different than me being impulsive, different than a midnight run to Don Q's. I apologized again. I hadn't wanted to hurt my sister, but I had.

It took a few days of talking it through, but Tara eventually booked her own flight—a direct one—and a separate room at the Hôtel du Petit Moulin. She said she needed her sleep, but I knew she'd always felt a bit outside of the bond Nicole and I shared. I didn't know quite how to fix that; I only seemed to make things worse. I hoped the charm and excitement of Paris would just magically sort things out. Besides, my ever-capable sister was already sorting things out for herself. She added an extra day to her trip and booked a beautiful hotel—Hôtel Regina Louvre—for her last night in Paris.

"If you can change your return date to the twenty-second, I would love for you to stay with me in my room. Just us sisters. My treat!" Tara offered generously.

A no-brainer, right? But I couldn't bring myself to immediately accept her kind invitation. Just going to Paris without my kids and being away from work when I undeniably needed money big-time was scary. I felt pulled in all kinds of directions, none of them quite right.

With the trip officially booked, I had just six weeks to find as many more potential soulmates as I could before Tara, Nicole, Penelope, and I landed in the City of Light. I had nine so far. If I'd been serious about doing this before, I was hell-bent on it now.

I ordered business cards to hand out to whoever seemed like they might help me. One side of the card featured me holding a 2 Novembre 1968 sign. The other side had my contact details:

Point of Destiny

natasha sizlo

@02novembre1968

I will always believe in Magic. And I will never give up on Love.

Then came a custom T-shirt from Etsy with 2 NOVEMBRE 1968 printed boldly in red across the front. I wore it on repeat around LA as I met with stagers to select a neutral palette of designer furniture for the pop star's listing, an odor-removal specialist to address the lingering smell of smoke, and my handed-to-me-from-heaven painter who would transform the dirty walls into a restful, soft white haven. I even wore the T-shirt when I met with the plumber. (All of our new seller's toilets needed to be replaced, even the talking Japanese one.) Maybe someone would know someone who knew my soulmate.

Finally, after dropping Dash off at school one morning, I decided to go for broke.

"Listeners! What's the craziest thing you've done after a breakup?" Amp Radio's morning DJ blared from my car's speakers. "We want to know!"

Dash had saved the dial-in number to 97.1 in my contacts while he was trying to win concert tickets the week before, and I saw it as a sign. *Maybe the universe is trying to help me,* I thought as my call went instantly through. I explained briefly to the screener about my search for every man born on November 2 in Paris. "They're gonna want to talk to you" is all she said as she connected me immediately to the DJs. And that's how my soulmate search was broadcast all over Los Angeles one bright and sunny morning.

I wasn't shy about asking for help or accepting offers at this point. I texted friends, told all my colleagues; I even sent DMs to media outlets like PopSugar and Refinery29. And I DM'd a bunch of random celebrities I thought would be into it. I was shameless. Why not? If any of them reposted or did a shout-out for me on their massive platforms, it could lead to true love! I had nothing to lose at this point. Of course, none of the celebrities or journalists responded. (Except for the majestic actress Kate Walsh, who reposted my call for all men born in Paris on November 2, 1968. Kate Walsh *is* the coolest.)

The following week at the office, I bumped into Boss Babe Keri, who immediately offered to shoot a promotional video about my search starring . . . *me.* (Promotional videos in luxury real estate are totally a thing, but I'd never made one because mentally I'd be back in kindergarten wearing a purple leotard and a top hat, no matter what.) Ignoring a flutter of nerves, I gratefully accepted and boosted the resulting video on Instagram and Facebook before I could think too much about it. Next, the creative director at the Agency designed professional-caliber posters advertising my search. A sweet new online friend who lived near Paris—Mercedes—volunteered to put them up in the streets and on the Métro before I arrived. I even wallpapered the glass walls of my office with the posters and randomly started taping them up around LA.

And then, like out of a dream, Ellen Kinney, the president of one of my favorite fashion brands, ALC, found my Instagram and offered to *outfit me for the trip.* I had to read her message several times before I took it in. Was this for real? Who wouldn't want a wardrobe of romantic new outfits for a week of hot dates in Paris? An intern bearing bags of going-out tops and flirty dresses arrived at my little yellow house. What a contrast to the twenty black funeral dresses earlier that year, none of which I had kept. A local jewelry brand, La Vie Parisienne, sent a selection of sparkly things. The brand Baacal gifted me a cashmere coat to keep warm. The LA-based French designer Tony Hamdan Djendeli sent me a couture velvet gown to be worn when I found "The One." A colleague gave me a necklace in the shape of a key to unlock love. Someone else gave me fancy French perfume. Each thoughtful gift was unexpected, beautiful, and useful. I saw them as signs that I was embarking on exactly the right journey.

"You're doing what you're supposed to be doing," Nicole repeated over a Reiki session. "This is what being in flow with the universe feels like. You're on your way to your point of destiny."

Nicole must have been right, because I was finding more and more potential soulmates.

Plus Fabrice and I had been texting regularly over WhatsApp. When I told him one night that Paris was definitely a go, he'd responded instantly: You've made my dream true, Natasha.

You don't care that I'm meeting other men with this birthday in Paris? He had to have noticed that part on Instagram.

No. They are only funny, he said. Tell me, how has your day been?

Of course Bob's ashes were coming with us to Paris. Not wanting to lose the golden scattering wand at airport security or in a dim French bistro (something that would surely happen to me), I drove to Remembered Forever Cremation Care to buy a memorial necklace. This time, I told Tara about my plans. Surprisingly, she gave me her blessing and joked that Bob would be like Flat Stanley, the paper-cutout children's character that travels the world. I had phoned my mother and told her I would visit after my errand, but when I pulled up to the mortuary, Edna was standing outside waiting for me in her crisp white trousers, jaunty denim jacket, and large sunglasses.

"Hi, Mom," I said, giving her a quick hug. "Didn't expect to see you here. Everything okay?"

"Why wouldn't it be?" Edna replied as we walked into the mortuary.

Edna trailed close behind me as I browsed the wide array of cremation pendants meant for a smidge of a loved one's ashes: ornate winged crosses, minimalist silver teardrops, diamond-encrusted orbs. Ken waited on us with infinite patience, as always. Finally, I settled on a simple gold heart: Dad and love. Edna elbowed her way between me and the display and said firmly to Ken, "I'm buying the necklace. It's a gift for my daughter."

Before I could protest, my mom looked me in the eye and said, "Natasha, I don't know if I believe in any of this, but I do believe in you." She reached into her bag and pulled out a second, equally beautiful piece of jewelry, a pale pink pointed crystal on a sterling-silver chain. "I think you should wear this beside Bob's heart. It's rose quartz, which, I'm told, attracts love. And you, my daughter, deserve all the love in the world."

"Thank you, Mom," I said. I felt Dad there with us then, and not because his ashes were now around my neck. "How about lunch? I can fill you in on all the cute Frenchmen I've found."

"How's it going?" Billy asked me a couple minutes before the weekly office meeting. We planned to announce the pop star's house that day as a pocket (meaning it would be exclusive to the Agency, not yet on the wider market).

"Fantastic. The painters will be done tomorrow. The house is becoming the stunning home it was meant to be. Cleaned up, it looks like it belongs on the cover of *Architectural Digest*."

"That's great news. And if the seller can crash at his buddy's pool house a little longer while we finish up, we'll be golden. I'll give the biz manager a call today. I think we're going to sell this one in record time. You've done a terrific job bringing the house back to its full potential."

Speaking of potential . . . "Thanks, Billy. On another topic, I guess you've seen the posters in my office?"

Billy grinned. "How could I miss them? I assume there's a story?"

I'd dreaded this conversation for months, and yet here it was, no big deal. Though I still wasn't sure what Billy's reaction would be once he knew the full scope of my far-out plan.

"Sounds like a movie in the making!" Billy said, smiling from ear to ear. "Just make sure I'm played by either Pitt or Clooney. When's the kickoff party? I'm in!"

A kickoff party. I *loved* that idea.

The Boss Babes and my besties helped me organize an anticipation-fueled send-off on the roof of the One Hotel. This time, I had no trouble designing the invitation. And I didn't send one to Philippe. My friends, family, and colleagues showed up to the Sunset Strip soiree in force. Even Michael and Anna came.

At the party, Michael greeted me by asking in confusion, "Wait, *you* have an astrologer?" But Anna, with the giddy enthusiasm of a teenager, came rushing into my arms. "This is *amazing,* Natasha! We're gonna find you a *man!*"

It felt good to hug Anna. My love and respect for the "Evil Stepmother" (a nickname proudly coined by Anna) had only grown stronger as I watched her relationship with Margot and Dash bloom. She was thoroughly invested in my family's happiness. Including mine, as evidenced by her showing up to this party. I was happy for Michael. Anna was a good person, and so was he. Seven years post-divorce, we had come full circle. *We're the lucky ones,* I thought. *It wasn't easy, but we did it.*

They made their way through the party; Michael wrapped his arm around Anna, and she embraced him in return. It was then

I noticed the sparkling diamond engagement ring on Anna's left hand, which was resting on the small of Michael's back. Of course I knew they'd gotten engaged. We had toasted together via Face-Time with the kids. But until that night, Anna hadn't worn her ring in public. Suddenly, I had the feeling that I didn't know what the fuck I was feeling anymore. There's something beautiful and yet bittersweet about your ex moving on so definitively, even years after the marriage is over. The official closing of one chapter pushed up against the blank page of the next. A physical reminder that people and situations change with time, often radically. And that's okay, I realized. I was filled with a profound happiness for both of them. I hoped that I too would be as lucky one day.

The rest of the night was a wild blur. I toasted my friends and family even as I was freaking out about being up in front of a crowd. Honestly, I'd been a wreck on the way over to the party, wondering if anyone would show up. But people did. Maybe it was hard to resist a party in honor of a totally oddball occasion. Or maybe, just maybe, that's what you do for the people you love. You show up. As it happened, the kickoff party fell a few days after my forty-fifth birthday, and for the first time in a long time, I fully, gratefully embraced one more trip around the sun. On the roof of the One Hotel that night, looking around at my friends, so many of us women gloriously in our prime, I felt the blessing of my years. Fittingly, we danced the night away.

Fighting a massive hangover the next morning, I started to pack my bags and coordinate inspections for the pop star's house. Billy had been right about the house being a quick sale. By some mira-cle, a serious buyer had materialized almost instantly and, after just two viewings, had made an offer above ask that the pop star ac-cepted with zero fuss. That almost never happened. But I couldn't focus on my clothes or the appointments. Something tugged at me: Philippe.

I sat down at my command central desk, took Philippe's poem out of my purse, and tacked it to the vision board in front of me. It was time I set a few things straight.

Dear Philippe,

As I'm sure you understand by now, I am on a journey to meet every man I can find who was born in Paris on November 2, 1968. Must sound strange to you. I would like to explain.

What I want you to understand is, everything I am doing right now comes from a place of LOVE. I promised my father I would never give up on love and I would always believe in magic, and that is what I am honoring.

When I started this journey, I secretly hoped it was you who I would find in Paris. I pictured myself sitting at a hotel bar, waiting to meet one of my maybe-soulmates, you walking in, telling me to cut this bullshit, us falling in love all over again and living happily ever after.

I realize now I've seen wayyyyyy too many romantic comedies for my own good. And that, although my love for you is the biggest love of my life, it's not necessarily the last, and it's time to accept that our story is over. And that's okay. We had a good story. A really, really good story. I am grateful for every moment of it.

Which is why it is so important to me that it doesn't end with any miscommunication or hard feelings.

I'm heading to Paris October 16. I always thought we would go there together, you showing me your home, walking the streets with me, telling me stories of your childhood. But, as we both well know, life doesn't always go according to plan. I don't know; I'll probably still look for you in the streets because, well, for better or worse, I will look for you in the streets the rest of my life.

Love,
Natasha

It was raining. I remember because it doesn't often rain in LA. I printed out the letter, folded it neatly into an envelope, and affixed two American flag stamps to the upper right corner to make sure it would get there. I didn't want to send this letter by e-mail. I didn't want Philippe to feel like he was obligated to respond. If he preferred to pretend he'd never received it, that was fine.

Two days later I received a text.

Hi, Natasha. Just read your letter. Thank you for sharing. This is very confusing. I thought LA was a lot easier than Paris . . . But what do I know? I guess you are on your own path. I hope this brings you what you are looking for.

The night before Nicole, Tara, and I left for the airport, I put more wishes into the blue jar:

Someone who's romantic
Emotionally available
Spontaneous
Makes me laugh
AMAZING SEX
Jenga partner for life!!
Dances with me even when there's no music

Sixth House

Coucou

Mercury rules the Sixth House; it casts a vigilant eye on what is needed and points to the most efficient manner by which to meet those needs.

The Sixth House is about small animals, gifts from the earth, and applying energy and intelligence to bring things both desired and needed into earthly manifestation. And since Mercury rules handheld tools, learning, intelligence, and sacred magic, one often encounters New Age practitioners who are oddly practical.

The Sixth House also includes those whom we pay for their services.

The sign of Leo fills my Sixth House. Stephanie says it's important for me to note that the sun is in Libra in my Eighth House of research and pursuits into the unknown. The more mundane aspects of life depicted by the Sixth House will be a bit like the home of the Munsters for people like me with Leo in the Sixth and their sun in the Eighth House. The Munsters are benevolent monsters, a *Leave It to Beaver* family of lovable freaks. Which, frankly, are my kind of people. But did that also mean even the supposedly simplest things in my life would be a little weird?

* ✳ *

I PRACTICALLY SAT ON NICOLE'S LAP IN A FROTH OF NERVOUS anticipation as our plane began its descent into Paris. We glued ourselves to her window, taking in what we could see of the city. Sun glinted off the green-gold water of the Seine. Cream-colored buildings with gray roofs lined streets that, to my eye, all seemed to lead straight to the heart-stopping spindle of the Eiffel Tower. *The Eiffel Tower!*

My soulmate. He's here. I know it.

I had insisted Nicole take the window seat, partly because I knew I'd never be able to sleep a wink, but also because it felt only fair, as her miles were why I was on the plane in the first place. And Nicole had to get some rest—at least one of us needed to be alert upon arrival. Tara, Nicole, and I left for the Los Angeles airport at six thirty that morning, and not only had I not slept well in days, I'd been up the entire night swiping, packing, and posting.

Punch-drunk with exhaustion, I'd bear-hugged Tara goodbye before she headed to her gate. Her direct flight meant she would arrive at our hotel hours before Nicole and me.

"Be good, sister!" Tara said. "See you in Paris!"

Nicole and I waved, giddy. We checked our bags, found our gate, and stopped for a quick breakfast.

"Tell me if you don't want to talk about this, but are you and Justin still on a break?" I said as we sat down at a table with our trays.

Nicole had called a time-out the week before when the "imbalances" (as she'd put it) in their relationship had become too great.

"It's fine and yes, we are. It's good for us. I don't want either of us to get hurt. I told him we shouldn't even text this week so we can recenter ourselves."

"I get it, but are you sure you're okay?"

"Hello, *Paris?*"

I laughed.

"I have an idea," Nicole said then, all seriousness but with that fire in her eyes that let me know *something* was coming. "What I think we should do is steal one of the bedsheets from the hotel and write on it ARE YOU MY SOULMATE?—with the birthday, of course—and then hang it off the side of the Eiffel Tower, kinda like when someone turned the Hollywood sign into the Holly-weed sign!"

"Brilliant! Love that!" We were so totally going to find him.

I had ideas too. I'd printed hundreds of 2 Novembre 1968 soulmate-search posters at my office and stashed the entire stack in my carry-on along with five rolls of clear packing tape and one of the crystals from my dad's bedside for good energy. The bag was now as heavy as a load of bricks. But not for long. Minutes before boarding began, I wallpapered the airport bathroom with my posters. The toilet stalls and baby-changing station were now one big ad for my soulmate. Because what if my soulmate's sister was about to board the same plane or a different one that day? It all seemed so cosmically right. Even though, yes, I was a formerly somewhat sensible forty-five-year-old mom of two who had never before done something like (temporarily) deface a public bathroom. I knew how bizarre my actions might look but I didn't care what anyone thought. No idea that Nicole and I had seemed too outlandish.

As I was flying over the Atlantic, my dad's promise to Tara and me felt closer than ever: I'll meet you there. Bob's voice floated in the air beside me, an otherworldly aural mirage. Our entire cabin was dark except for a few movies playing on tiny screens. Nicole slept. And I was finally on my way to meet my father. I'd missed him so much. I know it sounds out there, but I sensed Bob's spirit hovering just outside the window in the clouds. In the darkness. It was beautiful and overwhelming, too much and yet not enough. I wanted my dad to be able to hug me right then and there. Wishing I had the power to rip away the veil between the living and the dead, I opened my laptop and began writing. Some of my thoughts on love, grief, fear, and hope were for my Instagram diary. And some of what I wrote was just for me and my dad. I'd lost a big life. Embarked on an unconventional quest. I believed that I would find my soulmate, but I was also scared. What if the sparks flew only for me?

We landed at 10:00 a.m. Paris time on a Thursday, nine hours ahead of LA. Bright sunshine streamed through the windows at the Charles de Gaulle airport, and the French language all around us seemed like a subtle song of seduction to my ears. We're here!!! I texted Tara immediately. I refrained from crowing to her about the weather report, which had miraculously changed overnight from days of dreary rain to a week of mostly crisp blue skies. The heavens were obviously on my side. Tara must have asked me a million times before we left if I'd remembered to pack a rain jacket. "It's in my suitcase," I always responded. But no, I had not packed an ugly, practical rain jacket. Who meets her soulmate for the first time wearing black Gore-Tex? In *Paris?* Not me.

We loaded our bags into a waiting taxi and sped off to the hotel, the view slowly changing from the industrial outskirts of the city to the old-world charm of its heart. I couldn't wait to see the Marais neighborhood I'd heard so much about. My dear old friend and former neighbor Andy Fleming had recommended the area to us. As the director of a newly green-lit television series set in Paris that would debut sometime in the next year, he'd already scouted the city for the dreamiest backdrops. In fact, by lucky chance, Andy was also in Paris that October working on the show. I hoped he'd have time to meet up. I saw him as much as possible in LA, but it was never enough, never the same as living next door to him, as I briefly had at the end of my marriage.

I met Andy's assistant first. Michael had just moved out of our house. I was dealing with this new development by standing in my driveway late at night, drinking wine straight from the bottle and chain-smoking cigarettes, as one does. Every window of my house had been flung wide open and Amy Winehouse's "Back to Black" spilled out and down into the canyon. I'd turned the music up as loud as it could go. A nice-looking young woman (who turned out to be Andy's assistant) walked by on the way to her car and asked if I was okay. I laughed darkly.

"Oh, you know. My marriage is over, I'm short-selling my house, my business has collapsed, I'll likely file Chapter Seven, and my sweet Weimaraner's stomach twisted and he died suddenly last week. Good times!" I tossed my butt into the street and waved down my other dog—a tiny Chihuahua-Papillon mix—scooped him up, and continued.

"*But* I let the kids rescue a puppy, this sweetie. By the way, his name is Friday, for the day we got him, which turned out was actually a Saturday, because I suck at dates. And I found myself a superhot French guy. So I'm like five minutes away from living the dream."

The next day, the assistant called Andy, who had recently moved in next door. "I met your neighbor! You're going to like her."

Our taxi driver, who'd been silent for almost the whole ride, eventually asked in bored, halting English what had brought us to Paris. Holiday? Here for work? I'd already told the flight attendants and the currency-exchange clerk at the airport all about my soulmate search. Why not the taxi driver? He didn't look anywhere near fifty, but he might know someone who was. Just talking about my mission with an actual Parisian man *in Paris* felt freeing. Looking back, it's easy to see why. The last few weeks before I left LA for Paris had been a dizzying whirl of thoughtful gifts and positive vibes aligning for this trip, but I'd also been working around the clock and worrying about my bank account, my mom, my kids. Fires raged in the hills, the threat of evacuation ever present for friends and clients. Deep down, underpinning all that, was death. And grief. Those feelings were still an unshakable part of my LA. In Paris, I had just one thing to focus on: letting fate, destiny, and the stars lead me to true love. The driver nodded as I spoke, his general air of annoyance melting away.

"*D'ac,* you have come to the right city," he said with pride. "In Paris, we are in love with love."

"What a coincidence. As card-carrying Libras, we're in love with love too," Nicole replied, delighted.

The taxi slowed, pulled up to a curb, and stopped. I began to see why Andy stayed in the Marais whenever he visited Paris. The neighborhood was the stuff of fairy tales but *real*. Narrow cobblestone streets meandered around lush gardens, Gothic cathedrals, and medieval timbered houses. Museums and art galleries were nestled alongside the trendiest of shops and restaurants. I couldn't wait to explore it all with a 2 Novembre 1968 date by my side. I felt myself falling hard for the city, and we hadn't even checked into our hotel yet.

Speaking of the hotel, where exactly was it? Our taxi driver had unloaded our bags onto the sidewalk and wished us *bonne chance*. The address was correct. But we didn't see anything that looked like a hotel. No sign. No doorman. Nobody with suitcases. Just the extraordinarily charming black-and-gold little *boulangerie* storefront that was originally the oldest bakery in Paris, dating back to the seventeenth century, before the facade was renovated and the larger building housing it became a hotel. According to local legend, the famed writer Victor Hugo had bought his baguettes at this exact shop. I still couldn't believe we were here. In Paris.

There! Nicole pointed to a small white sign hanging above us, just to the right of the *boulangerie.* I squinted. An elegant curlicue script announced HÔTEL DU PETIT MOULIN. Yes! And then I noticed all the tiny, twinkling golden stars affixed to the ornate wrought-iron arm holding the sign. *Stars!* We were in exactly the right place. In through the black-and-gold not-a-bakery door we went.

A centuries-old petite jewel box bursting with color and whimsy—that was the only way to describe the hotel's lobby. We were definitely *not* in LA anymore. Pastoral scenes of a long-ago Paris decorated the ceiling. The walls and moldings were painted a light pistachio, and mirrored panels reflected space and light. White orchids and a glowing crystal lamp graced the check-in desk. And then we noticed the chic bar tucked into a corner, an eclectic mix of furniture both old-world and impossibly hip in shades of cerulean, orange, and forest green. Clearly Christian Lacroix had the same magical touch with interiors as he did with clothes.

Just one person, a young man wearing a quietly perfect suit, greeted us. He started at the sight of our luggage. Nicole and I had at least six bags between us: Two enormous, leaden suitcases we'd had to pay extra baggage fees for. A bulging wardrobe bag. My backpack. Her own overstuffed carry-on. Two purses. And a separate suitcase just for shoes.

"Your room is at the top of the hotel, which is floor three. *Voilà*, the junior suite! Ah . . . do you need help with your bags? I don't believe they will fit in the lift."

Nicole and I glanced at the elevator. It was only slightly larger than a telephone booth.

"Not a problem," I said. "We'll take the stairs. But I do have a question."

"*Oui?*"

Out came one of my flyers. What if someone with the right birthday had just checked in? Even if the concierge couldn't tell me, for privacy reasons, maybe he'd pass my message on.

A confused look crossed the young man's face as he listened intently. "*Je ne suis pas sûr,*" he said politely after he studied the flyer. "Sorry. I don't know. But I will keep this at the front."

We climbed a polka-dotted spiral staircase to the attic suite and opened the door to what would become home base for Operation 2 Novembre 1968. The cozy suite's slanted walls and exposed beams had all been painted cream, and there was a hit of boldly glam wallpaper here and there. The king-size bed with its white linens and luxurious fur throw would do nicely for Nicole and Penelope (due to arrive that afternoon). I decided to take the small red pullout sofa. Penelope, a newish mother, needed a real bed more than I did. Besides, I could already tell from the way my thoughts raced that I'd have trouble sleeping. A bed would be wasted on me. I had far too much to do.

Starting with unpacking. We had to get out of our gross plane clothes and into Paris-appropriate chic, pronto. I spun around the room, staring. One teensy set of apothecary-style drawers that might or might not be meant for clothing. Where was the closet? A door! That must be it. But no. The door led to a gleaming modern bathroom complete with a large soaking tub.

I poked my head out of the bathroom. "Nicole? Do you see a closet?"

"I see this." Nicole pointed to a metal rack with a few lonely-looking hangers.

We called the front desk. "Would it be possible to get more hangers, *s'il vous plait*?"

"But of course. How many? *Deux*? *Trois*?"

I looked at all the clothes spilling from our various bags—and Penelope had yet to arrive. "Definitely more than *deux*. We're gonna need . . . all the extra hangers you got."

I didn't know it, but I'd just had my first lesson in French. The older the building, the fewer the closets. And given Paris's long and storied past, there were plenty of rooms with no closets at all. Like our suite. But it did have the most enchanting dormered windows with deep cushioned seats and glass panes that opened like miniature French doors out onto a dreamlike view of the neighborhood. I swung open a window and peered outside while we waited for the hangers. *Wow.* I'd visited Paris only once before, at the age of nine, and I remembered little other than a double scoop of mouthwatering strawberry sorbet and my father having us all dash madly through six lanes of terrifying Arc de Triomphe traffic to get the perfect shot for a family photo.

I took in the creamy limestone exteriors of the buildings lining the block, the blue-painted window sashes, the flower boxes alive with cheerful blooms. Compact cars utterly unlike the ostentatious motor beasts of LA zipped purposefully along the lane, and well-dressed pedestrians strolled in and out of the shops. But when I finally looked up and out over the buildings, my heart leaped. There was the famed sea-gray horizon of zinc roofs we'd seen from the plane, but much closer now. A postcard-perfect Parisian view. Paris that October was cold and crisp, the kind of weather that woke you up and made you walk a little faster. Sitting in the window, I had that feeling one gets when the season is about to change. Like the world was on the cusp of leaving one thing and stepping into quite another.

After the accommodating concierge brought us every available hanger in the hotel (and possibly some from its neighbors) along with an iron and a luggage rack, Nicole and I tackled our bags. Once we finished, our suite no longer resembled a hotel room. It looked like a well-stocked fashion boutique, one that just happened to feature a giant bed and a mini-explosion of discarded clothes. Rows of sleek heels and sexy boots lined the floor. The bedside tables and the top of the minibar now boasted a glittering assortment of accessories. Dresses, tops, and skirts fluttered on the rolling rack. Nobody could say we weren't prepared. I changed into high-waisted jeans and tall sage-green boots and paired them with an off-white sweater and matching wool coat. Oversize white Celine sunglasses and a snakeskin-print cross-body bag completed the look. Nicole wore a classic trench thrown over a black silk blouse, slim jeans, and heels. We were ready to take Paris by storm.

Just then Tara rang to say she'd returned from exploring the neighborhood, and we went down one flight of stairs to her room.

"*Hiiii!*" We rushed into each other's arms.

Tara's room was smaller than our suite but an equally playful and pretty Lacroix fantasy. It was also extremely tidy. Where were her suitcases? The rows and rows of shoes and bags? How had she managed to keep things so bizarrely neat? "You made it," I said. "Are you happy with your room? It's super-adorable."

"Yes. I called before I arrived and they assured me that this room has less heavy drapery than all the others in the hotel. And it's just been steam-cleaned. My asthma should be okay. But I have a backup with hardwood floors booked at another hotel just in case the carpet—which can't be removed; I checked, ha-ha-ha—triggers anything. All good!"

My sister and I had different definitions of what constituted a *Let's get this party started!* conversation.

"We need an Instagram video together," I said. Tara's shoulders tensed. She still had only her private account with just five followers and no plans to ever change that. I videoed the three of us standing there: "Look at this cute room! So cute, isn't it?"

"So cute!" Tara and Nicole repeated in unison, on cue.

"Say bonjour!"

"Bonjour!"

"I checked out the area this morning," Tara said. "The Picasso Museum is just a five-minute walk from here. How awesome is that?"

"Translation: It's an *hour* walk because we're going to stop and ask any guy who looks even remotely fifty when and where he was born. Plus, I have all my posters to put up," I replied, not entirely joking.

"Right. Did you two read the e-mail I sent about all the historic sites in Le Marais we should visit? We don't have a lot of time here, so I thought we could hit a few museums this afternoon before they close, since Tash will have a bunch of dates this week and today is probably our only free day. How about we grab something to eat and go over it all? We might want to consider buying Paris Fast Passes. They'll give us priority access to more than fifty monuments and museums. We could squeeze in a tiny bit of sightseeing that way."

I glanced at Nicole. Weren't we here to look for love, not at boring old paintings?

Tara pulled out a map and tried to show us the location of a charming café she'd read about. But I wanted to get going. "Let's wander the neighborhood and find a place for lunch that way," I said. "Fate should lead us to where we're supposed to be on the almighty streets of Paris. Because I'm officially handing the reins to the universe!"

It felt good to let go, to say it out loud. I couldn't wait to see what would happen next.

My boots wobbled and caught as we set out on the cobblestone streets. How on earth did people wear heels in this city? I wondered. I considered turning back to get my sneakers but decided against it. I was determined to appear chic because the love of my life could be anywhere at any time. At the newsstand we just passed! Walking out of that adorable little *pharmacie* over there! But had I studied actual Parisiennes, I would have noticed that none of them wore high heels for serious walking. That first day, I saw only the story I wanted to see: Shop windows piled high with fresh baguettes. Beautiful people strolling, cigarettes in hand. Big lacquered doors. A line of yellowing linden trees along the Seine.

We walked the streets of Le Marais, filming every detail. Okay, Nicole and I filmed while Tara remained laser-focused on where it was that we were going. We practiced our French accents. Our smiles. We had endless patience for retakes. I wanted to document it all. Something was going to happen. Something good. I could feel it. I *believed*.

Soon, we stumbled upon a quintessential Paris café, one with a small terrace, round tables, and rattan chairs. We plopped down, famished.

After briefly studying the menu, Tara exhaled and smiled. "I can eat here. The salad with smoked salmon looks delicious *and* gluten-free. I'll just skip the bread."

"A bottle of this Sancerre, *s'il vous plait,*" I said to our waiter, who had greeted us politely with a *Bonjour, mesdames.* I wondered if I should give him a soulmate-search business card. Or maybe I'd see if the café had a community bulletin board. But wine first, love-life marketing strategy later.

My phone buzzed with notifications, questions, and encouragement streaming in from friends and strangers alike. We hadn't been here even four hours yet. The support felt incredible, like angels were on my side.

How's Paris?!

Was your soulmate sitting next to you on the plane?

Is he at the hotel?!

I can't wait to see what happens!

Keep posting! GIVE THE PEOPLE WHAT THEY WANT!

That I could do.

"What's your definition of a soulmate?" I asked Nicole, settling in with my wine and pointing my phone at her.

"I *love* this question!" Nicole sparkled, totally in her element. She lived for the camera and talk of anything even remotely mystical. She sat up straight and cleared her throat. "So, my definition of a soulmate is someone who can meet me on all four levels of my being: the physical level, the emotional level, the intellectual level, and the spiritual level. And if all four of those are going off, it's, like, *incredible.* But it's not just those four connections. A soulmate is also somebody who can compel me to want to be the best version of myself and, like, evolve and grow. And I would do the same for them. I could go on. But that's my definition for now."

"So good," I said.

"What's your definition of a soulmate?" I swung the phone in Tara's direction, putting her on the spot.

She chuckled uncomfortably, then replied, "Puzzle pieces. Click," making a cute little gesture as though fitting two puzzle pieces together.

"You two are the best wingwomen I could ever ask for," I said, posting the story.

"Okay, who is your first date with?" Nicole asked. Tara looked uneasy.

"Well, I haven't set them up *exactly*. I've been slammed these past few weeks dealing with that house Billy and I are selling soon, with any luck. Plus, I didn't know a lot about the neighborhood we'd be staying in or what our schedule would be. I told all sixteen that I would text them when I landed."

My sister deserved a gold star for remaining silent. She had sent me tons of information about our hotel, its exact location, and several proposed schedules before we left.

"What are you waiting for? Start texting!" Nicole commanded.

"Slow down," Tara said. "Who are these guys? Do you know their real names?"

"Don't worry. I have it all right here." I pulled a somewhat tattered paperback out of my purse. On my last night in LA, I had transferred all the critical items from my vision boards into a little book of poetry I already owned: *All the Boys I Never Kissed,* by Nicolette Daskalakis. I'd bought it years earlier, after Philippe and I broke up the first time. The title made me hopeful. Maybe there *were* a lot of boys out there worth kissing that I hadn't gotten to yet. I thought the book might bring me luck in Paris. Using a glue stick, some tape, and paper clips, I'd affixed not just the Tinder profiles and scribbled notes on each match but other things too. Like photos. Bob, of course, on page 1. My besties. Katie. Nicole. My sister. My mom. A fortune-cookie slip printed in green ink: *There are big changes for you but you will be happy.* A map of Paris. Basically anything anyone would need in order to track down her soulmate in Paris. But some of the poems I left uncovered. Like this one:

STAR-CROSSED
You asked me to look at the stars.
I wondered at their beauty and how the two of us were standing next
    to each other in the dark and
        somehow
still
        light
        years

apart

Pleased, I passed the book to Tara so she could marvel at my ingenuity and organizational prowess. Then I pulled up more photos of the fifteen men (and one woman, though it was her dad who might be my soulmate) on my iPhone, and we went over all the possible matches I'd found so far:

1. The Poet—Fabrice

Hot single dad of two kids close in age to mine and one adorable cat named Friday. (Which, come on, I saw as a total sign.) A teacher. His hobbies included writing poetry, traveling, nature, architecture, motorcycles, cooking, and museums. Father French and mother Scottish (!). Parents had been married for sixty-eight blissful years and counting. Romantic. Salt-and-pepper hair, amazing laugh lines, and the sweetest personality.

And of course, we'd been texting for months. Could anyone blame me for putting the Poet first on the list?

"One sec," I said to Tara and Nicole. I put the book down and quickly texted Fabrice.

I'm here in Paris! And staying in Le Marais. Where should we meet? I have until Monday morning.

Whatever Fabrice wanted to do, I was there.

2. The Spaniard—Mateo

Family from Spain, but born in Paris. Now lived thirty minutes outside the city. Thoughtful, curious about me in a nice way. Didn't speak much English. Great full head of hair. But maybe I'd been getting brother vibes? Only a real date would tell.

3. The Sexy Firefighter—Georges

I'd never dated a firefighter, but I'd certainly met some cute ones on the job back home (you'd be surprised how often the fire department gets called in my line of work, and not just because of the actual fires in California). Maybe it was time. No kids. Weathered skin. Aviator sunglasses and helmet in some pics, more than nice-looking without them in others.

4. The Devoted Dad—Maaz

Totally cool with a long-distance relationship (some of the other guys were unsure), lived in Paris. Had an app-development company, worked between Paris and Hong Kong, and the travel made dating a challenge. Two grown kids, involved in their lives. Married nineteen years, alone for ten.

5. The Pilot—Antoine

Sharp good looks, with a shock of white-blond hair. It would be great to have a soulmate with frequent-flier miles. He didn't say much and possibly just wanted to hook up. Great sex with my soulmate was *so* on my agenda, but there also had to be a deeper connection.

6. The Scar Guy—Jean-Luc

He had the right birthday. But in his profile pics, Jean-Luc looked angry. He had a lot of scars and tattoos, which aren't bad things, but Jean-Luc boasted often about his bare-knuckle-boxing hobby and "survivalist weekends" involving knives and fires.

"Hold up," Tara said. "Tash, I'm getting all the wrong vibes here. I don't think you should text that guy. He looks dangerous."

I expected Nicole to vigorously take the other side—Jean-Luc did have a certain smoldering appeal. But she studied his profile and said, "Tara's right. He's not aligned with your energy. I feel that."

One down so soon? I decided to go with it. The universe was guiding me. I crossed out Jean-Luc and continued down the rest of my list.

7. The Chic Writer—Chloe

This was the match that felt the most like fate. A drop-dead gorgeous writer and jewelry designer in her late twenties, Chloe found me after her cousin saw one of my targeted ads. Chloe's dad, whose name I didn't yet know, was born on 2 Novembre 1968, but she needed to check me out first before telling him about me.

8. The Sapiosexual—Benoit

He wasn't anything like the kind of guy I'd considered my type in the past. For starters, I was several inches taller than him. I didn't mind, but I'd found over the years that some guys did. And then there were the numerous shirtless bathroom selfies he sent. So many. He didn't drink coffee, listen to Beyoncé, or believe in marriage. I wasn't sure we'd have anything in common. Most concerning, Benoit identified as a sapiosexual, which I'd had to Google and therefore probably automatically disqualified myself.

9. The Sophisticate—Christophe

A fan of antiques, gardening, and tennis, Christophe seemed a little more polished than the others. Except he kept sending me photos of women playing tennis. Without any explanation. Were they his daughters? Was he part of a tennis swingers' club? I'd find out.

10. The Businessman—Laurent

There was something a little '90s Mickey Rourke about Laurent. Pathologically moody, even, but hard to tell. He had a son in New Zealand who did not speak to him for some reason (*did* I want to know why?). Laurent was in pharmaceuticals and traveled often. A lot of these guys traveled.

11. Mr. Marrakech—Thierry

Not a great communicator but he had a face like Colin Firth's and a body like Beckham's, so I'd decided to keep him on the list. [I'd kept any guy with the right birthday on the list, no matter what, until that first lunch in Paris, when Tara and Nicole made me cross off Jean-Luc. I would have been in trouble if I started looking for reasons to lose some of the matches before then. Because most of these men were not, for one shallow reason or another, people I would have been open to dating back home, I'll admit it. But caring about just one qualification, the birthday, had made me oddly more open. And it simplified things. Either they had the birthday or they didn't. And if they did, I was in.] Thierry was flying back from Marrakech the day before I was to return to LA and thought it might be too difficult to meet, but we'd see.

12. Monsieur Serious—Jacques

Blandly handsome, a lawyer. Never smiled in photos, never swore in messages (uh-oh). No jokes. Was it the language difference? I didn't normally date men without a sense of humor and I wasn't exactly getting butterflies about him, but that's why meeting in person was important.

13. The Documentarian—Max

A passionate fan of travel, excellent restaurants, and good wine. What's not to like? Except I wasn't sure if I wanted to fall in love with another cameraman. I swore I'd never do that again. But Max, who made serious documentaries, seemed like the opposite of Hollywood. Clean eating mystified him; never once did he ask if I'd "seen his work"; and his teeth weren't bleached Clorox white. He even said he liked me as a brunette.

14. The Talent Agent—Alcide

Alcide's hobbies were cinema and work. How was *work* a hobby? His schedule was extremely busy as well as unpredictable, but he said he'd do his best.

15. The Sweet Chef—Gael

Cheerful. Always dressed in T-shirts and fleece, sort of like a happy toddler. Some kind of chef. Loved cooking, feeding people, and parties. If it was true love, I wouldn't mind doing all the dishes.

16. The Bike Guy—Amir

A tech guy, but spent most of his time on a fancy bike. Extremely fit, with the pics to prove it. Funny. No kids, but had been married briefly. Obsessed with cycling and French politics. I could learn to love those things too, right? There was a Lenny Kravitz vibe to Amir, so I was determined to give it my best shot. Plus, let's be real, I could use the tech support.

Our food arrived and as we ate and drank more wine, I texted the men and Chloe on WhatsApp. Mateo shot me a message back immediately. Welcome to Paris! How's eight tonight?

OMG! Was this happening? Could it be that easy?

"Is that too soon?" I asked Tara and Nicole. "Should I make it for tomorrow? I haven't slept, plus Penelope isn't here until five thirty and—"

"Tonight!" Nicole practically shouted. "You have fourteen men and one woman to meet and just four days to work with. What about second dates? Or thirds? Or *sleepovers*? It's a lot to fit in. And

hey, I just thought of the perfect use for Tara's backup hotel room."
Nicole grinned with wicked delight as Tara gasped.

Oui! Great! I wrote Mateo back, reading aloud as I typed. Will
figure out a location and text you shortly.

"What's the best bar for this date? One where we can sit near
you but not so close that it's weird. Do you have a safe word or
signal for us?" My sister had many questions, ones I didn't have
answers to. My stomach suddenly felt a bit queasy.

Tara read the situation instantly. "Don't worry. I did a ton of research. I'll look at my date locations spreadsheet when we're back
at the hotel. I sent you a copy too. But just going by memory, I
think the Little Red Door bar will be perfect. It's a ten-minute
walk from the hotel."

Ping! Fabrice had replied.

My heart is ecstatic. Sunday I am yours in afternoon and I wish for
us someplace romantic. Do you know Versailles? It has a garden I
would like to give to you.

I showed the phone to Nicole. "It's working!" she said.

Oui! Versailles sounds perfect! I typed back to Fabrice. (*Where
the hell is Versailles?*) This was so much fun. Why hadn't I ever tried
dating in Paris before?

I continued down my list, texting the rest of my potential
matches as quickly as I could. Not all of them spoke English. And
my French relied heavily on Google Translate, so there was a lot
of toggling back and forth between apps. I'd just sent a note to
Jacques when a bird flew over my head and slammed into the café's
window with a loud *thwack* directly behind Tara and Nicole. The
glass rattled. We all jumped, even people sitting inside the café. The
poor bird, a fat gray pigeon, lay stunned on the sidewalk for a few
seconds before it struggled to its feet and flew unsteadily away.

"Holy shit! That was freaky! Is this an omen? *Dad?* Is that you?"
I said.

"It could be a message from your guides," Nicole calmly interjected, looking up the meaning on her phone. "A bird hitting a

window is a message that you may need to overcome some difficult obstacles in the near future. This marks the end of a phase in your life, a sign of things improving after a difficult period or an important relationship ending, allowing space for a new person to enter your life."

Oooohhhhhhh.

"Well, it's that or this French bird is just a fucking idiot," Tara said and I laughed. It would all be okay. We were in *Paris.*

Ping! Another text. But this one was from Billy.

How's Paris? The inspections are going great. Buyer is thrilled.

Amazing, I replied, adding a fingers-crossed emoji. Anything could still happen with the sale, but this was looking better than good.

"Listen, I know we all want to get to the Picasso Museum before it closes," Nicole announced as we were finishing up our lunch, "but I have a minor emergency. I need to find a curling iron. Mine totally died back at the hotel. And obviously, my hair can't look like crap in Paris."

Tara's face fell for a brief second before she recovered her smile and gamely agreed to the curling-iron hunt. It's not that my sister didn't understand. She also curled her hair daily, with hot rollers worthy of Rita Hayworth herself (which was the whole point). But if she'd had to choose between replacing her rollers and an extra hour at the Picasso Museum, there would be no contest. *Vive le cubisme!*

It was much harder to find a curling iron in Paris than one would guess. By the time we arrived at the Musée Picasso Paris, just fifty minutes remained before it closed. Located in the grand seventeenth-century Hôtel Salé, the museum's four floors of galleries brimming with paintings, letters, sketches, sculptures, and poetry took my breath away. To breeze through it in under an hour felt wrong. Now I understood Tara's impatience. And yet I had a hard time focusing on the art.

I excused myself and went to sit outside in the museum's

courtyard. Drifting inward, I thought about my date that evening. Would we even be able to have a conversation if his English was as nonexistent as my French? Hopefully, language wouldn't matter. It would be a dream, obviously, if that turned out to be the case. I'd be beside myself with all the good feelings. But would I cancel the rest of the guys? And then invite Mateo back to my hotel with a roomful of women? Go with him somewhere? I made a mental note to remember to wear the sexy lace thong that night. And shave my legs. My head swam. Maybe wine with lunch hadn't been the best idea.

I couldn't help but think about Philippe too. Paris *was* his city. Hearing the French language all around me, seeing men on the street with a way of carrying themselves that seemed so familiar, breathing in the scents of cigarette smoke and fresh bread, I felt like I was wearing a memory of him.

I tipped my face up to the sun, meaning to close my eyes and recharge for a moment, but the Paris sky captured all my attention. It had turned from pale cornflower to the most arresting Tiffany blue. Gold light edged around wispy clouds and I knew there had to have been a famous painter who'd specialized in exactly this version of a Paris sky. Probably one of the museums on Tara's list had the paintings on display. But as far as I was concerned, this real-life, real-time sky was more special than anything in any museum. My brain quieted and my pulse calmed. The boundary between me and the air blurred. My dad's spirit came whispering in just then, a tendril of ease and love telling me not to worry.

"Penelope just landed," Nicole said, coming up behind me and snapping me back into reality. "Tash? You okay? We need to head to the hotel so you can get dressed for your first date. But we have time for a disco nap too. You look wiped."

Back at our hotel, I nearly knocked down the bellman at the sight of Penelope. I wrapped her in a huge hug, realizing in that moment how deeply I'd missed her steadying presence in my life. Nicole had introduced us years ago, when I was still married, and we'd hit it off instantly. Then my world fell apart. Penelope, just a few years older than me but with decades of real estate experience, stepped up in a way that made my desperate second act possible. In order for a new agent to join the Agency, that newbie needs a mentor to supervise all aspects of her first three sales. It's not easy to find a willing mentor. Penelope, then a successful agent in LA, did that for me. We became even closer and I counted her as one of my best friends. When she moved to Ibiza for love I was over-joyed for her, but my heart broke a little too.

Penelope's mouth fell open in awe as she stepped into our suite. "This is insane. I can't believe the clothes you brought!" She dropped her one small duffel bag onto the floor and immediately began flipping through the rack of colorful dresses and curve-hugging skirts.

"I haven't shopped in almost three years. These dresses! I've packed all wrong. Like, *beyond* wrong. Most of my clothes at this point are black, stretchy, and machine-washable." Penelope had been on bed rest for almost her entire pregnancy and then busy with her twins, who'd just turned two. Fashion understandably came last.

"Look around this room, Penelope. Borrow something! Wear anything you like," I said. Her eyes lit up.

"I'm taking you up on that, Tash. Thank you. I love that we're all here. It's a dream for me to be back in Paris."

Penelope's father was French, and thanks to his family, she'd been coming to Paris her whole life. She knew the city, its language, and its men in a way I could only hope to.

"It's the least I can do. Because I'm gonna need your help, P.," I said with a laugh. "For starters, I'm a little lost on some of the texts from my guys. Google Translate only goes so far. I *think* Georges is planning to meet me tomorrow for coffee."

"We'll sort all that out, don't you worry."

Nicole synced her iPhone to the Bluetooth speakers in the room. "What do we want to listen to?"

"My Get Up playlist?" I suggested.

"*Get* Up?" Nicole rolled her eyes. "Girl, you're officially *up*. How about Get *It*!" She fiddled with her phone for a few minutes before "Girls Need Love" by Summer Walker and Drake filled the room with its gauzy R and B beat. "Next up: bubbly." She grabbed a couple half bottles of Veuve Clicquot from the minifridge. "We're gonna need more of these."

Trying on dress after dress, drinking champagne, and dishing with my girlfriends, I felt like I had climbed into a time machine and zipped back to the most fun parts of LA in the early '00s. I must have changed clothes twelve times. I couldn't remember when I'd last been so worked up about a date. At one point, I stood in front of Nicole and Penelope in a skirt, one boot, one stiletto sandal, and no top.

"Which shoe?" I asked.

"Oh my God, you have perfect boobs" was all Nicole could say. "How is that possible after two kids? Like, they are *perfect*-perfect."

I mean, I knew I'd had cute boobs—if tiny ones!—but that was before breastfeeding two babies more than a decade ago; I wasn't so sure anymore. I lived in LA, the land of gravity-defying giant fake breasts. And it wasn't like other women commented on your boobs every day.

"They are soooo cute!" Nicole kept gushing. "Can I touch them? Wait, is that weird?"

Penelope raised her glass in a salute to me and my good boobs. She and Nicole had met years ago as young models in Miami. Nudity did not faze either of them. Or me. I burst out laughing.

"Sure! Touch away. The ladies could use a warm-up for all the action they're gonna get this week."

I eventually settled on an outrageously fluffy angora sweater that just begged to be petted along with a slinky skirt. Heels, of course. Nicole chose a lace-trimmed camisole and black leather pants. But Penelope took our breath away. Dressed in a black-and-emerald-green midi-dress with sexy side cutouts, she'd resurrected her siren self and then some.

"You're one hot mama in that, P.," I said, raising my glass back at her. This was fun. And ridiculous, but in the best way. Why had I waited so long to have silly fun with my friends?

"The dress is magic!" She smiled. "Tash, I love it."

We were *so* ready for the Little Red Door. But first, I thought, I'd better do something for Instagram. I'd snuck a peek at WhatsApp earlier to see if any more of the potentials had replied to my *I'm here!* text. Only Devoted Dad and Mr. Marrakech had, and their answers were vague. I wasn't worried, though. Penelope would help me with texts later. For now, I'd put some more positive energy out there into the Paris universe. Like attracts like—wasn't that the rule of attraction?

"I have no idea how to do this but we're going live on Instagram!" I announced. How hard could it be? Nicole and Penelope were totally in. I took a deep breath and tapped my phone. I told my friends and followers I was just about to head out for date number one, that I was excited. Hopeful. We posed and toasted. And then Tara popped her head in our door.

"Oh my gosh! It's my sister! Tara, say hello! You're live!" I turned the phone toward Tara, who now had a look of horror on her face. She shook her head slightly, put her hand up, and backed out quickly as she mouthed, *See you downstairs.*

My sister. She was funny. I wondered briefly why she hadn't joined us to get ready. But maybe that was for the best. I was pretty sure she would *not* have been into Nicole admiring her boobs.

Tara was sitting quietly in the lobby, studying a map and marking it with a highlighter, when the three of us came clattering in. *Click-clack, click-clack.* Nobody could miss Nicole, Penelope, and me. Though we tried our hardest to look quintessentially French, we were undeniably LA with our sky-high heels, snakeskin bags, sculpted eyebrows, and blonder-than-blond hair.

Tara smiled and stood. She too looked stylish, though oddly sporty. Ready for the kind of action that had nothing to do with hot French guys and trendy Parisian bars. She had a functional cross-body bag strapped on tightly to protect against pickpockets, and she wore shoes made for running, the ones I knew she'd specially ordered because they fit her orthotics.

"Okay, ladies." I pulled a bundle of business cards out of my coat pocket. "I have plenty more cards upstairs, so feel free to let me know when you need to restock." Penelope and Nicole each took a thick stack.

"What *are* these?" Tara asked.

"My soulmate-search business cards. To hand out tonight. I need as many people on the ground helping me in Paris as possible."

"You can't be serious. There is no way in hell I'm handing out business cards or talking to strangers." She peered at the card in my hand. "Is this your picture, Instagram, and *phone number*? This isn't safe! You're going to get kidnapped!"

"Oh, come on. It's fine. What's the worst that can happen?"

"What? You don't want me to answer that. I have a whole spreadsheet of all the things that could go wrong."

"You're freaking me out, sister. You don't have pepper spray in your bag, do you?"

"No! Though I'm starting to wish I did have some."

"I'll loan you my pineapple vagina spray. We'll fight them off with a tropical blend," I said with a wink. "Relax, Tara. It's all going to work out."

"Your pineapple spray made it past customs?" Tara's voice softened with a giggle. "Ahh, the French." She'd realized she couldn't win this fight—not tonight. Resigned, Tara accepted the soulmate-search cards and we pushed our way out the door.

"You do remember that spray is not gynecologist-approved, right?"

"It's a *joke*!"

Tara and I walked arm in arm down the street, a little ahead of

Penelope and Nicole, the shops and restaurants aglow all around us. I felt shaky. And excited. Overwhelmed. What did I know about Mateo, a Spaniard whose mother happened to be in Paris in the fall of 1968? Not much, but the stars were on our side, weren't they? I pulled out my phone and began recording. "Oh my God. I'm *freaking* out! We're on our way, I'm meeting this guy for the first time. My sister and girlfriends are going to be incognito in the bar somewhere close." I turned to Tara. "What am I going to talk to him about? Just 'Hi. Is November 2 your actual birthday? Are Scorpios really the bad boys of astrology?'"

"I don't know about that. How about 'What do you do? Who are you? Are you creepy?'" Tara laughed nervously.

Destiny, here I come.

Seventh House

Bonjour, Are You My Soulmate?

The Seventh House rules relationships and other people; marriage and partnerships. It asks us to shift away from the self and orient toward a partner or partners with the purpose of creating or achieving something greater than we could alone. Since I was born with an empty Seventh House, the key is to understand its ruler. The planet that rules the sign on the cusp of a house is its ruler. I have Virgo on the cusp of the Seventh House. Mercury rules Virgo.

Mercury is in my Ninth House of adventure, teachers, spiritual guides, purpose, foreign lands, and the pursuit of truth. It tells me how to unfold my story and also how to share my story. Mercury coincides with Scorpio in my Ninth House, and this energy floods my Seventh House of partnerships. Mercury and Scorpio push me to choose a spiritual path toward the greater truth of my story and my eventual partner in marriage or otherwise. This path had to include an adventure to a country foreign to me, and that adventure would be one ignited by a spiritual guide, according to Stephanie. Also: Nicole signed up for this trip a (very) long time ago. Our charts are almost identical.

* ✳ *

"DOES MATEO HAVE ANY IDEA THAT YOU'RE BRINGING ALONG a group of women who might be videotaping him on this date?" Tara asked. She'd been worried about permissions.

Mateo did *not* know about my sister, Penelope, or Nicole. But I wasn't going to think about that now. I had far more pressing concerns. Like what if this "romantic bar" Tara recommended turned out to be a brightly lit café conveniently located next to the Préfecture de Police de Paris? I wouldn't put that past her.

But the Little Red Door, a speakeasy tucked away on a quiet street in Le Marais, had me at bonsoir. A line of understated but dead-chic people waited to get in. They looked nothing like the plumped and trussed clubgoers in LA. A handsome, muscle-bound bouncer sat at the door. With so many people trying to get into what seemed like a Prohibition-era hole-in-the-wall, how would we snag the two strategically placed tables that I needed for this date? I bit my lip anxiously. Tara began fiddling with her cross-body. At least Mateo wasn't with us. He'd texted that he was running late, which gave us time to figure out a plan. We inched our way to the front of the line, my pulse quickening with each step. Finally, it was our turn. The bouncer looked us up and down. Tara and I began speaking over each other.

"We need two tables, please."

"A cute romantic one with perfect lighting for me. And not so loud that I can't hear my date."

"Plus another nearby so I can keep an eye on my little sister in case this guy's a serial killer, but not so close that we scare him off."

"Because he might be my soulmate. At least, according to my astrologer."

"But I don't want her to die finding out. Neither does Penelope or Nicole. They'll be here in a few minutes."

The bouncer rolled his eyes, thoroughly confused. "Eh, *répéter?*"

It was clear we had to slow down if we wanted this guy to help us. I took a deep breath and explained all about 2 Novembre 1968. A few people behind us came closer, listening intently. The bouncer pulled out a cigarette, snapped his finger against the flint wheel of an old Zippo, and looked me straight in the eye, skeptical.

"You flew here all the way from America to meet a stranger with a birthday? And astrology? Why not come to Paris to simply find love, whatever the birthday? Open your eyes. *Cueille le jour.*" He tapped his chest, perhaps throwing his own hat into the ring. He had a dark, brooding Marlon Brando vibe and looked to be roughly the right age, so I asked the bouncer for his birthday.

"This is real," I said, handing him a soulmate-search business card, "and I have to find him."

The bouncer, whose birthday unfortunately was not a match (though he was born in '68; I was getting good at spotting men of the right age), stared at the card, turning it over and back again. Then he looked up at us and his face cracked into a wide grin.

"I've never heard such a story. And I see people look for love night after night. Or something like it. Wait here." He tossed down his cigarette and rushed inside.

I passed out more cards to the people in line with us, all of whom were asking questions, wishing me luck, and following me on Instagram right there. Within five minutes, it seemed everyone in the line was invested in the evening's outcome.

The bouncer returned to the door and said he'd moved some patrons so that I'd have the romantic corner table and Tara, Nicole, and Penelope would be visible but not obvious. "And when your man gets here, I will make sure he's *cool*. I'm an ex-bodyguard, so don't worry." Ex-bodyguard? Tara was now officially this guy's biggest fan. We followed him into the cozy interior and through a maze of small tables. LA bars were cavernous by comparison. In my unfamiliar layers and heavy coat, I felt like a rhinoceros in a dollhouse made of glass; I was sure I'd knock something over and then of course I did: someone's champagne coupe. My cheeks burned. I was so clumsily American, and I couldn't even apologize in proper French, though I tried. The man whose drink I'd spilled graciously refused my offer of a replacement and seemed oddly amused. It was then I noticed the curious glances, encouraging nods, and knowing smiles from most of the staff and customers— the chicest group of twenty- and thirty-somethings I'd ever seen. A few of them even raised their glasses to me in silent toasts.

I realized that our new bouncer friend must have told the whole bar what we were up to. Strangely, I found I didn't mind the stares and smiles. The vibes were all good.

The bouncer sat me on a petite red velvet sofa tucked into a quiet nook, a swoon-worthy setup for any date. *Is this the scene where I fall hopelessly in love? Please let it be.* Next he installed Tara at a large table across the room all by herself; the two of them talked conspiratorially before he went back to his post at the door. She was too far away to hear me, but she could see me perfectly. Tara waved excitedly and gave me the Sizlo thumbs-up. I smiled back weakly. A text from Mateo arrived: Almost there, looking for parking. *It. Is. Happening.*

My phone buzzed, beeped, rang, and flashed constantly with questions from my LA friends and so I posted an update, the briefest of stories on my Instagram. "I'm here at the bar waiting for potential soulmate number one," I said as quietly as I could while still being heard. "So nervous! And excited." And then I shoved the phone deep into my bag. I couldn't have Mateo thinking I was one of those phone-obsessed people, unable to focus on the moment. That would be a terrible first impression. Penelope and Nicole arrived and blew kisses at me, then greeted Tara and sat down. More people filed into the bar, making it harder to see my life-preserver sister and friends, but I knew they were there.

I felt like I waited forever for Mateo, but it was probably less than ten minutes. People chatted all around me, catching up, ordering cocktails, falling in love. Mostly in French but some English too. Then, suddenly, the sea of strangers standing near my table hushed and parted. The bouncer appeared with a tall, well-dressed man by his side. "This is Mateo," he announced as he adjusted his herringbone cap and scrunched his face like he wasn't sure if he approved. "I'll be checking on you."

Mateo looked just like his photo: salt-and-pepper hair, bright blue eyes, a quietly gentle face. I stood as he approached and we gingerly said our bonjours.

Mateo leaned forward, touched both my cheeks with his own, and made a kissing sound in the air. My first official French kiss with a man born in Paris on November 2, 1968, who was *not* Philippe! It wasn't the steamy kind of French kiss, but it was a start.

"I'm sorry I'm late, I don't know this area," he managed. "And my English, I'm sorry. It's no good." Mateo glanced hesitantly around the room. *Oh! He's nervous too.*

"Your English is perfect," I said, trying to put us both at ease. "I can't thank you enough for meeting me. *Merci beaucoup!*"

It was an awkward beginning, as many first dates are. Only my date with Mateo was on another level. On first dates back home, I observed the same rule that many of my fellow Los Angelenos did: I'd drive twenty minutes, max, to meet someone (the city's stultifying traffic meant dating by zip code was just what most people did to stay sane). But I'd flown across the world for Mateo. I peeked through the crowd and saw Tara, Nicole, and Penelope contorting their bodies and craning their necks to get a look at him. At us. As were some other people now seated with them at their table—three decidedly handsome men. *Who were they?*

"The drinks here look amazing," I said, focusing on Mateo, trying to get my flirt on. *He could be my soulmate!* "But I'm a Libra," I continued, touching his forearm gently, "so I'm having a hard time deciding. Though, uh, Libras are also hopeless romantics, so maybe that cancels out how indecisive we are."

"Quoi?"

I wasn't sure if Mateo had understood anything I'd said. The bar rang with laughter and the sound of clinking glasses. It was hard to hear. I knew I'd spoken too quickly and too much. I worried Mateo would think I was a complete basket case, and who could blame him? I couldn't remember if I'd brushed my teeth after lunch. What if I had garlic breath? Or stinky-airplane breath? Mojitos. I'd order mojitos with lots of mint for us both. *You got this, Natasha,* I told myself, subtly adjusting my sweater in a way that I hoped would reveal some cleavage. But instead, tiny puffs of angora wafted into the air like dandelion fluff, and Mateo sneezed. This was absurd. My date gazed at me, puzzled. Then he pulled a small piece of paper out of his pocket.

"It is, how do you say, my *l'acte de naissance,* my paper of birth?"

I couldn't believe it. "You brought ID?" The sepia-colored paper in Mateo's hand was old—fifty years old, to be exact. It had long been folded into four equal squares; its creases and edges were crumbling with wear. Mateo carefully unfolded the document and offered it to me. I couldn't help thinking of my dad. *Just make sure you check ID,* he had told me. I touched the heart pendant around my neck. *I love you, Dad.*

"This feels like a dream," I said, studying the document. "You are so thoughtful to bring your birth certificate. Thank you. And thank you for meeting me in person for this date. I know it must seem strange."

"Yes, it's strange." He laughed. "Can you explain it to me?"

And so I did. The whole thing. Slowly, so he could understand. We settled in, ordering a second round of drinks. Mateo was just so *nice.* I began to feel more comfortable. This was okay. I wanted to remember him exactly, and almost before I knew what I was doing, I retrieved my phone and filmed us for a few seconds, somewhat to Mateo's surprise. But he went along good-naturedly. Understated, soft-spoken Mateo didn't have much in the way of game—not like the kind I was used to in LA, at least. He seemed like a guy who would be happiest behind a desk in a library with a steaming cup of tea at hand.

"I was so surprised when I saw your profile, you holding a sign with my birthday. It felt—I couldn't believe it. It was like you found me," Mateo said when I finished explaining how I came to be sitting across from him at the Little Red Door.

Mateo was thoughtful. Warm. Open. He told me about his family, who lived in the Basque region of Spain. His English was awful and my French nonexistent. "Have you ever been arrested?" I finally managed, remembering the French phrase Colette taught me. "*As-tu déjà été arrêté?*" He laughed and looked confused.

"No, not yet." He smiled. "Are we many?" Mateo asked. "Are you meeting with more men with this birthday?"

"A few."

"Ah." The look in his eye told me he understood.

Mateo was a thoroughly decent man, but no electricity crackled between us. No magnetic pull like . . . I didn't want to think about him, but I couldn't help it. It wasn't like it was with Philippe.

"Do you have friends in Paris?" Mateo asked.

"Yes! They are sitting across the bar. Right over there! Want to meet them?"

I grabbed Tara first, then Penelope. Mateo visibly relaxed when she spoke to him in fluent Spanish. Nicole came over too. Mateo chuckled softly as he took in the four of us. It was clear the date was over, and although I hadn't met my soulmate, I'd at least made a friend. We left Mateo at the table, our goodbye short, sweet, and sincere.

"I'm happy we met. And I hope you find him, Natasha," Mateo said, kissing me again on both cheeks in parting.

"He's *cute*," Tara whispered in my ear.

"But probably not The One," I whispered back. Then, noticing her jewel-cut martini glass with a sprig of pink flowers: "Um, what are you drinking and who are those adorable guys at *your* table?"

Tara lit up. "Taste it. The bartender said it's infused with *magic*." She laughed. "And talk about fate! Your bodyguard bouncer sat these guys down with us and one of them was born on November second! For real!" I eyed the dark-haired stranger at the end of the table. "Okay," my sister whispered in my ear, "so he was born in

LA, not Paris, and in 1986 not 1968. But maybe destiny is dyslexic! And directionally challenged! He *is* supercute. And how cool is it that he's from LA too? You wouldn't have to move anywhere."

I wasn't sure if Tara was under an actual magical spell or simply jet-lagged and drunk. I smiled at my possible dyslexic destiny and made my way to the table.

"Your sister gave me your business card with my birthday," he said, grinning at me. "This is weird. I've always wanted the perfect meet-cute. Which is something I've never said out loud. But, my parents had one and . . . yeah." He stopped talking and blushed, hard.

I stared in disbelief at Tara. *She* was handing out my business cards now? But I wasn't surprised that this stranger had instantly confessed to secretly wishing for a meet-cute and a happily-ever-after. Though each man, correct birthday or not, that I'd connected with so far on this search was unique, there was one thing that almost all of them had in common once we'd made it past the pleasantries (having a batshit mission makes it much easier to get real, oddly enough): They wanted to find true love. Wanted it desperately, in some cases. I hadn't expected that vulnerability from men when I started this. It gave me hope even when the match wasn't right.

The guys at my sister's table were friendly and funny, but they were also young enough to own hoverboards. It was time to settle the tab, grab a late bite, and *finally* head to bed. I'd been awake for more than twenty-four hours at that point. We said good night and thanked the accommodating bouncer. He leaned against the door, a mischievous glint in his eye.

"Your date. Obviously, he is not your Prince Charmant. Perhaps I am the better man and you should all come back again sometime!"

"Maybe we will!" I replied gaily. Paris was proving to be just what Stephanie had promised: fun.

Outside in the street, Nicole insisted on filming a recap for Instagram. She pointed my phone at me. "So, Natasha, is he The One?"

"I don't think so," I said wistfully. "He was sweet, though."

"Right," Nicole chimed in. "What we have learned here is that the birthday is not everything. If it were *only* about the date, then you would have immense chemistry with any person who had that date. So the date is part of it, but it's not the whole thing. There are many other elements. Any serious astrologer would say we need these guys' exact times of birth, for starters. But I see this as the nature-versus-nurture conundrum. What truly makes us who we are? Astrology is one map of our incarnation in one lifetime, but that incarnation is also influenced by our early childhood conditioning and how we choose to respond to our individual circumstances. It isn't just the stars and planets that dictate our destiny."

"Date number one is done," I said to my friends back home. "Wish me luck for date number two tomorrow at lunch."

"*Déjeuner d'amour.*" Penelope smiled, linking her arm with mine.

"Who's tomorrow's lunch date with?" Tara asked.

"Destiny," I said. Which was true. There were still thirteen guys plus Chloe on my list.

Back in our little attic suite, I pulled out the sofa bed and accidentally smacked my head hard on the low ceiling's slanted beams. *Ouch!* But I didn't care. Nothing could ruin Paris with my sister and best friends. I changed into pajamas and grabbed my phone. First I checked in with the kids and Edna. All good. Then Tinder, Instagram, Facebook, WhatsApp, and e-mails needed my attention. There were dates to set up, friends to fill in. I somehow had almost three thousand followers now, and that meant something to me. Of course I knew a social-media professional would find that follower count hilarious, to say the least, but I didn't think of the people following me as numbers. They were (and are) real people and I didn't want to go dark on any of them. Not when they'd been so unexpectedly supportive for months, checking in and cheering me on. But as the night wore on, I felt myself both there in the moment and also online in a surreal and overwhelming way. I swiped, typed, texted, scrolled, and, eventually, fell into a fitful sleep.

Penelope slipped out for a long solo walk hours before I woke the next morning. Tara too; there were countless monuments and museums on her lists. She would meet up with us later. Sleep, her text read. That was a big night.

I glanced over at the bed. Nicole hadn't moved yet, so I turned back to my phone. Maybe some of the potential soulmates had answered overnight. I needed to set up a lunch date, a coffee, and a dinner. Bring it on, universe! I crossed Mateo off my list, but even though he wasn't The One, our date had taught me something important: *I can do this.*

I checked WhatsApp. Antoine, the pilot with clean-cut good looks, had replied. True, just Hey, but that was a start.

Hi back! Could you meet for a coffee or even lunch today in Le Marais? I typed.

No.

When are you free?

Where.

In Paris. I'm in Paris. I'm staying in the Marais but could meet for coffee anywhere.

Not interested in coffee.

Maybe a drink later in the day? An *apéritif* at Bar Hemingway? Or we could go for a walk along the Seine?

Not interested.

You don't want to meet to talk? To get to know each other?

My sex is very thick and measures 22 cms would you try to taste it?

Wow. Right to the, ah, point. So Antoine did just want a hookup. Which definitely had a certain appeal; I won't lie. But I also knew my soulmate would want more. I was here for that, damn it, not just random French D.

No. No, thank you. I'm pretty sure we're not soulmates. Wishing you love and light and all the things!

He typed for a few seconds. Then—nothing.

I crossed Antoine off the list in my notebook. Mateo and Jean-Luc had been scratched out too. Three down, thirteen left. None of the others had replied yet to last night's texts. Maybe they were still waking up or busy getting ready for work. They'd get back to me soon. I wrote again to my favorite—Fabrice, aka the Poet.

My friends and I went out last night. Wished you were there. Can't wait for Sunday.

As much as I believed that I'd shortly (possibly even within the hour) have more dates than I could juggle, just waiting around for the men and Chloe to reply didn't seem like the wisest plan. Not when I had only three full days remaining to work with. I thought about where most of my Princes Charmant had come from: Tinder. What if I looked for my soulmate on Bumble too? Couldn't hurt. The app was already on my phone; I'd used it in LA before. Katie had set it up for me while we were bored out of our minds looking for "hot smart guys" at a Book Soup event. *Okay, Bumble Paris. Let's see what you got.* I reviewed my old profile, swapped a couple blond photos in, and adjusted my description to reflect my soulmate search. Then I checked my date filters and, like a flash-bulb, something Margot had said a few months ago popped into my head.

She'd just come into the kitchen for a study-break snack and saw me pinning something new to my vision board. Probably one of my potential matches' Tinder profiles.

"Mom. You do realize your weird astrologer only mentioned the date and place, right? Have you ever considered that maybe your soulmate is *not* a guy? Like, love is love. What if your soul-mate is a woman? Or nonbinary? Are you open to that?"

When Margot asked that question, I still believed that my soulmate would probably be more like Philippe than less. Also, let's be real. I'd only ever dated men in a serious way. But when I thought about it that morning in Paris, I realized I *was* open to meeting a woman as my soulmate. I didn't know yet how my search was going to work out, but I had learned one thing from letting go of looking for love in all the same-old, same-old ways: My dad was right. Anything was possible. If I found a woman with the birthday, maybe we'd be like sisters. Or best friends. Or maybe something more. I opened my heart to the universe and began swiping on *all* fifty-year-olds who, regardless of gender or sexual identity, might possibly have the correct birth date.

I also DM'd Chloe again. We were destined to know each other. I could feel it. Though she had yet to commit to so much as a coffee, saying she was a little unsure about meeting a stranger with a mission like mine.

Then I roused Nicole by pointing my phone in her face and recording a video. "Good mor-*ning*," I sang brightly.

"Noooooooo," she replied, pulling a pillow over her head. Even my always-camera-ready bestie needed a minute in the morning before I began rolling tape.

My phone buzzed. Could it be Fabrice or Chloe? No— Penelope had sent a selfie. Fresh-faced and wearing a cute striped top on the streets of Paris. How did she look so awake so freaking early? Let's all meet at Verlet in an hour, her message read, with the location attached.

A photo from Tara arrived immediately after Penelope's. My sister glowed with contentment inside an old chapel. Lighting a candle and saying a prayer. See you there soon.

Nicole and I needed to get moving, fast. We curled our hair and threw on sneakers (we'd learned), and I shoved a thick sheaf of soulmate-search flyers into a bag. Outside the hotel, I immediately began lifting cars' wipers and placing my flyers on windshields.

"Let me help," Nicole said, taking a stack, and we moved quickly down the line of Citroëns and Vespas. Soon, the streets were papered with my soulmate's birth date and birthplace. COME FIND ME, IT'S OUR DESTINY black-and-white posters read, some in French, others in English. We couldn't stop smiling. Or taking pictures. Or talking to people who walked by about my search. I was sure someone would tell me I was straight-up *insensée,* but not a single person did. One young woman who stopped to read my posters said to me, "All three of my serious lovers have been the Taurus sign. Two is a coincidence. But three? I think there is something to it."

By the time Nicole and I made it to Verlet, a bustling, charming, centuries-old café, Tara and Penelope were already seated. I'd been looking forward to visiting this particular café, as Penelope's aunt, of the famed Verlet family, had once owned it. Being there with Penelope made me feel connected to the city, as if I were somehow more than just a typical tourist. *I could get used to belonging in a place like this.*

And I could get used to dining in Paris with Penelope. Her fluent French made everything easier. Including deciphering texts from Georges, who rarely wrote in English. Was he meeting me this afternoon like I'd thought? I showed her my phone. She laughed.

"Natasha, dear Georges lives in Provence. He will need to take a train to Paris. That's what he's trying to tell you. He wants you to pick a time for tomorrow."

"Where's Provence?"

"About four hours south, maybe a little more, by train."

So Georges wanted to do this. A four-hour train ride was a commitment. I liked the sexy firefighter even more for that.

"P., what would I do without you? Thank you. Let's tell him three o'clock tomorrow. Oh, wait. No. It should be a glass of wine instead of a coffee. It's more romantic. Five? Yes, five. Ask him if that works, please!" This was so exciting.

Penelope tapped away for a minute and then handed me my phone. *"Voilà,"* she said. "When he writes back, let me know."

Gael had messaged to say he would love to show me his restaurant that afternoon, and Thierry thought a late dinner could work. Both said they'd confirm soon. And I had several other men to hear from. Plus Chloe. So far, so good.

"Is it okay being back at Verlet?" I asked Penelope.

She stirred the foam on her cappuccino. "You know, I was wondering if it would be as I walked here this morning. But the story has unfolded in a lovely way. I have an ending now. A happy one."

Paqui, as everyone called Penelope's Paris aunt, the one who'd owned Verlet years ago, had doted on her niece. She'd forever promised Penelope that if she spent her junior year of college in Paris, one of the apartments above the café would be hers. Penelope gratefully accepted, but only months before she was to arrive, Paqui died of cancer. Her uncle had a lover (as the French do), and it seemed he no longer especially wanted a non-rent-paying relative of Paqui's in the apartment. Perhaps the memories combined with even a slight financial strain would make it harder for him to move on. But Paqui had promised, and so Penelope stayed for an indelible year, learning the city of her father, grandparents, and aunt as only a resident can. Still, her uncle and his lover made things awkward from time to time. Not enough to ruin Paris, not even close. But it was unsettling to feel even slightly unwelcome. Whenever Penelope traveled to Paris in the decades that followed, she had avoided Verlet. Until that October morning, almost thirty years later.

Penelope spoke with warmth of the cousin she'd reunited with—Paqui's son, who still lived across the street; how about that!—before we joined her. She'd learned that her uncle (not in truth a bad man, just sad at the time) had long since passed on, and the café had been sold to a company devoted to preserving its legacy. Minute by minute, Paris was returning an essential piece of Penelope to herself, reviving the long-ago young woman figuring out who she would be in the world and reconciling her with the tired but grateful mother and businesswoman she was today.

"Awww. I love this story, Penelope. It's like you're here picking up a trail of bread crumbs. Integrating misunderstandings and re-claiming pieces of your former self," Nicole said.

We took a photo of the four of us standing outside Verlet, Penelope at the center embraced by her friends. Tara suggested we map out a specific plan for the afternoon, one that included museums and monuments, but any of my potential dates could answer me at any time, and then we'd have to be off to meet him. Was it worth it to buy tickets or wait in a line? We settled on just walking the streets. It seemed like the most practical solution. Penelope and Tara led, Tara recounting historical details of the city and Penelope chiming in with her memories. I heard them say "Louvre" and "Tuileries." But I had no clue where we were headed. Honestly, I didn't care. All of Paris was equally fabulous to me. Mostly I was concerned with WhatsApp. Because what was going on? None of the guys still on my list, not even Gael or Thierry, had confirmed a date for today yet. Was it going to be harder than I had anticipated to set up actual dates? If that was true, then I had no time to waste. I could message these guys and sightsee at the same time, right?

First up: Max, the documentary maker, the one who described himself as a fan of travel, good restaurants, and wine. I love history and countries, he wrote to me in the days before I left LA for Paris. I love nap and make love.

Me too! I'd shot back. I mean, let's be real, who doesn't love *The Crown* followed by great sex and an afternoon nap? Throw in some pizza and I'd be his for life.

I messaged Max, trying not to bump into my sister, who was going on about some famous French sculpture nearby that she hoped to find because it had reminded her of Dad when she read about it.

Coucou, Max, I typed, proud of myself for properly using the informal French expression for "hello." Sorry to keep messaging you. Can you meet for a drink today?

Hi, Natasha, I work in Deutschland all this week and next too. ☹
Fuck.

Oh no! So sad! I thought we would meet!

Yes, me too, but my company changed my schedule. How long do you stay in France?

I leave on the 21st. Monday.

You only stay so short a time? ☹ Please send me a picture of you in Paris.

Shit! Four crossed off the list. Shit, shit, shit.

"Tasha. We found it! Look at the sculpture. It's a huge golden thumbs-up! Like Dad. Joe Cool! Get off your phone and look up." Tara tugged at my sleeve.

"I'm sorry, what? Tara, just give me a minute. I can't look right now. I'm freaking out a little bit here." I never did see the golden thumbs-up. I walked right by it, blind with the first inkling of something that felt like the opposite of magic.

My phone didn't stop. Texts and DMs were piling up by the second and none of them were from the men I was supposed to be meeting or Chloe.

Date number two??? Details, please!

Did you find him?

Do you have a date tonight?

And so on.

"What's up?" Nicole asked, picking up on my concern.

"I don't have any dates, Nicole. All my potential soulmates are theoretically so close by . . . it's weird. I came all the way here, but I'm not sure if I'll see even one of the guys tonight. Should I make other plans? Should I just go to a bar by myself and see what happens?" She could see I was getting emotional. "And then my Instagram—I had so many questions last night, this morning, right now. People are following this journey, hoping for something to happen. But *nothing* is happening today. I don't know what to do."

"Come on," she said, grabbing my arm. "It's going to be okay."

As we strolled through the Tuileries Garden, Nicole pointed to a crowded walkway near a grand arched monument. "There!" Nicole said.

Tara read aloud from her guidebook: "'The Arc de Triomphe du Carrousel is one-half the size of the Arc de Triomphe. Built between 1806 and 1808, the arch commemorates Napoleon's military victories.'"

"Victory. It's a sign," Nicole said confidently. "Hand me some of those flyers. Penelope? How do you say 'Do you believe in love' in French?"

"Croyez-vous en l'amour?" Nicole's voice rang out over the courtyard as she held a flyer aloft, attracting the attention of the people passing by.

"Give me some of those too!" Penelope said, reaching into my bag and grabbing her own stack. *"Croyez-vous en l'amour?"* The phrase rolled off her tongue.

We began passing out soulmate-search flyers to whoever would take one. In broad daylight. Like it was a normal thing to do. I couldn't help but smile and then laugh. I felt my panic melt away, and the buoyant mood from earlier that morning returned. Action is the antidote to anxiety, right? Or so I'd heard while listening to a podcast on one of my hikes at home.

Tara stood apart, uncertain. Amusement flickered in her eyes as she watched us, but she didn't join in. She'd always preferred to survey the action from the sidelines, ensuring nothing went wrong. It was an older-sister habit, an understandable one. I got up to trouble of all kinds when we were younger. Tara's watchful eye had literally saved my life before, when I was seven and almost drowned in a public pool. The lifeguard had been on a break when I decided to jump into the deep end for the first time. Nobody noticed but my sister. But we weren't at a pool now. I wasn't seven. Or even sixteen and off to Don Q's.

"Tara!" I called over to her. "Take some flyers!"

Tara shook her head no, but she got out her phone and began recording video, a genuine smile blooming on her face. Nicole, of course, played it up even more for the camera. Penelope chatted with strangers in French. I approached old couples, young tourists, families, men, women, a teenager. Anyone who might take a flyer. When people accepted, I did my best to thank them in French. I didn't mind when they refused. After a moment, I too stood back. I watched my two best friends in the world embracing rejection and embarrassment in a busy city, passing out flyers emblazoned with my personal information and a call to action for true love. A student carrying a cello set up on a bench and began playing an absolutely gorgeous song. We all stopped briefly to listen, transfixed. The musician's arrival was nothing more than a coincidence, but it felt predestined, as if what we were doing was supposed to happen exactly like this. If only my dad could have seen and heard it.

The four of us walked a little farther, handing out more flyers. Soon we arrived at the Louvre and its iconic glass pyramids.

"Come on, Tash! Climb onto that pillar over there. And here, take a flyer. I'll hold your bag," Nicole said.

"Oh my God, *no*," I said, snapping back to reality. "No, no, no." My stomach went funny. *Oh no.*

"This is about getting outside your comfort zone. You've come so far. Literally. It's time to tell the universe exactly what you want—out loud! Be specific. You can do it! Think of this as an exercise. As practice."

Practice for what? I didn't want a career in public speaking. I just wanted my happily-ever-after. And I didn't talk out loud to the universe in public where people I didn't know could hear me. Who did? It seemed more than a little loopy. I hoped Nicole knew what she was doing.

I took a deep breath, scrambled onto the waist-high pillar, and stood tall. Nicole stared at me, expectant. "Well?"

Some people in the square stopped and looked up at me. Others went about their day. But it was busy. Busier than the arch, even. *Crap.* I closed my eyes. I wasn't sure I knew how to do this.

Then I remembered what Stephanie said the first time we spoke: that when a person undertakes the precious journey to her point of destiny, she receives support from the universe. *Well, I've undertaken a journey. So here I go.* I imagined myself alone in a sacred space, the bustling square around me falling away. It was easier than I thought it would be. My breathing calmed, my pulse settled. I felt my feet grounded on the stone of the pillar (it was a big pillar), which, I reminded myself, came from the earth. I pictured my children content and in good health. *Thank you.* I pictured my mom, my sister, my ride-or-die friends. My dad. *Thank you also for them. But there's one more little thing . . .* I opened my eyes.

"Is there anyone here born on November second, 1968?" I called out tentatively.

"Louder!" Nicole yelled encouragingly. "People can't hear you! The universe can't hear you either!" A crowd gathered. *Oh God.* I held up a flyer.

"Is anyone here born on November second, 1968?" I yelled.

"Louder!"

"I'm trying!" I said, embarrassed. But I also felt good. Energized. I took a huge breath. "I'm looking for someone born in Paris on November second, 1968," I shouted as loud as possible. And then: *"Hear that, universe? I am ready to meet my soulmate!"*

"You do you, boo!" Nicole cheered, joyful.

I hopped off my Parisian soapbox and hugged Nicole, then Penelope and Tara too. It's hard to describe the jubilant high we were all on just then. That moment in the Paris sun, yelling for my soulmate to show up already while my best friends metaphorically lifted me up, up, up, will forever be among my most treasured memories. Afterward, we continued exploring the streets around the Louvre, all of us cracking up, spinning and skipping. And then I checked my phone. Fabrice had written back.

I hope you are having a good time in Paris. I am writing poetry, thinking of you and our meeting Sunday.

Un murmure de moi
Un allusion de toi
Pour devenir nous
Nous ne pouvons pas le savior
Mais déjà nous aimons

I tapped Google Translate and pasted in Fabrice's poem:

A whisper of me
A hint of you
To become us
We can't know
But already we love each other

Had my plea to the universe worked? Or maybe destiny had been working all along for Fabrice and me. With him, there'd been no playing hard to get, no games. The man wrote me poetry. *Original* poetry. He sent GIFs and emojis of angels, hearts, and doves without shame. I surprised myself by finding it sweet and then sexy even. Back in LA, I might have considered all the emojis kind of dorky, to be honest. I probably wouldn't have given him a chance, even though he fell into "the beautiful category," as Margot would say. I wished yet again that Fabrice's busy schedule would magically let up and allow us to meet in person before Sunday, but I also had a gut feeling he was worth the wait.

Neither Thierry nor Gael ever got back to me to confirm plans for later that afternoon or evening. I told myself it didn't matter and gave them both the benefit of the doubt. Maybe Thierry had gotten stuck in a roundabout and Gael had lost track of time at the *fromagerie*. Who knew? But I still had all of Saturday and Sunday. Plenty of time for my soulmate to make himself known. In the meantime, I wouldn't be sitting around. Not only was that not my style, but I wasn't without options. Because there *were* two men in Paris who definitely wanted to see me that night.

My director friend Andy, the one I used to live next door to and who was the big-souled, crazy-creative, loyal older brother I never had, invited the four of us to the set of his new TV show. He suggested our second night in Paris as the best time to visit, because they'd be filming a scene at the Paris Opera House. Andy thought we should see it—the building, the costumes, the scene itself. Even though I had no idea what he was talking about, I said *oui*. Andy's taste is always impeccable, but more important, I missed him. The only catch, according to Andy, was we'd have to arrive around midnight, which was when they'd be ready to shoot. But that turned out to be perfect timing.

François, Nicole's ex-fling who'd generously met with a private investigator on my behalf several months ago, had also been in touch. François was French. And not just French, but Parisian. He'd asked us to dinner. François had found out about my search early on through Nicole and surprised us all by becoming one of my staunchest champions. I hadn't known François well before I started looking for my 2 Novembre guy, but I considered him a true friend by the time we bought our tickets to Paris.

I have the perfect restaurant, François WhatsApp'd us. And you'll never believe it. I am bringing a man born on November 2nd '68 in Paris. He was right—I didn't believe him for a second. François had an impish sense of humor.

The four of us returned to the hotel to change for dinner, which that night meant finery worthy of an opera house. Yes, we'd packed that too. Nicole and I were both big believers in the idea that if you had the outfit, the occasion would come. I zipped myself into a black lace dress with three-quarter-length sleeves. Nicole chose a black, almost sheer bodysuit overlaid with a cutout panel skirt. It was modern and daring and she looked fantastic in it. Tara's short cocktail sheath draped beautifully over her curves. But Penelope, still reveling in all the clothes we'd brought that *weren't* a practical cotton blend with an elastic waist, selected the showiest piece of all: a one-shouldered, puffed-sleeve skintight leopard-print midi-dress. She wore it with stiletto ankle boots and her blond hair loose around her shoulders.

By the time we arrived at Sur Mer, wolfishly handsome François and his equally attractive friend had already started on a bottle of wine. The two men were hard to miss in the tiny restaurant, a tiled galley with a handful of wooden tables and an exposed kitchen.

"I ordered for the table," François announced, greeting us warmly, kisses on both cheeks all around. "The food is magnificent. You California girls are going to love it."

With his suntanned skin, amber eyes, and shirtsleeves rolled up to expose sexy, tattooed forearms, François seemed like a man who was used to pleasing the women in his life. But I saw Tara stiffen slightly. Because of her food sensitivities, she preferred to carefully examine restaurant menus and speak with the staff before ordering. But before she could ask even a single question, an onslaught of small plates—all meant to be shared—began filling the table. Shimmering oysters, goose barnacles, and sardines topped with beetroot puree and bloodred peaches. Escargots on a bed of garlicky greens. More wine. Sublime crusty bread. And that was just the first course.

As an enthusiastic omnivore and a Libra who can't ever make up her mind on what to order, I couldn't wait to try it all. But Tara, a Leo who didn't care to know a single thing about her sign, waved down a waitress. I watched out of the corner of my eye as my big sister tried her best to discreetly determine which dishes were gluten-free.

"What's the problem?" said François in his playful way. "You're *so* LA." This to Tara. And then, to me: "Your sister, she might want, I don't know . . . to relax."

"She's *so* relaxed. It's Paris," I responded. "But poor Tara's gluten-free diet is serious, not some LA trend. Though all four of us might be guilty of some of those on occasion." I didn't want Tara to feel singled out.

"Sadly!" Tara said lightly. I knew she'd noticed the way we'd embraced François like an old friend and how Nicole, who'd had a beachy, harmless fling with him ages ago, sparkled in his undeniable light. "Celiac disease is torture in Paris. All the croissants and baguettes I can't eat are calling my name."

"Maybe," said François, pushing a plate toward her with a smile, "it's all about just trying new things on occasion. That is what I recommend."

Tara's eyes flashed with a spark of true irritation that would ignite if this conversation continued. *Uh-oh.* Where was this dinner going?

"François!" I exclaimed. "Where are my manners? I should have started tonight with a toast to you. For inviting us to dinner. For being the first French person to believe in my search. For meeting with a private detective, even. *Merci,* my friend."

Tara poured herself more wine.

"In France, a woman never pours herself a glass of wine. That's a man's job," said François sagely. "And never more than half full."

Did I mention that François was as old-school French as Frenchmen come? It was part of his charm. Most of the time.

"Well, it looks like we're making women's history tonight," said Tara, rolling her eyes and filling her glass right to the top.

Penelope laughed. "Pour me a glass too, will you, Tara?"

"I'll take your helpful advice, thank you, François," I said, holding out my almost-empty glass to him. Frankly, he had probably saved me from a major faux pas on any number of my Paris dates to come, because I'd been known to pour myself a glass of wine. Or three.

"François, did I hear that you met someone? Tell us," Penelope said.

François leaned back in his chair and surveyed the table. He cleared his throat to get our attention. "As you know, I've been following Natasha's quest from the start. It has made me believe in love again. I *have* just met someone. And it could be love, it's true. What Natasha is doing, sometimes it's a little bit ridiculous because she's so like"—he began waving his hands about, searching for words—"she *wants* it. Sometimes it's a little *too* much for the Frenchman, is what I am saying. But I think if I was that guy with the November birthday, I would respect her and I could fall in love because it's admirable to be so brave like Natasha. And all her friends here to help her—that is beautiful. All of you together, it's love. Natasha, though, I think she has balls. And you know, as a man"—François proudly gestured to his crotch—"I like that. Sometimes men might be afraid of a woman this strong. Natasha needs a man with balls." He turned to me. "You do, you know. Someone who can handle someone like you. So bravo!" He clapped. "And I think," François said, raising his (half-full) glass of red wine high, "cheers to balls!"

Well, who wouldn't toast to that? We all clinked our glasses to balls, friendship, and true love.

François looked at me and tapped his glass on mine. "Cheers, Natasha. I believe you will find him."

"Thank you. Cheers, François."

François turned to the other people sitting in the little restaurant, raised his glass again, and said to the room, *"Excusez-moi d'avoir interrompu vos diners, mais est-ce que quelqu'un ici est né à Paris le deux novembre 1968? Cette belle déesse californienne cherche son âme soeur! Non? D'accord, bon, santé! À l'amour!"*

The diners lifted their glasses back to him, to us. But no soulmate came forward.

Another round of dishes arrived: Briny sea urchin. A plate of shaved fluke with lime and flowering herbs. And a tangle of grilled octopus.

"Oh no, no, no," Nicole said with dismay. "Did you know that the octopus is among the most intelligent of animals? They have *personalities.* Also, they don't share DNA with any other being on the planet. Octopuses are basically aliens. Which is something I deeply relate to. I could *never* eat an octopus."

"More for us, then," François replied good-naturedly. "Ladies, would you like to try this delicacy?" he asked Tara and me. But the waitress, who turned out to be an accommodating woman well versed in special diets, had shaken her head no to Tara about that particular dish.

"I'll stick to my grilled fish. It's wonderful," Tara said.

"You should live a little, is my advice," François offered. "The dish, it will not kill you. Loosen up! Have a good time. Maybe I should pour you more wine, yes?"

Tara stared straight at François. "Or maybe not. When I have a little too much wine, it kinda makes me want to tell everyone to just *fuck off.* Know what I mean?" She grinned, truly enjoying herself now.

I could tell François wasn't used to having a woman tell him to fuck off, even indirectly and in jest. And even when he kind of deserved it. He didn't seem angry, though, just confused. Maybe more like: *Ooof!* I laughed, doing my best to dispel the slight undercurrent of tension that had formed. It seemed to work. All of us at the table truly loved or at least liked one another, and we didn't want to be anywhere else, no matter how tired we four travelers were by that point—not that we realized it. Paris had us under a spell, one that made us believe that we could go on forever fueled by anticipation, magic, and wine. We shared our thoughts on fate and destiny late into the evening and on dating and love in Paris versus the United States. François's friend turned out to be a considerate young American (with entirely the wrong birthday, as we'd suspected) and he and Tara hit it off well. Finally, it was time to say good night, pay the bill, and head to the Palais Garnier to see Andy on set. François bade us farewell and promised to look out for my soulmate.

In the cab, I stared out at the darkness and the city's twinkling golden lights. *Did* I have an unusual amount of courage? I wasn't used to thinking about myself that way. Well, one thing was for sure. "Date or no date, I had dinner tonight with a cute Parisian man, just like I wanted," I announced, rolling down the window so the stars could hear me. "But, ah, still send me my soulmate, okay, universe?"

"It was nice to see François again." Nicole sighed. "There's no one quite like him."

Penelope smiled slyly. "Well, except perhaps for half of Paris." Then she turned to Tara. "Hey. Just checking that you're okay. I saw how François talked to you. I hate it when men tell women to loosen up. They wouldn't say that to a guy."

"I know," Tara said with a laugh. "It's so predictable sometimes. But I honestly liked him a lot. It was sweet how much he supports Tasha. He just wanted us all to love his favorite spot. And he likes being in charge."

Penelope scoffed. "Many Frenchmen do. Tash, you sure you want to sign up for a Parisian man again?" Of course she knew all about Philippe.

"I'm sure I want to find my soulmate," I replied.

COME TO THE SET, Andy had texted, anytime after dinner. We wrap at 4 a.m. Can't wait to see uuuuuuu!

We'll be there. What's the show going to be called again?

Emily in Paris.

Right! Love. See u soon.

None of us knew much about this new show Andy was working on. This was long before anyone except for the people making it knew about it. And I didn't truly understand what he'd meant when he told me they were filming at the Paris Opera House. I didn't know about the grandeur of the building or its magnificent history. Or that the entire place would be shut down for filming.

A woman with a walkie-talkie met us at the entrance and led us inside. The opulence of the interior was almost impossible to take in fully; I'd never seen anything like it. Gilded moldings and glowing chandeliers, glittering mosaics, winged statues, antique mirrored panels for operagoers to see and be seen, a sweeping white marble double staircase. Even the modernity of the film crew buzzing around us couldn't break the spell of an enchanted past. Extras, gorgeously dressed and dripping with jewels, waited in their places. I remembered then that Andy had told me Patricia Field designed the costumes for the show. *Patricia Field!* I loved her! Once, years ago, I'd even interviewed her for *Detour* magazine about her work on *Sex and the City.* And there I was, not simply watching her genius on my television but surrounded by it in real life. *Breathe, Natasha.*

When we finally found Andy, I was more than a little starstruck.

"Hey." Andy greeted us coolly, like hanging around shooting a TV show amid the splendor of the Paris Opera House was no big deal. Andy stood at least six one, had a big mustache like almost nobody else had in LA (or Paris, for that matter), and a head of silver hair. That night he somehow managed to pair Texas cowboy boots with a chic French silk scarf and make it look like that's what all men should be wearing.

"You're in Paris, yay," Andy said, deadpan, kissing me on both cheeks.

Andy sat us in an assortment of director's chairs placed behind the monitors—what's known as the "video village" on a set.

"Stay put, Lily is in the next scene, and after that I can come hang out. Oh." Andy turned to a man sitting near us. "And this is Darren. Darren, this is my friend Natasha I was telling you about. The awesomely crazy one who came to meet every man she could find with some ridiculous birthday."

Reader . . . this is the moment I met Darren Star. Here in front of me was the man responsible for the Paris happily-ever-after scene to end them all: the one from *Sex and the City* where Big comes for Carrie. Was this a sign? Was my Big just around the corner?

"Nice to meet you, Natasha," Darren said, smiling and shaking my hand. "How would you feel about being in this next scene?"

Um . . . what?

Other than my extremely recent, perhaps somewhat unhinged, affinity for Instagram stories, I was never the person in front of the camera. Which was fine, because I'd never wanted that. But now Darren fucking Star was suggesting that I be an extra on his new show. In a scene at the Paris Opera House. It's a good thing I had no idea in that moment what a phenomenon *Emily in Paris* would one day become, because that layered with *Sex and the City* mashed up with the actual home of *The Phantom of the Opera* would definitely have been enough to make me faint. As it was, I couldn't speak for a few seconds. Things like this did not happen to single moms well past forty. Or maybe in Paris they did? *I knew I overpacked for a reason!*

Luckily, my job was easy: take the arm of a devastatingly handsome extra dressed in a tux and follow the actress Lily Collins up the white marble staircase. I worried I would trip or otherwise ruin the scene. I couldn't help but think of the stranger's champagne glass I'd accidentally shattered the night before. But somehow, we glided up the stairs as if we'd done this a thousand times. Of course I turned to my "date" and asked him his birthday. But the night's magic extended only so far.

After my star turn on the staircase, Tara, Nicole, and I hugged Andy and said goodbye so he could get back to work. Penelope, exhausted, had returned to the hotel shortly after we'd arrived on set. Though it was now past two a.m., the three of us thought we should have a quick look around the rest of the opera house. When would we ever have a chance to do it again quite like this? Never. That just wasn't my life. Or any of our lives. Eventually, we headed for the exit, ready for bed. In the foyer, we stood soaking in the hushed grandeur for one last precious minute. There was no music, but I bowed to Tara. She smiled and curtsied back. Nicole spun theatrically, her arms aloft. Suspended somewhere between the splendid moment right then and the memories of dance-offs long past, we twirled and swooped and danced in the mellow light of the chandeliers, three operagoers bidding the Palais Garnier good night.

Eighth House

Merde!

I love the Eighth House. It rules connection, integration, spies, secret missions, soulmates, partners' values, sex, betrayal, death, detachment, and the willingness to face the unknown in pursuit of fulfillment. It's just really me.

The sign of Libra (also my sun sign) fills my Eighth House. Libra rules the part of ourselves that we give up at about seven years old in order to appease those around us. This is the alter ego. Like a vessel, it holds all that we no longer identify with. It calls us into self-actualization by showing us these qualities in another so that in the process of falling in love, we see those "lost" aspects of ourselves and reclaim some of what we sacrificed.

When Libra is in the Eighth House, it can show up as obsessive yearning to find what we feel is missing from our lives. Of course, nothing is truly missing; it is just temporarily repressed, waiting to be seen, known, and reintegrated.

There's a lot besides Libra going on in my Eighth House. I have the sun, Venus, Mars, Uranus, and Pluto all there. Uranus urges me to connect to my psychic ability and know that anything is possible. When Stephanie told me this, I got the chills. That's what my dad always said to me: Anything is possible. And so I wasn't surprised when she said next that people with an Eighth House like mine will find that those who have passed on are likely to want to participate as a team in their efforts to find what is missing from their lives.

MY EYES WERE CLOSED BUT I COULD HEAR THE WORLD AROUND me in motion: Cars in the street. The clink of a spoon on a saucer. A hanger on a metal rack. The whizzing sound of the room-safe motor. The quiet tapping on an iPhone followed by *swoosh,* an outgoing text. The purr of a zipper. *Zzzzziiippp!* I rolled over and opened one eye. Penelope had already dressed for the day, and Nicole lay in bed scrolling on her phone.

"Want some coffee?" Penelope asked softly.

"Sure," I said, sitting up, clearing my throat. "Yes, please. Thank you, Penelope."

"Morning, sunshine," Nicole sang, parting the drapes behind her and letting in some light. "How'd you sleep?"

"Great," I said, stretching my back, which popped and cracked even more than usual. Truthfully, I hadn't slept all that well. My whole body was out of sorts from constantly hunching over for fear of hitting my head on the sloped ceiling in our room, trying to position myself nightly on a tiny pullout mattress, and carrying twenty pounds of posters across the world and around the city. Not to mention staying up until almost four in the morning for the past two nights. I felt physically wrecked as I woke to our third day. Still, it was Paris, so no (out-loud) complaints from me. "Like a French baby."

"*Un bébé français,*" corrected Penelope in perfect French, handing me a cup of coffee on a delicate tray. "I'm going to have to give you some French lessons if you marry *un Parisian.*"

After I drank my coffee and adjusted to the morning light, I checked WhatsApp. One of the men had to have gotten back to me about meeting up today. It was Saturday, and didn't Parisians go out on the weekends like we did back home?

The first message I opened was from Jacques, a man I had, in my head, nicknamed Monsieur Serious from the start. This guy never joked. And he asked a lot of questions. Which didn't bother me; many of the men I matched with were curious about my search.

Bonjour, Natasha. Explain again why 2 Novembre 1968? It cannot be astrology. It doesn't make sense.

So without thinking twice, I sent him my Instagram handle and suggested we pick a time and place for later that day. His reply came a few minutes later.

And you're writing about us all? Online? I'm not interested in a foolish charade with many men. Ciao.

Shit. One more crossed off the list. I opened the next message, this one from Laurent, the melancholy businessman whom I never could quite get a read on. Laurent's message was partly in French so it took me a minute to puzzle it out, calling over to Penelope when I came across a phrase I didn't know. He did want to meet! Were things looking up? What did *vendredi* mean? Oh, Friday. He was free on Fridays. At eleven a.m. Because that was the hour at which his wife had agreed to allow him to engage in what he called *petites aventures*.

I send to you the address to my apartment and wait for you in my bed. This in English.

I sighed to myself and deleted Laurent from WhatsApp. I wasn't judging anyone, but I knew I wanted my soulmate all to myself. I crossed Laurent off the list too. The page was looking a tad bleak. Only eight potential soulmates left. And maybe nine or even ten if Gael or Thierry ever got back in touch? But no date yet for today. Just like yesterday. I was starting to wish I'd had time to do a little more prep work before leaving LA. After all, these guys were not on vacation like I was. They had kids, jobs, and lives (*wives,* even!). Had Philippe been trying to tell me something crucial when he said early on in our relationship that there was no word meaning "date" in French? That in France, dating is not a thing? It insulted me in the beginning. I wanted him to take me on formal dates.

The spontaneous picnics were dreamy, don't get me wrong, but it would have been nice to occasionally be picked up at a specific time arranged in advance and taken to dinner and a movie, to be less *laissez-faire* about it all. But what if Philippe hadn't just been making excuses?

Clearly, I needed fortification in the form of carbs and a lot more caffeine before figuring out my next move. We all did. It had been a late night. Noting the cooler weather today, I threw on a striped turtleneck, a navy trench coat, and—channeling my best inner French girl—a swipe of my brightest red lipstick. Downstairs, the girl at the front desk offered me an umbrella, pointing out that it had begun to lightly drizzle outside. Tara met us moments later wearing a trail-ready rain jacket and smart waterproof boots.

We settled in at a cozy table by a window in the back of Breizh Café and drank coffee as we perused the menu. The café specialized in organic buckwheat crepes both savory and sweet. Comté cheese, French ham, an egg sunny-side up, and lots of butter wrapped in a warm crepe sounded like heaven on a plate to me. Plus a salted-caramel crepe for the table to share.

My mouth watered at the sights and smells inside the café, but my nerves were beginning to feel raw. I glanced at the time on my phone. Ticktock.

"I'd love to make a real plan for today," Tara said. "Tasha, any news on dates? We could schedule our sightseeing around the guys."

"Not yet. I'm trying, though." I'd had my phone out since we sat down, and I'd barely looked up from it.

"I wish you'd been able to schedule some or even most of these dates before we got here so we'd know how to organize the days. We'd be able to get so much more done." Tara sighed.

"I wish it were that easy. Honestly, I was beating myself up about it earlier this morning. But not only was I working like a maniac on that deal, like I said—I did try to set up some dates with these guys before we left and they were all like, 'Kiss-kiss, can't wait for you to get here, text me when you arrive, we'll figure it out then.' The truth is, setting up dates too far in advance is pretty much always pointless. It doesn't even work in LA. If I make a date for more than a day or two out, it's almost guaranteed the guy will flake. It's like I gave him a hall pass to do it. Dating is such a game, it's exhausting."

"We'll figure something out," Nicole said. "And I have a good feeling about Fabrice tomorrow."

So did I, but I couldn't bet solely on Fabrice, no matter how perfect he seemed on paper. Or text. As I'd discovered, meeting someone in person, even a someone you were on fire with on-line, could upend it all. Chemistry mattered. Mateo had reminded me of that. And when it was there, sometimes it wasn't enough. Philippe had taught me that, again and again. Dev too.

Dev continued to check on me after our steamy weekend in LA, but in a protective-friend kind of way. He followed my Insta-gram and texted regularly. Be careful putting those signs up every-where. There's a lot of crazies around, he'd write. And, when I was on my way to meet Mateo at Little Red Door:

Please be careful, Natasha. Go for it, but be extra-careful.

You'll be happy to know my sister is with me. She's an even bigger worrier than you. What's the worst that can happen? Creepy guys? Same thing in LA, so . . .

Please just be smart and safe. Watch your ass.

I wished someone were watching my ass that morning at the café. I'm sure Dev thought I'd be meeting other Devs in Paris, having more hot hookups. But things hadn't turned out that way at all so far.

As Tara, Nicole, and Penelope discussed shops and museums, I lost myself in my phone while my breakfast grew cold. Swipe right, swipe left, type, tap, send: Bonjour, are you born on 2 Nov. '68? Can you meet tonight? Yes, a few days does make a difference . . .

"What do *you* think, Natasha?" Penelope's voice pierced my ris-ing panic.

"I'm sorry?" I said.

"Do you want to go to the museum with Tara and Nicole or come shopping with me? Paris has the cutest baby clothes in the world, trust me."

Shopping for rompers and booties? Museums? I was supposed to be falling in love.

I wanted to spend as much time with Penelope as possible. She would be leaving the next morning to go home to her family. But I couldn't shop for baby clothes or anything else. I didn't know for certain if the deal Billy and I had would go through. If it didn't . . . best not to go there. The reality was, I couldn't afford to shop recreationally. I was already worried enough about the cost of the mini-bottles of champagne in our room, the dinners, the taxis. Those things add up. And I was too embarrassed to tell Penelope any of that. Only Tara knew how precarious my financial situation was.

"The museum?" I said, thinking that at least I could easily monitor my phone there.

We hugged Penelope goodbye, agreeing to meet up later. I put more signs on the windshields of cars outside the café and tucked a few into the back pockets of our taxi's front seats, just in case my soulmate caught the next ride. Then I posted a photo from dinner the night before (François was too handsome not to!), trying to fill my feed and distract my friends back home from seeing the truth: my potential soulmates didn't seem all that excited about my arrival in Paris.

We pulled up to the Centre Pompidou, home to the globally renowned National Museum of Modern Art. Here was a starkly different Paris style from the nineteenth-century Haussmann buildings and the medieval streets of Le Marais we'd been admiring since we'd arrived. Built in the 1970s, the massive Centre Pompidou was famous for its "inside-out" construction. All the museum's mechanical systems were worn boldly on its exterior—a feast for the eye of color-coded pipes, white-painted stairs, and permanent scaffolding—leaving the entire interior of the building for art and people.

"I wish Dad could see this," Tara said, staring in awe.

Bob, with his civil engineering degree and fascination with architecture, would have flipped for the Centre Pompidou. Except for the long, slow-moving line to get in. It stretched on for what seemed like forever. Just when we were regretting not having Fast Passes, we overheard someone say the line had to do with increased security, and no pass could help with that.

As we inched forward, I studied my phone. My follower count had ticked up yet again. Friends and strangers peppered my feed with questions. Had I found him yet? When was my next date? Any hot hookups? (That was Katie, of course.) *No, no idea, and, depressingly, none,* I replied in my head. I opened WhatsApp. Thierry, aka Mr. Marrakech, had written back at last. I'd wondered what happened to him after he disappeared on me yesterday afternoon. He'd been so keen on meeting, and then . . . poof! Maybe he'd confirm a date for later today. I was due for a little luck. I tapped his message.

Bonjour, Natasha, what timing is this. I must admit that I have fallen in love myself with a beautiful woman. I wasn't expecting, but it has happened. And so with regret I leave you.

So yesterday's silence wasn't because of escargot poisoning or a Métro accident. I wanted to be happy for Thierry. Love should be celebrated. That was the whole damn reason I was in Paris. But all I could think was: *What the fuck?* Another potential soulmate evaporated, just like that? That made three disappearing acts so far today and we'd only just finished breakfast.

In the best of times, waiting in a molasses-like line would be a challenge for me. But now, with almost *half* of my candidates off the list? A manic urge to escape overtook me. In hindsight, I wish I could say I had been more subtle about it.

"I have to get *out* of here!" I said loudly, waving my arms frantically. "Right now! Waiting in line for a museum filled with tourists and Play-Doh sculptures that Penelope's kids could have made is literally my definition of *hell*." One or two people ahead of us turned to stare. It did not occur to me that I was one of those tourists I was complaining about.

Tara's face fell. Of course she also found the line tedious, but her wish in Paris (aside from me *not* being abducted) was to see as much art as possible. I knew that because I knew my sister better than anyone, but I was hardly my most selfless (or self-aware) self in that moment.

"I wouldn't mind ditching this line and getting a few gifts for my girls," Nicole said quickly. "And then maybe have a bottle of wine somewhere, watch the world go by?"

I liked the sound of that. I just wanted to *be* in Paris. To soak it in, walk for a while, then sit in a spot for locals and imagine what it might be like to live here one day. "Fine," Tara said, "let's go. We'll figure out something else to do."

We walked a short way along the rue des Archives and Tara spotted the Patrick Roger chocolate shop, which was reputed to be among the best in all of Paris. We stepped inside the emerald interior and were met by the scent of cocoa beans, vanilla, and sugar. As I browsed the chocolatier's signature flavors (lemon with basil? Dash would love to try that), I checked my phone. And got an unexpected jolt.

Jules Perreault: Hello, Natasha, I know this sounds crazy, but were you just now near the Pompidou wearing a Marine T-shirt?

What? What were the odds? Jules was Philippe's childhood best friend. Jules was funny, carefree, and just a blast. I adored him, but we'd lost touch after Philippe and I broke up for good. What did this mean? My pulse quickened.

Me: YES!!

Jules: Ahaha! I saw you then but I was not sure

Me: C'est moi!;) I'm here until Monday.

Jules: Looking for someone born in November, right? If you have some spare time, let me know.

I decided not to respond after that, at least not right away. I was having a heart attack that Jules had randomly seen me on the street in Paris and that, unbeknownst to me, he was obviously following my Instagram. I knew that's how IG worked, but it felt too much like Philippe himself had walked by, like the ghosts of heartbreaks past were closing in.

I considered leaving both Nicole and Tara and venturing out on my own right then. I'd run straight to Philippe's family's apartment (I knew the address by heart because his father had listed it for lease with the Agency). He had shared so many stories of the Paris of his youth with me. I wanted to see the real settings of the scenes I'd imagined: Philippe shopping hand in hand with his mother for vegetables at the farmers' market near their home; the hushed classroom where, as a young boy in Catholic school, he'd been forced to memorize poetry whenever he misbehaved; L'Entrecôte, the historic steak frites restaurant his friend's family owned where he'd spent his adolescent years smoking cigarettes, drinking red wine, and flirting with girls. I'd go have a drink there myself. I wondered what it had been like for him to come back to Paris after his divorce to visit his parents in that elegant family apartment near the Champs-Élysées and rue du Faubourg Saint-Honoré. What did the streets smell like? What did the local butcher sell? What Métro had Philippe taken? What was the view from his bedroom? I wanted to find the park from his poem, to take in all that I could. I wanted to understand what had made Philippe who he was. Because maybe if I understood that, I could understand how to let him go once and for all.

It was, for sure, a stupid idea, and not the only one I'd have that day. But I didn't see that then.

I said nothing about Jules's text or how I was feeling to my sister or Nicole. They certainly didn't want to hear any more about Philippe and I couldn't blame them. But I hadn't been exaggerating in the letter I wrote to him before I left. I was looking for him down every street, in every café window. It was more painful than I'd guessed it would be.

We finished up at the chocolate shop and headed back out into the soft gray drizzle. Tara decided to check out the Musée des Archives Nationales, and Nicole and I planned to find a few more souvenirs for her girls before parking ourselves at a café. I was convinced that between the two of us, we could get at least one potential soulmate to appear in the flesh today.

Before we parted, Tara asked once again if I would stay an extra day with her. "Let me think about it" was all I could manage. I felt the pull of work, Margot, Dash. My mother. I missed our puppy, Friday, even his barking. But I felt the allure of one more sparkling day in Paris keenly too. More time to find my person. I didn't know which to choose. I'm the kind of person who makes—and cancels—plans at the last minute, a combination of never being able to decide anything and a terror of being hemmed in by a bad decision. This behavior has driven my sister crazy, understandably, for decades. I've tried and tried to be better. Sometimes I'm successful. But it's how my brain is wired.

There was also a part of me that just wanted to go home to LA and hide. To give up. Remember that little voice in my head? It had come creeping back in on that third morning in Paris.

After wandering the streets for a little while, Nicole and I found ourselves outside an unassuming bistro in the third arrondissement, the perfect spot to sit and watch Paris go by. Not that I did that. No, I got out my phone. I checked Bumble first—plenty of new matches, but none with the right birthday. Same with Tinder. My DMs and Facebook groups teemed as usual with questions, suggestions, and messages of support. It would be impossible to go through them all.

"I think I need an assistant to help manage all these accounts. It's a lot," I said without looking up.

Nicole didn't reply.

I opened WhatsApp next to see if any of the remaining men on my list had responded. They hadn't, not even Georges, who I thought was meeting me later that night for a drink. But *I* sure had been busy.

"Nicole. Oh my God, I just realized that I've messaged one of these guys *ten* times since I got here, and he hasn't once responded. *Ten times!* I've lost my mind."

Nicole sipped her rosé. "Which guy is this?"

"Christophe. The fancy tennis-playing one."

"You suck at tennis. Cross him off the list."

I felt like a failure. I was fully prepared to have awkward dates, bad dates, funny dates, even potentially dangerous dates. But almost *no dates*? That possibility honestly hadn't even occurred to me as I made plans for Paris.

"What do I do? *Eight* men have ghosted or canceled on me and I have only one other date set up. This is humiliating. I can't believe I announced my soulmate search on live radio. Plus all over the internet. All these people who think I'm some kind of fearless love goddess are waiting for me to do something amazing! I'm just going to let them down. That's what I do. Fuck things up. I don't know, maybe I should fake a date so I can keep the story going and not die of embarrassment."

Fake dates. In an instant, fake dates seemed like a *brilliant* idea. Like, one of my best ever. Intriguing, sexy men were everywhere in Paris. All I had to do was go to a bar that evening dressed for a date and talk to one of them. About anything. Hadn't Katie and I done that countless times before in LA? Nicole could sneakily snap a picture here in Paris with her phone. And *voilà!* I'd have the perfect cover until I figured out what was going wrong with my real search.

Nicole put her glass down and stared at me. She didn't look happy. "Whoa. You're being way too hard on yourself right now. Fuck things up? Fake dates? That sounds like your ego talking, trying to make you feel small for things that are completely out of your control. And now you're panicking. Slow down. I think people back home are probably more inspired by the courage it takes to live in your truth rather than some hope of a fairy-tale ending. You never promised to deliver one of those, by the way. It's time to listen to your higher self. I'm not saying that what you want can't change, but you should think about what started you on this journey in the first place."

"Stephanie?"

"Nope. She helped you find a path, but she didn't suggest you travel across the world and run around the streets of Paris chasing down people who have your ex's birth chart. You did that all on your own. Why?"

I shifted uncomfortably in my seat and thought back, not to the dizzying months leading up to Paris, but to the two years prior to that, when my family first learned of my father's illness and how it would progress. I thought about how, though ending my pregnancy was the right choice and one I'd make again, the abortion had laid bare all that would never and could never be with Philippe. What I'd wanted back then, besides Bob to miraculously live forever, was to find my person. My other half. Someone I could plan a future with. The fact that I wasn't with that person in a committed relationship, in a *marriage,* terrified me. I wished it didn't, wished that I could say (and mean), "Who cares? It's 2019 and I don't need a partner." But it felt like an emergency that I had no idea who would hold my hand on a Saturday night and snuggle with me while we watched movies and ate ice cream. Who, I wondered, would tell me I was beautiful at eighty? Who would be there when the financial chips were down? Who will hold my hand when the plane takes off and go camping with me? Who would love me no matter what? *Nobody* was an unacceptable answer, one I couldn't live with.

"I want love. True love. My soulmate. I believe that person—*my* person—is out there. I have to believe that. But I don't know why it's been so fucking hard to find that person."

"Yup. That's where you began. And now you're sitting in Paris—

Paris!—thinking about faking a date for Instagram. You can't put away your phone for even ten minutes. I'm not hating on social media, but as your friend, I'm telling you this doesn't seem good for you. What about your point of destiny? Do you even care about that anymore? Because if you do, I guarantee your point of destiny has nothing to do with the Gram. But hey. You know me, I love a good scene. I'm an actress. A producer. Your best friend. I'll help you fake the best fucking date this city ever saw, but only if you are honest with me about what the hell is going on with you so I can adjust my expectations for the rest of this trip."

Nicole's words stung, because she was onto something. And it wasn't pretty.

Likes, re-Grams, shout-outs, follows—I'd somehow become a person who increasingly craved them. I hadn't meant for that to happen, but the attention made me feel seen. Made me feel like I mattered. Like I wasn't a flailing divorced mom barely keeping it together in a city full of success monsters. Which is how I still felt a lot of the time, despite the life I'd so carefully rebuilt for myself and my kids. It's not always easy to get your inside reality to match the outside one. The online validation made that friction feel less fraught. Or gone altogether, even. But playing to an audience, even an audience of the nicest people you could imagine, had also, little by little, made me blind to what had felt so good about my soulmate search in the first place: that I was finally speaking my truth. I, Natasha Sizlo, wanted to find true love.

When you speak your truth out loud, even just part of it, something shifts in you. It's powerful. Because soon after I'd spoken my truth, I was going after it. I had to do it. It was almost as if a force outside of me made it impossible not to. Which was fucking terrifying at times. And huge. This was my journey, not someone else's. And not something that had happened to me by accident. I'd chosen this path with intention and purpose. I remembered the quote on my dad's whiteboard above his hospital-issue bed.

Success is not final; failure is not fatal: it is the courage to
continue that counts.
—Winston Churchill

I knew then I couldn't lie about dates, no matter how good that
stupid idea had sounded to me. There were still eight potential
soulmates out there that I knew about. I promised Nicole I'd do
my best to stay focused on my purest intentions, to pay attention
to the signs that mattered and not the noise. I said I'd use social
media as a tool, not a crutch. Because even if I wanted to throw
my phone into the Seine, I couldn't. I no longer knew how to
entirely separate dating from the internet. Did anyone? It might
be possible, but it definitely wasn't practical. I'd simply have to be
smarter about it all.

Just then an elderly couple caught my eye. A man and a woman,
elegantly dressed, carefully crossing the street, each of them
stooped with age and leaning in toward the other. She'd taken
his arm and he used a polished cane. I saw her smile in response
to something he said softly into her ear. They seemed as if they'd
walked this exact route together thousands of times, and perhaps
they had. I picked up my phone and began filming them. I saw my
mother and father, the embodiment of a great and everlasting love.
I wondered if somehow they'd find each other in another lifetime.
Stephanie, I knew, would say yes. I silently pointed out the couple
to Nicole and she smiled, seeing exactly what I saw.

"I want that," I said.

"I know, Tash." This time, all the love was back in my best
friend's voice. Later, I'd realize it had never left.

Then I turned the phone on myself.

"Reality check. If you're wondering when I'm going on my
next date . . . well, so am I. Because I'm being stood up left and
right. Turns out you can get ghosted in Paris just the same as in
LA. But I still believe in magic and I'm definitely *not* giving up on
love. I'm gonna find that motherfucker."

After posting my (non) story, I sent a quick note to Stephanie, filling her in on the unexpected roadblocks I'd encountered
thus far. Maybe she'd have celestial guidance for me in the days
I had left in Paris. She might be too busy to reply in time, and
it might cost me money I didn't have, but it was worth a shot.
I scrolled through the rest of my DMs, dozens of them, until an
unusual handle caught my eye. Someone named Shayna Klee @
PurplePalace had written to me.

Hi Natasha! This may seem out of the blue but I came across
your story today on Facebook and I felt an urge to react! I am an
American artist living in Paris. I run a YouTube channel (The Purple
Palace) and oftentimes I interview people, do short films, etc. I love
your mission. Maybe you would want to share it and be interviewed
for one of my Paris vlogs (just a low key discussion, nothing Barbara
Walters or anything hahaha)? I have a pretty large YouTube following.
An interview might not only inspire people but also help get the
word out about your search. In any case I think it is both romantic
and courageous what you are doing.:) Let me know! xx Shayna

"What do you think?" I asked Nicole, who read the message
and then studied Shayna's exuberantly stylish feed.

"I think connecting with fellow dreamers and travelers like
Shayna is *exactly* what you need to be doing. That's aligned with
your truth. I like her vibe—confident and quirky," Nicole said.
"Shayna has followers all over the world, so if your Mr. November
Second lives in another city now, she might be able to help you
reach him."

So, although I knew little about YouTubers in general (Dash and
Margot watched YouTube; I watched good old-fashioned television), I gratefully accepted Shayna's invitation to the Purple Palace
and made plans to meet her the following day at a bookstore.

The four of us met back at the hotel to rest and then change our
clothes. Earlier in the afternoon, Andy had asked if we could have

dinner with him that night at Le Dome du Marais, a French-Asian fusion restaurant in our neighborhood. As I still had exactly zero dates lined up for the night, we were free.

Can't wait to see you, I texted Andy.

Me too, he replied. Hey, my friends Ashley and Lucas are joining, hope that's okay.

Of course! I replied. Friends of Andy's were friends of mine. Plus, the name Lucas sounded French.

Andy, in part because of the location scouting he'd done for *Emily in Paris,* knew every cinematic space in the neighborhood. Le Dome du Marais was no exception. The neoclassical building, erected in the late eighteenth century, was once an auction house. Tara, having done her research the minute Andy invited us, told us the restaurant's history on the walk over. A glass-and-gold-leaf dome added in the nineteenth century was considered one of the finest examples of circular skylights in all the city. We entered the restaurant and spoke with a gracious maître d' who immediately led us past the packed bar to a long table directly under the famous dome. Above us, the Paris night sky. Andy had chosen this setting for a reason. He might have liked to appear gruff and slightly nonplussed about my soulmate search, but I knew better. Andy wanted me to find my person the way he had found his in his longtime partner, Eric.

Lucas and Ashley turned out to be Lucas Bravo and Ashley Park, two of the leads in *Emily in Paris.* Ashley, we learned, played an irrepressibly upbeat au pair named Mindy with a hidden talent for singing and a to-die-for wardrobe. Ashley told us that what drew her to the show and Mindy's character was how the script celebrated women's experiences. Mindy and Emily's blossoming friendship moved her deeply, especially the way they openly centered each other's happiness. Ashley beamed as she spoke. With her shining cascade of dark curls and magnetic smile, I had a feeling that Ashley's Mindy would be a hit. We were already her number-one fans at the table that night. Lucas, a young French actor and model, had been cast as the romantic lead, the hot chef Gabriel. Yes, Lucas Bravo is indeed as stunningly handsome in person as he is on television. The sea-blue eyes, thick wavy brown hair, chiseled features—it's all as advertised. Plus he's charming and considerate. But no, tragically, Lucas Bravo was *not* born on November 2, 1968. Not even close. Neither Ashley nor Lucas had been on set the night before, so meeting them at the restaurant was something of a surprise.

The almost-too-pretty-to-eat food arrived and the wine flowed, and our conversation turned to love. "Tell them your wacky plan," Andy suggested offhandedly, like what I was doing was both stupid-crazy-LA-girl-nonsense *and* the most brilliant idea he'd ever heard.

I told my story, a much shortened version, though I was nervous to do so. Here were these incredibly accomplished actors—Ashley was a Tony Award–nominated Broadway star!—and I was, well, me. But Ashley listened intently as I spoke. Lucas seemed taken as well. They didn't laugh or roll their eyes, and their questions came faster than I could answer them. Ashley even asked our waiter for his birth date and gave him one of my soulmate-search business cards. He didn't laugh either. Instead, he told us he'd been married twice and both his wives had exactly the same birthday. Then he wished me *bon chance* and said he'd pin the card up in the kitchen.

"What's the craziest thing you've done for love?" Ashley asked the table. "Let's all go around and share."

I was curious. *Was* I doing something especially strange or brave, like François said last night? Or does love make all of us, no matter our personal histories (or even zodiac signs), a little crazy sometimes?

Nicole jumped immediately in with a response: "I flew to Paris with my best friend to find her soulmate!" We all laughed. But I squeezed Nicole's hand under the table. *Thank you.*

My sister told a tale about high-school hair loved and lost. Back then, Tara had showstopping honey-brown hair that fell in soft waves to her waist and an all-consuming crush on the cutest boy in school. So when Mr. Take My Breath Away mentioned casually to Tara one day in math class that he thought she would look totally awesome with shorter hair á la Kelly McGillis in *Top Gun,* Tara took it as a hint that he had "that lovin' feeling" for her just like Maverick did for Charlie. After all, it was 1986 and *Top Gun* was the greatest love story of all time. Tara rushed to the salon, chopped off almost eighteen inches of hair, and got a poodle perm.

"I looked like Kelly McGillis if she were forced to ride on the back of a motorcycle for ten hours," Tara said. "Needless to say, my crush never did ask me out and I spent the rest of the year under a hat I bought at Casual Corner."

All of us at the table that night had at least one story. But in the end, Lucas won.

About a decade earlier, when Lucas was in his early twenties, he studied theater at the American Academy of Dramatic Arts in Los Angeles. Born and raised in the South of France, Lucas had a lot to learn about his new city, but he was motivated, because he'd fallen hard for an LA girl. When she invited him to come over to her place one night to watch *Gossip Girl* (a detail we all found hilarious), Lucas looked at a map and did what any Frenchman without a car would do: he set out to walk there. It looked like a bit of a trek, but doable. In France, people walk everywhere. But Lucas lived in Laurel Canyon and his new love was in the Pacific Palisades. To anyone who knows LA, this is completely insane. *Nobody walks in LA* is a real thing. But Lucas did it. He walked and walked and walked. (This was in the days before Uber, and you don't see many taxis in LA.) He went down the Hollywood Hills and spent hours walking Sunset Boulevard, hot in the hot sun, all the way through Beverly Hills, Bel Air, and Brentwood; he finally arrived long after *Gossip Girl* was over. He never gave up, though the walk took almost five hours.

Incredibly to all of us gathered that night, the young woman in question was not even remotely impressed by Lucas's show of devotion. In fact, she was straight-up annoyed: it was past her bedtime.

As the dinner came to a close, I felt relaxed, happy even, surrounded by my sister and friends both old and new. I hadn't checked my phone once all night, hadn't thought about the questions I couldn't answer, the promising updates I didn't have. Could it be possible I was exactly where I wanted to be at that moment, date or no date, soulmate or no soulmate? Maybe. But I had no idea what to do with that knowledge, and I didn't trust it.

Walking back to the hotel, the streets now wet from the evening's rain, I noticed the flyers I had placed earlier on windshields starting to disintegrate. Other flyers had been layered on top of mine. And parking tickets. Some leaves. All wet. It broke my heart a little. And filled it too. My whole night had been rich with love. None of it the heart-pounding romantic kind I'd come to Paris to find, but love just the same. Something about the dissolving flyers made me think of Philippe and the feelings I still had for him that had been surfacing all day, a dark seal appearing and disappearing in the waves. Intoxicating love like I'd had with him seems utterly perfect and fresh when first discovered. That's part of what makes it irresistible. Then life happens; real problems layer and settle in. Leaves fall, rain comes down. And sometimes, the flyers fucking disintegrate.

In the hotel's lobby, we hugged Tara good night and then she went to her room and we went to our attic suite. I curled up on my little red couch and opened Instagram to post some shots from the restaurant. And there it was on Margot's feed.

My mom's in Paris looking for her soulmate. Check her out @02Novembre1968—she's a real snack! Margot had reposted a photo Nicole had taken of me near the Arc du Carrousel holding a soulmate-search sign.

Was I finally being supported by my über-cool fifteen-year-old daughter? It was a miracle. Bigger than Kate Walsh, even. This was *Margot Barrett.*

"Look! Margot did a shout-out for me on IG!" I showed Penelope and Nicole my phone.

"What does she mean, you're a snack?" Penelope asked. "Is that an American thing? Is a snack a good thing?"

"I think so. But wouldn't it be better if I were a whole meal?" I half joked. "Should I look it up on Urban Dictionary?"

"It's a good thing," Nicole interjected. "You know, like someone you can sit and watch a movie with and . . . nibble on."

Ohhh, Margot. The three of us burst out laughing.

By this time, it was so late, it was early. But I couldn't wind down. As Nicole and Penelope took off their makeup and readied themselves for bed, I pulled on my boots.

"Where are you going?" Penelope asked.

"I need a minute to myself," I said. "I won't be long." I might as well admit it: I wanted a cigarette.

I didn't smoke anymore back home. I gave that up with Philippe. But . . . goddamn it, what was it about Paris? I had turned into the American who fell for all the clichés. Blue-and-white-striped sweater? Check. Crepes for breakfast? Check. Hanging out almost exclusively within a two-mile radius of the Eiffel Tower? Check. Gitanes cigarettes? Okay, check. But just one pack, which I'd secretly purchased while we were out hunting for a curling iron our first day in Paris. That was it. I doled those cigarettes out to myself like gold.

I stood outside the hotel under my umbrella, the rain falling heavily now, the street silent and dark. Still, the city looked beautiful to my eye. I pulled out my phone. Tired of the ghost parade, I hadn't been on WhatsApp since before dinner. But I thought I'd better see if any of the guys had come through and were waiting on me.

Devoted Dad, Maaz, had written back. We'd been messaging since I'd first arrived about dinner tomorrow night, but he hadn't committed. Maybe now he would. I opened his message.

My daughter is sick and it's my week to have her. My ex will kill me if I make plans. I have to cancel. Sorry.

Wait a minute. Wasn't his daughter an *adult*? I closed WhatsApp, tapped Tinder, and scrolled back through weeks of messages. Yes—she was out of college and working. This guy had probably been recycling the sick-kid excuse for *years*.

Hope she feels better. And I hope you find your match. What else was there to say? Nine down. And then there was the fact that several of the men technically still on the list—Benoit, Alcide, Christophe, and Amir—had not replied at all to my very first "I'm here in Paris finally" messages. Or my follow-ups.

Was I trying too hard? Or not hard enough? Did my potential soulmates all secretly think I was a fool and that I'd never *actually* come here, and now that I had, they were on the run? Was François right that I was a little bit too much for Frenchmen? Or maybe I'd been reading whatever signs the universe had been sending all wrong. For the thousandth time that day, I doubted myself, my search, and my ability to be in tune with my higher self, let alone higher powers. And then I wondered: What if I just stopped? Not my soulmate search, because I truly believed that there was something built into my spirit that would respond to the right match. But what if I shut down the doubts about how and when it would all happen and whether or not I'd accidentally fucked it up? What would that feel like?

Hey, universe, I thought, *I got this. Yes. I do. Hear me? I. Got. This. You don't want to send me my soulmate right now? FINE. We're still going to find that motherfucker. Also, we're still going to have FUN.*

Pushing back with intention felt good, like I was getting somewhere. All the effort, love, and understanding I was so busy sending out to the Devoted Dads of the world began to crystallize into something clearer. Harder. More beautiful.

I thought of how my best friends, the women who now lay sleeping upstairs in the hotel and those who were awake in sunny

Los Angeles half a world away, had been there for me uncondi-
tionally, year after year, when divorce or Philippe or dating in general or anything else got me down. And how I had returned the
same kind of love and support to them whenever they needed me.
It was a type of powerful magic that I knew for certain existed,
no signs or crystals required: Friendship. Sisterhood. Even if my
soulmate hadn't appeared yet, I had them. That's what inspired me
to do what I did next.

I opened Facebook and wrote a post in Paris for Her, one of
the groups for expats living in Paris I'd joined over the past few
months (I thought the members might have suggestions).

My name is Natasha and I'm an American here in Paris looking for my soulmate. It may sound strange, but an astrologer
told me someone born in this city on 2 Novembre 1968 is in
line with my point of destiny. For a lot of reasons, I believe her.
I flew all the way from Los Angeles to see if she's right, with the
goal of meeting as many men born with this birth chart (and
one woman, whose father might be my soulmate) as I possibly
could. I made a promise to my dad before he died that I would
always believe in magic and never give up on love. And, as I
see it, a promise is a promise. One of the last things my dad
said to me before he died was "I'll see you in Paris."

So here I am. In Paris. Hi, Dad.

I'm far away from my home in LA for sure. And some people have told me I'm crazy or worse. But I gathered my courage and came here because, well, something bigger than me
took over. Something that felt a lot like FAITH. Like HOPE. Like
LOVE. Like DESTINY.

Long story short, it's been a disaster. I've been stood up and
ghosted. I've failed miserably at finding The One. I feel more
than slightly lost. But it just occurred to me, standing alone
here at 2 a.m. in the rain, maybe I've been missing something.
Maybe I've been doing this all wrong.

For my last night in Paris, I would like to invite you—THE WOMEN OF PARIS—to join me and my best friends for a drink.

For anyone out there who believes in love and magic, living fearlessly, following dreams, and keeping promises . . . I would love to have a date with you.

I will be at Le 1905 bar in the 4th Arrondi at 7 p.m.—yes, seventeen hours from now! See you there! Love, Natasha

I hit Post before I could change my mind. If the men of Paris refused to show up for me, maybe the women would.

Ninth House

We're Gonna Find That Motherf✳%ker

The Ninth House rules foreign travel, adventure, and risk. Also, philosophy, religion, good fortune, growth, humor, higher education, mythology, and experiencing the largeness and generosity of life.

The Ninth House is our entry point into our alignment with our higher selves. It guides us to discover the answers we have been searching for. We encounter gurus, big-idea people, spiritual teachers, publishers, travel guides, comedians, religious leaders, philosophers, and pathfinders of all sorts through the planets in our Ninth House or the ruler of our Ninth House.

Scorpio fills my Ninth House, and both Mars and Pluto rule Scorpio. Because of this, my teachers tend to spring from the occult. Both of these planets strongly influence my journey, and both want me to find myself through a partner. But not just any partner—a soulmate who is my equal. Easier foretold than done. Reaching one's point of destiny isn't supposed to be effortless.

THE VERSION OF ME THAT TOLD THE UNIVERSE *I GOT THIS* evaporated like mist as soon as I checked my phone the morning of our fourth day in Paris. Instead of twenty or thirty new messages, which had been unnerving enough on previous mornings, *hundreds* of people had somehow found my Instagram overnight. It didn't make sense. The last story I'd posted, the one I'd filmed with Nicole yesterday, had been about how I was failing at all of this so far. But now some for-real famous people like Busy Philipps were following my search. How could my life be even remotely interesting to them? There were countless messages of support and requests for updates in the comments and my DMs. Sitting up on the little red sofa, I scrolled and scrolled, ping-ponging between gratitude and *Oh, shit!*

A modern-day fairy tale! Keep goingggggg!!!!

OMG, this is the best thing on social media. Better than any Netflix show!!!

Fairy tale? Netflix? If this was a fairy tale, then I was Cinderella at one a.m. walking barefoot through the streets, no coach or prince in sight. That terrible feeling of two selves coexisting uneasily—the social-media me beholden to an unexpectedly large audience and the scared me, flailing and uncertain in real life—came roaring back. My heart began to race. Any perspective I'd gained the day before seemed like a distant memory, someone else's epiphany.

Across the room, Penelope busily folded clothes into her little duffel bag. She'd be leaving for the airport in an hour. I wanted her to stay, even though I knew she had to get back to her family. Penelope had always been able to point calmly to the steady path whenever I felt like my life was about to go off the rails. Which was how I felt right then. Objectively, I knew I was being absurd, that I was worrying about nothing. In the middle of Paris. But I couldn't shake it. It was like that feeling you get when you are on a roller coaster (speaking of rails), going up, up, up a horrifying incline, wondering why you'd asked to be strapped into the ride in the first place. Knowing the ride, though safe, was *way* outside your comfort zone. As anyone dealing with anxiety knows, you can't simply will it away. Not that it stops people from trying.

I flopped back down onto my pillow and tried to calm myself for the day ahead. First I texted Dash and Margot a cute note for them to wake up to in a few hours: Bonjour, les enfants! Je vous aime! Being with my kids, even virtually, always helps center me. Then I sent positive thoughts about Fabrice out into the ether. I still wasn't sure I believed in manifestation, especially after the past two dateless days, but it couldn't hurt. *The stars will align today. Fabrice is handsome, kind, and smart. He's from a loving family, has grown children, and is even willing to come to Los Angeles. He's practically flawless. He's The One. It has to be him. Has to.*

"It's going to be okay, Natasha." Penelope could read me like a book. "So what if you don't know yet how it ends? That might be a good thing. The best love stories have a little mystery, trust me."

"If you say so," I replied, sitting up. "Thanks for coming all the way to Paris, P. I wish we had longer together."

"So do I. And I wouldn't have missed this, Tash. I love how you are chasing your destiny out loud. Thank *you* for sharing your journey with me."

Just then, the rolling rack jammed with fluttery, satiny clothes caught my attention. The dresses! Ellen Kinney, the generous president of ALC who'd gifted me the über-sexy dating wardrobe, would want me to pass that magic on, girlfriend to girlfriend. I wasn't sure about much that morning, but I was sure of that.

"P., you have to take the two dresses you rocked here in Paris home. Even if just for dates on your balcony after the boys are in bed. Wait until Teunbart sees you in them. He's going to want you to come on my stupid missions more often." I took the black-and-green dress and the ruched leopard one from the rack and handed them to Penelope. "Here. They were meant to be yours."

Penelope's face lit up. "Are you sure?"

"Yes. Nobody could look more gorgeous in them. I'm going to miss you."

"We'll see each other soon. Promise. How else will I get out of diaper duty and have a screwball adventure like only you could dream up?" Penelope winked at me and zipped her bag shut.

"I think I might be good on adventures for a little while after this."

"Hmm" was all Penelope said in response. And then: "Don't you and Nicole need to be downstairs to meet Tara for breakfast?"

"What is that?" I said, grimacing and pointing to the sad, solitary brown lump on Tara's plate. My own plate overflowed with *pain au chocolat,* brioche, fresh yogurt with granola, and fruit.

"Gluten-free bread. I don't want to talk about it."

"What's the plan today?" asked Nicole as I scrolled through more DMs and WhatsApp messages.

"Before we get to that, I have a favor to ask. For tonight." I looked hopefully at Nicole and Tara, both of whom sat expressionless. "So, I made plans to meet some people at Le 1905, a bar in the fourth, at seven."

"Made plans with *who*?" Tara asked, spreading some creamy Brie on the brown lump.

"Well, I'm not exactly sure yet. I posted a call to action in one of my Facebook groups last night—don't worry, Tara, this is a women's Facebook group. No scary Frenchmen. Anyway, I basically invited all the women of Paris to come meet me to celebrate love and magic and shit. You know, since the men haven't exactly been showing up for me."

"Oh God. You can't be serious." My sister stared at me.

"I swear it will be quick. We can just pop over for a drink, see who shows up, then go get a bite at one of the restaurants on your list. Our last big dinner together before Nicole and I leave tomorrow. Just a quick cocktail? Pretty please?"

"Aren't you meeting Fabrice at Versailles this afternoon?" Tara asked. "And Shayna at the bookstore for your YouTube interview?

How will we fit all this in? Versailles is a forty-minute cab ride away."

I checked my phone. It was only a little after eight a.m. "We have *so* much time. It'll all work out. But just in case the stars don't align for the poet and me, I thought this morning we should pass out flyers on the Métro? Oh, and maybe hit up a couple of hospitals for birth records? One of my followers suggested that."

Nicole and Tara exchanged tired glances. Anyone else would have told me I was on my own that morning. But my sister and best friend had made a promise to me, and I looked like I was about to lose it. My hair hung flat; the old T-shirt and tennis shoes I'd worn to breakfast were more appropriate for a day of housework than finding love in Paris. I'd barely slept since we'd arrived—none of us had (except Penelope). The only color on my face was an uneven swipe of the red lipstick I'd gotten in the habit of putting on no matter what.

"Tasha, remember I went to the archive museum yesterday?" my sister asked. "You know what else was there besides Marie Antoinette's secret love letters? Lots of beautiful people. All walking around solo, from what I could tell. None of them looked like tourists. So maybe museums here are like Equinox or Twenty-Four-Hour Fitness back home—undercover pickup spots. The Musée d'Orsay is right near the bookstore where you're meeting Shayna. What's more romantic, riding in circles on the Métro underground or bumping into your soulmate in front of a Renoir?"

Just then Penelope swept into the breakfast room, duffel bag over one shoulder, her long hair pulled into a tidy bun. She looked rested. Content.

"Do I hear talk of the Musée d'Orsay? You have to go, Tash. It's one of the most special spots in the city. Something good will happen there. You'll see." Penelope hugged us all, and I noticed she squeezed my sister extra-tight. "I'm glad we got to spend some real time together, Tara. Find a magnificent painting for me today, okay?" She blew us a dramatic kiss before rushing to her waiting cab.

With the mood lightened, I saw Tara's logic. The museum opened in an hour, which meant I had just enough time to change my clothes and fix my hair. I wanted to look pretty in case the Musée d'Orsay was filled with cute, cultured Scorpios looking for a date.

"Le 1905 *is* on my list of cool places to visit," Tara said, leafing through her notes.

"Let's do it," Nicole said, in a way that seemed forced for a split second and then not at all. "We're going to find that motherfucker today. I *know* it."

If I'd had any kind of a grip on reality, I would have called a time-out. I would have asked myself: *What are you doing, Natasha? Your best friend is exhausted and your sister is politely gnawing at a saw-dust brick. Do you have any idea what they might want to do in Paris? It's Nicole's first time here! And it might as well be Tara's too.* I would have put my phone away. I would have crawled back into bed for an hour. I might even have eaten breakfast.

But I didn't do any of that.

The Musée d'Orsay, perched on the Left Bank of the Seine in the seventh arrondissement, was once a grand turn-of-the-century train station meant to impress visitors to the city. The building still bore two showstopping clocks left over from its railroad days: an enormous black metal and glass one on the facade and a fancy smaller gold one in the main hall. Some people go to the museum just to see those clocks. But the Orsay also holds the best collection of Impressionist art in the world. Sunlight streamed through the vast, arched skylights—enough glass to cover five football fields—as we entered the lobby, awestruck.

For a few minutes, even I was captivated by the masterworks surrounding us. But my phone called to me like a drug. Plus, Tara turned out to be right—there were plenty of ridiculously attractive people milling about the museum. I started guessing their ages in my head, listening for French accents, and holding my flyer casually by my side, hoping someone would recognize the birth date. I tried to look sexy but approachable. But not one person noticed. It was nothing like Runyon Canyon or Whole Foods on a Friday night. People were at the museum for the reason on the door—art. *Shit*. I needed to set up more dates. And I thought I should post something soon, let people know I hadn't fallen into the Seine. I began scrolling through messages and DMs, oblivious to the people and art around me. Which was exactly what I'd told Nicole just the day before I *wouldn't* be doing.

"I don't get it," Tara said with real confusion. "How can you be in the middle of all this and not look up from your phone?"

She gestured to a painting directly in front of me: a Monet featuring a woman standing in a field of red poppies, holding a parasol and gazing into the distance.

I held up my phone and pressed Record. "She's looking for her soulmate too," I said to Tara and, of course, Instagram.

Tara rolled her eyes. "See the small child sitting next to her? I think that's Monet's son, and the woman is his wife."

We stopped in front of Renoir's *Dance in the City,* which showed a dancer looking searchingly over her partner's shoulder. "Is her soulmate here?" I said into my phone. "Nope."

Tara said nothing.

I wandered a little farther, and a Degas painting caught my eye. In it, a sad-looking woman sat alone at a café table staring at a glass of bile-green absinthe. "Oh no . . . he didn't show up for their date," I said into my phone.

At this point, my sister drifted farther and farther away from me in the galleries. And Nicole—where was Nicole?

I noticed her sitting alone on a bench, staring up at a colorful Renoir painting of people drinking and dancing at an outdoor party. Nicole looked upset.

"They're all so beautiful, aren't they?" Nicole said softly as I sat down beside her. I thought I knew what was wrong. Nicole had been working feverishly for several months on an independent film, a supernatural thriller that drew on the shadows of her past. It would be her debut as a filmmaker and I was so proud of her. She'd been frantic with edits right up until the minute we'd left for Paris, and they weren't finished. Major work stress waited at home for Nicole just like it did for me, so I thought that's what I saw on my best friend's face. I should have asked her, though. And remembered I wasn't the only one with a bruised heart on this trip. She and Justin hadn't spoken or texted once since we arrived in Paris. Their break from each other seemed to be turning into something coldly real and not so temporary after all.

Much later, Nicole told me that the painting's overwhelming beauty and romantic subject had unexpectedly hit her raw nerves like a ton of priceless Old Master bricks because she'd begun to realize that her feelings for Justin ran deeper than she wanted to acknowledge.

Also, both of us were fucking exhausted.

A few minutes after I sat on the bench next to Nicole, my head began to hurt so badly that spots appeared before my eyes. My back throbbed and I felt horrible all over, like I might faint.

It turns out, jet lag gets progressively worse if you don't sleep, hardly eat, and drink buckets of wine and coffee while stressing out over things you can't control. I needed some water. And Advil. For starters.

"I'll be right back," I mumbled to Nicole and made a beeline for a café I'd noticed earlier. My pulse began to slow and my headache faded a little after I downed a bottle of water. I'd like to say it was then I took stock of the situation and went back to our hotel for a nap. But, once I was semi-revived, I could focus only on the ticking clock. I had the rest of today, tonight, and tomorrow morning (at the airport) left to meet my soulmate in Paris.

Something Nicole had said to me months ago popped into my head just then: *Don't forget, Tash, he's looking for you too. I know it doesn't feel that way right now, but soulmates look for each other.*

I hoped to God she was right, that someone out there was

working just as hard as I was to find *me*. Maybe I simply needed to trust more in that.

Just then my phone pinged. WhatsApp. Fabrice! I felt a little zing in my chest. A good zing, not the freaking-out kind. Some-one out there *was* thinking about me! I tapped on his message.

Papa's heart has a crisis.

Wait, what? I read Fabrice's message again, trying to make sense of it. I saw the little green *typing* under his name. Another message appeared.

I'm sorry to cancel. I must go to my mother now.

I closed the app. I needed to walk. Find my sister and my best friend. The pain in my lower back picked up again.

"Tasha?" Tara said when I met her and Nicole by the giant clock. "You look a little peaky. Should we go back to the hotel?"

"Look. Fabrice—lovely, amazing, perfect Fabrice—is bailing on me too. Surprise." I handed my phone to Tara so she could see for herself.

My sister's brow knit as she read his messages. "Did you read all these? I think Fabrice's dad just died."

I took my phone back. Fabrice had written more. His father had collapsed as he'd gotten out of bed that morning. It was, the doctors thought, a sudden massive heart attack.

I felt like such an asshole. Fabrice had taken a moment to write to me on what I knew from grim experience was one of the sad-dest days of his life. He wasn't bailing on me; not even close. And yet I'd gone there immediately. What was going on with me to-day? This wasn't the love I wanted to put into the world or what I hoped to receive in return. I needed a neon Post-it on my phone, Sizlo-family-style, that said *Don't be a total shit*.

Fabrice, I am so, so sorry. I'm here if you need to talk. If you need anything, I typed.

"That's awful," Nicole said. "It's strange . . . you and Fabrice have some major things in common. Your dads. Your parents and their long happy marriages. I believe this has something to do with his birthday, with November second. But then, you also aren't meeting in real life, though you are trying. I wonder what an astrologer would say."

It was then I remembered that I'd written to Stephanie the day before for advice. *Please, universe, let her have written back.* I opened my e-mail.

Stephanie's reply was long. Really long. I tried not to imagine the associated Venmo request. I scanned for highlights, reading aloud.

> It doesn't matter that some of these men are ghosting you. That just shows that Saturn is doing its job. You were born with Saturn in Cancer in the Fifth House of love and romance. Saturn wants you to find love in the world. Cancer only wants the real and authentic. So, Saturn behaves like a screen door to your open door. You open the door to love and the screen door is there to filter out the riffraff.

> I understand that this is a quest for love in the physical world, but even so, this quest is about inner peace for you and is, at its heart, a spiritual quest. The key is to know that you are not looking for someone to add to your life to make it complete, but rather you are activating the part of you that is ready for this spiritual experience.

This was not what I wanted to hear. I looked up at Nicole and Tara. "Um, I think Saturn might be cockblocking me." I smiled uncertainly, trying to laugh.

Nicole sighed. "I'm not so sure that's what Stephanie meant."

Tara simply looked confused.

"And what's this *spiritual* quest? I don't want spiritual anything. I want someone to hold my hand. Someone to kiss on New Year's Eve. My other half. An actual, living, breathing person here in the flesh. Fuck Saturn." So much for celestial guidance on demand.

"Maybe we should get some air," Tara suggested.

I said I'd meet them outside, that I wanted to get another bottle of water. I needed a minute alone to gather my thoughts. With Fabrice suddenly out of the picture, the day felt even more off-kilter. I sat on a bench and pictured stars aligning in my favor, good energy, and everyday magic. I told myself to be cool, Joe Cool. But that dark little voice crept in: *What if nobody is out there looking for you? What if nobody ever looks for you specifically ever again?*

"Shut up," I muttered. "Go away." Fuck those bad juju spirits. If they wouldn't go away, I'd go someplace else. I began walking quickly toward the exit, where the gift shop happened to be. Something in its window caught my eye: an elegant candle in black glass. I hurried inside the shop and picked up the candle, taking in its hyacinth and woodsmoke perfume. UN SOIR À L'OPÉRA PARIS the label read above an illustration of a black swan wearing a diamond-encrusted crown. I shouldn't have been buying a pricey, heavy candle. But nothing bad ever happens while shopping and I needed to escape something bad. And for some reason, I just had to have it. After shoving my purchase deep into my bag, I stepped out into the sunlight to meet Nicole and Tara.

"So where's this bookstore again?" I asked Tara.

"It's not just some bookstore, it's Shakespeare and Company. One of the most famous bookstores in all of Paris. Maybe even the world. It's right across the river from Notre-Dame. Could we maybe visit a chapel after your interview to light a candle together for Dad?"

I felt a lump in my throat. "Dad would love that. I'll light a candle for Fabrice's father too."

Shakespeare and Company's green-and-yellow facade and weather-beaten sidewalk book bins telegraphed old-world charm. Inside, thousands of books both new and used lined the shelves that stretched from floor to ceiling. More books were heaped on tables crammed into corners. I'd never seen so many books packed into a space. Tara had told us on the way over that this English-language bookstore, founded in 1951, had long been the center of expat literary life and that many famous writers had visited and even slept there over the years. Looking around the store, an extraordinary tribute to reading and writing as surely as the Musée d'Orsay was to art, I could see why.

I ran my fingers absently over the spines of books, picking up one classic novel and then another. A tattered copy of S. E. Hinton's *The Outsiders* caught my attention. It looked just like the one I'd been assigned in boarding school long ago. As I leafed through it, the words on the page brought me powerfully back not to the lessons in the classroom but to the countless letters I'd written to my friends in those years. What happens to you as a teenager matters. Sometimes, the intervening decades can feel all but gone.

It's easy to get kicked out of most boarding schools. All you have to do is break just one of the cardinal rules: no leaving campus without permission, no alcohol, no drugs of any kind, no cheating, no sex, and, above all else, no breaking of the school's beloved honor code.

I'm a born rule-breaker. As a child, when someone said sit, I would always stand. I'd refuse to go to bed, flush my sister's Weebles down the toilet, and insist on wearing Christmas dresses in summer photos. And that's just for starters. I knew I'd get in trouble and, strange as it may sound, I *hated* getting in trouble. Eventually, I felt bad about myself all the time. I never seemed to be able to be good like other kids. My brain said yes when someone told me no, and vice versa. In my twenties, I received a diagnosis of attention deficit disorder, which helped me make sense of some of my childhood behaviors, and I began to chart a healthier way forward. But as a teen? I was in the dark. As were my beleaguered parents.

But that's not why I ended up at Thacher, an elite boarding school in California, though my trouble with rules did contribute to why I got kicked out. Our parents sent my sister and me there because education was *everything* to them. Bob, born into a working-class immigrant family in Detroit, saw how his degree from MIT opened doors. And Edna, whose schooling finished in Scotland when she was fourteen, vividly understood the advantages that the upper classes in Edinburgh enjoyed because of the higher education that was their socioeconomic birthright. Securing the best education for Tara and me felt urgent to Bob and Edna; the stakes were high. Boarding school, a concept that neither of my parents had heard of before, became a Sizlo family obsession after a star student in Tara's class left for supposedly greener educational pastures that included a dorm and a big tuition bill. Also during that time, my dad overheard another parent say that the Sizlo sisters would never fit in at a school like Thacher. Talk about a red flag and a bull. The die was cast. With a little luck, plus some serious sacrifices and generous financial aid, my sister went to Thacher. I followed three years later.

Thacher turned out to be a bewildering, often terrifying world to a thirteen-year-old girl with undiagnosed ADD in 1988. Official rules and consequences structured nearly every minute of our existence at Thacher. I knew upon arrival I'd never remember them all, that I'd slip up regularly. Anxiety consumed me. After that came anger as I slowly realized a much bigger problem loomed there: The unwritten rules, which were meant for female students. First and foremost: Be ladies. And remember that boys will be boys. Ladies should be attractive and never question authority, especially not the authority of men. If the headmaster compliments your appearance, say thank you. If he smells of alcohol, say nothing. If he drops his napkin at Formal Dinner and asks you to put it back on his lap, do it. While wearing a dress. But not a black one. Ladies don't wear all black. Only girls looking for trouble wear all black. And so on.

In 2021, in a series of bombshell reports, the *Los Angeles Times* revealed Thacher to be a nightmare of sexual harassment and assault for many teens, most of them girls, who were preyed upon, consequence-free, by male teachers and students alike in the late

1980s through the 2010s. I couldn't have put into words all that I sensed was wrong about the school back then, but the blatant hypocrisy between the rules for the students and the actions of the adults who were supposed to protect and care for us ate away at me. I credit the friends I made at Thacher, friends I still have to this day, for saving me from total despair. We all saved each other.

In the spring of my sophomore year, six of those friends and I snuck out after check-in to an off-campus party where there were older boys who didn't go to our school. There was beer and weed too, lots of it, as we soon discovered. I knew we might be expelled if anyone found out where we were. But I couldn't stop myself. One beer, one drag turned into more beers, more weed. I don't remember much about the party, but I do remember one thing: I lost my virginity. And not in a romantic the-stars-are-aligned kind of way.

Only the sun coming up alerted my friends and me to the fact that we should try to sneak back *into* school. Unsurprisingly, we were caught, still drunk, and quarantined for discipline. My expulsion was abrupt and final, a lonely, shaming experience. I tried to tell myself none of it mattered, that since some of my friends had also been expelled and Tara had already graduated, I didn't want to be there anyway. That part was true—I didn't want to be at Thacher. But fifteen-year-old me couldn't think of an acceptable way to express that, so I had let myself out the only way I knew how.

In an instant, I found myself home in Rockcreek, Oregon, far away from the Ojai sun and my friends. I wasn't allowed to talk to any of them on the phone. I said nothing to my parents about what I had been through or how difficult my time at Thacher was. How could I? Bob and Edna had downsized to a small two-bedroom apartment and lived on credit cards to afford to send us to the school. I had failed them, just like that parent my dad overheard had predicted. I began writing letters to my closest classmates, scribbling my feelings of sadness, isolation, rage, and confusion in Bic pen onto lined notebook paper.

What started as an urgent means of communication quickly became my lifeline and passion. Writing was difficult and painful sometimes, but it also felt good. I needed something to make me feel good about myself back then for lots of reasons, but a big one was that I never managed to finish high school. Not the traditional way. It's still hard at times for me to tell people that. Finishing high school can seem, in our status-obsessed society, like a low bar. But for some of us, it's not. Eventually, I got my GED.

I studied screenwriting in college and afterward jumped at an entry-level job at a magazine. But soon, I switched to the fashion and wholesale industries. It paid more. I promised myself I'd write on weekends. Then I met Michael. We got married, had Margot four short months later, and I quit my job as a sales rep for a denim company and my freelance writing, which I'd been doing on the side. Soon I stopped writing altogether. I didn't even keep a journal.

There was this idea in my head that good mothers and wives devoted themselves entirely to their families. I was determined to finally be good at something, to stop hopping from thing to thing and *focus*. I loved being a mother; loved little Margot right from the minute I laid eyes on her. But writing had been my way of working through ideas and emotions dark and light. Without it, all those feelings had no place to go. Sometimes I think that's why postpartum depression hit me so hard in the weeks after Margot's birth. I still want an explanation for the wild and terrible darkness I felt other than "Sometimes it just happens." I didn't ever reach for my computer back then. Even after my divorce, I didn't think about writing. If I'm being honest, I dulled the rare moments alone I had after the kids were asleep with alcohol. A glass of wine. A shot of tequila. The kind of writing I'd been best at was too raw and vulnerable to contemplate starting again. Dig into my feelings, the events of the past few months and years? No, thanks.

Instagram changed that, probably because I didn't think of it as writing. Not at first. A post isn't an article or an essay or even a proper letter to a friend, and that's what let me dip my toe back in.

But at Shakespeare and Company that October afternoon in Paris, I wasn't dwelling on Thacher or the past; something else kept grabbing my attention. The books. I looked at all the words and pages and books surrounding me on the shelves and wished for the first time in a long time that some of them belonged to me. And not in an "I just bought this" way. Maybe Nicole wasn't entirely right when she said that Instagram had nothing to do with my point of destiny. Stephanie said that my point of destiny was to tell a story. I couldn't deny I was now in the middle of doing that, albeit unconventionally. What if I kept going? Then I shook my head. What was I thinking?

"Shouldn't we get ourselves to the café? I think that's where we're meeting Shayna," I said. I still wasn't ready to own the writing part of my dream, not even to Tara and Nicole. Why I found it infinitely less challenging to blast a bald request for my soulmate, a man born on a specific day in a specific place per my astrologer, across the internet and *in person* in two major cities, only a good shrink could say.

After settling in at a table tucked up against the bookstore's exterior, Nicole and I devoured the bagels we'd gotten at the counter. But Tara sat with just a mug of tea before her.

"Aren't you hungry?" I asked.

"I'm okay," Tara replied.

It dawned on me then that the café must not have had any appealing gluten-free options. Crap. Tara hadn't eaten anything since that sad lump back at our hotel hours ago. I didn't know what to do. This YouTuber with well over a hundred thousand followers would be here any second. *We'll be quick,* I thought, *and then we'll find Tara some food.* Nervously, I reapplied my lipstick. I wasn't exactly used to interviews.

When I looked up, Shayna stood before our table. Just twenty-two and almost impossibly fresh-faced, she wore her shiny platinum-violet hair tied in a loose ponytail. Her eyelids had been dusted in bright orange sparkle, her lashes dipped in white mascara, and her lips painted a maraschino red. Her electric-blue trousers, silver vest, and whimsical duster printed with zebras, peacocks, and butterflies were the upcycled opposite of LA's flashy-logo and fast-fashion trends. Black platform Mary Janes paired with striped tube socks perfectly punctuated the look. Shayna's entire being was a canvas for ecstatic self-expression. I loved her immediately.

"Hiiiiiii!" she sang, brimming with kinetic energy. "It's fantastic to meet you finally!" Shayna sat down next to Tara at our table, camera in hand, although she wasn't recording yet. "I want to know *everything.* From the beginning! What you are doing is radical! How did this even happen? I have so many questions!"

Usually, when I told someone new about how I came to be searching for my soulmate in a foreign city, I went heavy on the Philippe and Stephanie parts. On astrology, magic, and love. That's what we'd all been doing as we explained to taxi drivers, waiters, and strangers on the streets about 2 Novembre 1968. But that day, sitting across from Shayna, for the first time, I talked a lot about Bob. I told the story of being at his bedside with Tara in the last few weeks of his life and promising to meet him here in Paris. As I spoke, Shayna nodded, rapt. But Tara's face fell. Were those tears in her eyes? I couldn't tell, because my sister hastily got out her sunglasses and put them on.

I should have stopped. Tara had just left a sunlit museum filled with paintings of ballerinas and wildflowers, and I had taken her back to darkness. A private darkness. Those hours at our father's bedside as we'd together made whatever decisions we could about how he'd leave the life he'd known with us had been only ours. It was the three of us against the world in a way, a sacred expe-

rience. Bob was old and he was sick and it would be fair to say
we'd known this was coming. Still, none of us were ready to say
goodbye. And while there were moments of levity because that's
how my family rolls, death isn't funny or fun. Without question, I
should have stopped talking. But I didn't. Not because I wanted
to tell Shayna or her followers a great story but because I couldn't
help myself. It all just came out.

Sensing Tara's distress, Nicole gently placed her hand on my
sister's back. Tara stiffened. The look on her face, even behind her
oversize sunglasses, told me it took every bit of restraint she had
not to punch Nicole. We were Sizlos. Or, rather, Henrettys—my
mother's side. The Henrettys, Scots to the bone, don't want your
sympathy or your condolences or your comfort or your help. We
carry on. Not much does us in. Except for a hug or a rub on the
back. We can't take that.

Tara stood abruptly and said she needed to stretch her legs.
After watching my sister walk quickly away, Shayna turned to me,
worried. "Is she all right?"

"She will be," I said, mostly to convince myself it was okay that
I didn't go after Tara.

We did the actual interview on the quieter park benches nearby.
It didn't take long, or so I thought. It was easy to talk to Shayna,
with her sparkling gray-blue eyes and the bubbly twang of her
voice—a blend of France and Florida, which she'd moved from all
by herself at just nineteen. Wrapping up, she asked one final question. "If he's out there listening, what would you like to tell him?"

No one had ever asked me that.

"'I'll wait for you,'" I said, the words spilling out almost before
I knew what they would be. "'I'll wait for you,'" I said again.

Tara returned as Shayna was shooting some B-roll of me in the
bookstore handing out flyers and tucking my business cards into
old books. "Tasha, don't forget that the chapel has limited hours.
We need to go."

"It's right there. Relax." I gestured to the imposing glorious cathedral shrouded in scaffolding that loomed just across the river. If I were a bird, I could have flown to its gates in less than five seconds.

Just then I noticed a red-painted staircase leading up to the store's second floor. How had I missed it earlier? I knew we needed to leave, but the staircase was the perfect Instagram backdrop. "Nicole, can you take a quick picture of me on these cute stairs?"

"Amazing idea," she replied. "Should you be holding a stack of books about love?"

Tara stared at her watch. And then at me as I posed on the stairs. Shayna took a few more shots, then declared herself satisfied.

"I'm so inspired by your ability to live in your truth," Shayna said as we parted. "Hey—imagine if you find your soulmate because of this video? How cool would that be?" We hugged goodbye.

"We've got to run!" Tara said. "It's four twenty-five and the chapel closes at five."

"How long does it take to light a candle? Three minutes? We're fine," I said, silently praying to the universe that I was right.

We picked up our pace as we headed across the Petit Pont to Notre-Dame.

If I'd been paying attention, I would have known that we *weren't* going to Notre-Dame. The cathedral was still closed to the public since the devastating fire that had destroyed much of the interior and the building's structure earlier that spring. No, we were going to a smaller Gothic chapel just five hundred meters from Notre-Dame: the Sainte-Chapelle. It was, Tara said, where the kings of France used to worship.

Even though we arrived with more than twenty minutes to spare, the doors to the chapel were shut and locked. The sign affixed to them read PAS D'ADMISSION APRÈS 1630. What? Tara opened Google Translate.

No admittance after 4:30 p.m.

Oh no. I banged on the doors. "Hello?" I called. Nothing.

I turned to Tara, who stared at me with sadness and disappointment mingled with exhaustion and a flinty spark of fury.

"I'm sorry. R–really, really sorry," I stammered, "but at least you got to light a candle for Dad at that other church you visited a couple of days ago. He knows that, sis." *Right, Dad?*

"I lit that candle for *you*. To find true love. We were supposed to light a candle for Dad together. Because we promised him we'd meet him here, *together.* You and me."

Shit. Shit. Shit. My sister's face had turned to stone; her lips were pressed thin. Back on went the dark glasses, even though the sun would soon set.

"It's fine," Tara said flatly as the three of us piled into a cab. We'd go back to our hotel to change before heading to Le 1905.

We were running late by the time we left for the bar. I was a wreck. Uneasy and then downright negative thoughts ping-ponged in my head. Here's just a partial list: I was a thoughtless jerk for not lighting a candle with Tara for Bob. With my flight so early the next morning, we wouldn't get another chance. I didn't know how to make it up to her. Then there was Georges. Remember how he was going to take a train from Provence to meet me for a drink? I thought he'd ghosted me, but he hadn't. I'd missed his last reply, a DM lost in a flurry of DMs, trying to confirm the time. I saw it twenty-four hours too late. I apologized, but he must have thought I was a flake or worse. And Fabrice. His first night without his dad. Thank goodness Fabrice hadn't seen how self-centered I'd been when I'd first read his message. He definitely wouldn't have wanted me for his soulmate then. I worried about things back home and about the night to come. What if my last-ditch effort to meet with the women of Paris was an epic fail? What if some of them showed up early and we missed them? I'd already messed up so much that day. I wanted to get something right, get things back on track. But we were late.

The helpful concierge, now thoroughly our friend, assured us that Le 1905 was a short walk away and that no Parisian would take a cab there from the hotel. "*C'est simple.* Just two blocks this one way, and then a block the other, and up the street, and *tu es arrivé.*"

Or was it two blocks the *other* way? Once we'd walked a few blocks, we weren't sure. Tara consulted the map on her phone. Yes, we'd accidentally gone the wrong way.

"We should still be okay if we hurry," I said to Tara and Nicole. I had on boots with my skinny jeans. Tara in her practical shoes could follow me easily, but she kept turning to look behind us as I charged ahead because Nicole had worn an exquisite pair of Christian Louboutin heels, and they were most definitely not made for walking.

Every sparkling thing about Nicole's beauty that night was turned up a little higher. She'd gotten ready with an almost meditative level of focus, so absorbed in her process that she hardly spoke. Her hair fell in gleaming waves, her makeup was an expert blend of subtle and smoky, and her slip dress channeled an elegant vibe. On just about any other night, I would have recognized all this as Nicole's personal form of Xanax and checked in with her, especially after what I'd seen at the Musée d'Orsay that morning.

But I had been on a call with Billy as I'd thrown together my own far more casual look. The sale of the pop star's house was off. The buyer, a man who prized privacy and efficiency above all else, had backed out. Drama spooked him. As did delays—he'd wanted a quick, hassle-free close, but that was no longer an option. The night after the final inspection, the pop star decided to let himself and his buddies back in to say goodbye to all the good times. At 3:00 a.m. Forgetting the code to the keypad door lock, the pop star broke in by smashing one of the plate-glass windows in the game room with a deck chair. That's where the police found him:

sitting on a formerly pristine fur beanbag, alternately smoking a bong and eating the staged candy, surrounded by vintage Pac-Man and Donkey Kong machines (none of which were his; these were staged too), and gushing over how incredible the house looked. *Just look at my place!* he said to the cops. *See how cool it is?* Since it was indeed his place, the cops left. And the party raged for the next twelve hours. About the only thing that hadn't happened to the poor house was the reinstallation of the taxidermy decor. The pop star simply hadn't had the time.

Billy and I were fucked. All the many hours we'd spent prepping the place and then managing the sale up to this point were wasted. As were the thousands of dollars fronted by Billy for a top-notch promotional video of the property. (I'd promised to reimburse him for half the cost after we closed.) The painters, the tile guy, the deep cleaners—they all needed to return. We'd need to reshoot at least part of the video. And fucking up staged furniture is an expensive no-no. We'd have to explain to the pop star that it now belonged to him, or at least it would after he paid for it, which he had to do, an uncomfortable conversation with a client no matter the circumstances. Gone was the promise of a timely commission that would allow me to exhale for a few months while I hustled more listings but with a gold-star celebrity sale to my credit, which would hopefully make attracting new business a little easier. We were almost back to square one with the house—if we were lucky. Because the manager had ended his last call with Billy with the words no real estate agent wants to hear: "If we can't find another buyer right away, maybe we'll just lease the house." Agents handle leases, but we prefer sales. The commission for a sale is ten to twenty times what we earn on a lease.

Fuck, fuck, *fuck.*

To say I was distracted that evening as we set out would be a gross understatement.

"I can't go this fast," Nicole said as she teetered on the cobblestones, stumbling a bit. "Damn it." Nicole removed one of her shoes and studied the heel. The tip had come off, exposing a thin metal spike. "Go on without me and I'll meet you there. We're close. Just a block or two left, right? I'll walk at my own pace."

I looked up and down the street at the darkened art galleries, the scattered Parisians in their wool coats leaving offices. It seemed perfectly safe, if strangely quiet for this time of evening. I didn't want to leave Nicole, but I also didn't want to be a bumbling, rude host.

"We're not far at all, Nicole's right," Tara said. "We're going to be late as it is."

"Are you sure you're going to be okay, Nicole?"

"OMG, go already. I have my phone. I'm fine. I'll see you in five minutes!"

Tara and I soon discovered we were more than just a block or two away from the bar (we'd gotten totally turned around somehow), but once we decided to hurry ahead, we went. Nicole would catch up.

When we finally arrived at Le 1905, a cozy and chic cocktail bar tucked above a buzzy bistro, it was dead empty except for the bartender. I checked my phone: 7:27 p.m. Where was everyone? Was this even the right place? The bartender confirmed it was. I asked her if maybe a bunch of women had already been in, looked around, and left? She shook her head no. We ordered a bottle of champagne and twelve glasses. And then we waited. And waited.

A text arrived from Nicole. Stopped in a store. Be there soon.

I've got a glass of champagne waiting for you. No rush, I replied— the understatement of the week, because I was being stood up. In a big way. Tara and I sipped our drinks in silence. How could I have been so dumb as to think that all these women would come to a random bar to meet a stranger from LA? A stranger who, by her own admission, was an embarrassing failure?

My sister tried to make the best of it. "A quiet night isn't the worst idea. Why don't we order an appetizer here and enjoy our aperitifs while we figure out where to have our last fabulous dinner together in Paris?" Tara studied the menu. "I still wish you were staying tomorrow, but I know you have to get home."

Then I felt a warm hand on my back. I looked up and saw a petite young woman with dark hair and kind brown eyes behind cat's-eye glasses.

"Natasha?" she asked quietly. "I'm Mercedes."

"Mercedes!" I jumped off the barstool and wrapped my arms around her. Forget formal French hellos. "I can't believe you're here! This is my sister, Tara. And my best friend Nicole is on her way. OMG!"

I couldn't believe my eyes. Mercedes was the thoughtful, generous stranger who had reached out to me on Instagram many months ago, the one who had suggested I join Paris Facebook groups and had printed out hundreds of my posters and wallpapered Métro stations and street corners with them. And now here she was. In person!

"We'd just decided nobody was going to show up," I said.

Mercedes laughed shyly. "Well," she said in her soft voice, "perhaps you did not know that in Paris, it is still early in the evening to be out at a bar?"

Ah. We did *not* know that. The night took on a different cast and my spirits began to lift. I poured a glass of champagne for Mercedes. "I've been dying to ask: What's your story? Are you single? Also looking for love? Like, why on earth would cute-young you be following dusty-old me?"

"I'm not single. My boyfriend and I have been together for years. I don't know exactly why I am so moved by what you are doing. I just knew instantly that I needed to be a part of it."

Tara smiled warmly as Mercedes spoke, the two of them connecting immediately. And then Nicole appeared beside me. Something about her seemed slightly off. Her hair wasn't quite so flawless as it had been, and, for the merest second, she had a look on her face like I'd never seen before: haunted, drawn, and gray, all her usual sunshine snuffed out. But that look disappeared almost as soon as I noticed it. Maybe I was seeing things? It had been a long day.

"You okay?" I whispered as I handed her a glass of champagne after introducing her to Mercedes.

"Fine," Nicole replied. I wasn't sure I believed her, but before I could find out more, the door to Le 1905 opened again. And then again and again as one by one, women who'd seen my invitation began filling the room. With each arrival, the good energy in the bar rose higher and higher. Most of the women were not Paris-born; they'd come to the City of Light for work or love or family. They were seekers and risk-takers of varied ages and backgrounds. None of them knew one another. But they all wanted to. And they wanted to know *me*.

There was Dominique, a hilarious and wry gorgeous older woman totally rocking the off-duty-fashion-editor look with her slim black jeans and blazer. As she later confessed, Dominique wondered if she'd come to meet an insane woman and her equally disturbed companions (was she Colette's secret sister?). Tara, especially, found this funny. It was the first time she'd realized that some people might think *we* were the ones to be wary of on this trip, not the potential soulmates. As a divorced single mother herself, Dominique had given up on the dating scene but thought it might be time to try again. She wanted to know how it had all been going for me. Then there was no-nonsense Magritte, a nanny turned teacher who, in her spare time, expertly ran a Facebook group for au pairs living in Paris and devoted herself to helping them thrive. A nurse named Anabelle fervently followed astrology; Anita the thirty-something feminist scholar had dating stories so funny, they brought us to our knees; and tiny Beatrix carried a violin and a bulging backpack. Just nineteen, she had stepped off a bus from Budapest and come straight to the bar. When Magritte discovered Beatrix had nowhere to sleep that night, she immediately offered her a safe place to stay until she found work. Yes— that happened right before my eyes at Le 1905.

Over champagne and tapas and stories, all of us eventually crowded around a large table on the terrace, and strangers became immediate, intimate friends. The women wanted to know: How was the search going? What did I think of Paris? Of Frenchmen? Had I found him yet?

"Honestly, I have been ghosted or canceled on so far by all but one of my potential soulmates. It's been a huge failure."

Magritte shook her head. "That's so like Parisian men. They were probably intimidated by you. I swear, whenever I have asked a Frenchman out, he *seems* excited by it, but then it falls apart. Frenchmen can be too macho."

"It's true," said Rosalie, a sophisticated Dutch woman in her thirties, "and there is also the problem of how meeting someone usually happens in Paris. French people tend to socialize within their own circles, with friends of friends, et cetera. There's very little talking to people at cafés or bars like I experienced when visiting the States. And forget blind dates. Which is one reason I think dating apps have been exciting for some of us in France, though off-putting for others. My favorite is AdopteUnMec, where you literally drop dudes in a shopping cart. If only!"

"You should be getting the birth times from all the possible matches," said Anabelle knowingly. "Timing is everything in astrology, as in life."

"I can't even get most of them to answer me about a coffee now that I'm here in Paris," I said, laughing, "but you make a good point."

"You won't give up, will you?" one of the women asked.

"No," another immediately answered for me, confident. "She won't. Look how far she has come."

For once, I didn't refuse the compliment. Instead, I stood up, raised my glass, and made a toast to all the women gathered at the bar. I thanked them for coming to meet me, for showing me that Paris was full of love after all. They were right, I said. I wasn't giving up. As I spoke, I noticed something bizarre: I, Natasha Sizlo, was up in front of people, talking, and I wasn't scared. This had never happened to me before. What was going on? I had no idea, but I liked it.

We drank and laughed for almost three hours. Dating could be hard, we concluded, no matter one's geographical location. But mostly, we didn't talk about our disappointments. Instead, the women opened up about their own wild dreams for themselves, strange coincidences, and gut impulses. Beatrix pulled out her violin and serenaded us with songs of love, heartbreak, and soaring joy. There seemed to be no emotion she couldn't conjure with music.

Eventually, all the brilliant women had to get home to children or bed or off to their own dates. Hugging everyone goodbye, I promised to let them know what happened next. Nicole and I had already checked in for our flight home in the morning, but my soulmate could be at the airport. *Right?*

We waited on the street for a cab.

"Okay, wow. Like, *wow*. I can't believe they all showed up." As low as I'd felt on the way to the bar, this was the opposite of that. "*Wow*."

"What just happened?" Tara asked, almost as awestruck. "Tasha, I had no idea how much your search meant to the people following it. Or how cool and awesome they are. Did you?"

"I don't know what I was expecting tonight, but that was beyond anything I could have hoped for." It was a lot to take in. My thoughts swirled. I couldn't stop smiling.

"I'm ready for bed," said Nicole quietly.

"No. Not yet," Tara pleaded. "We should have dinner. It's our last night together in Paris. Let's not end it just yet. Besides, none of us had much beyond a few bites of cheese at the bar. Aren't you hungry? I could eat."

Tara was being kind. She hadn't had a full meal all day. She must have felt faint with hunger by then.

"Of course we have to have our grand finale," I said. "Steak frites? Nicole, what about you? Think you can find your second wind?"

Nicole agreed to come with Tara and me once she remembered there was no kitchen at our sweet little hotel, which meant no room service. We ended up at a restaurant very close to the Hôtel du Petit Moulin so that getting back there would be easy on all of us, especially Nicole with her busted shoe. The nondescript bistro we found wasn't at all what we'd have chosen for our last meal in Paris, but at least it was open. Partially, anyway. The host led us through an empty front room where a young man was busy turning up chairs to a dimly lit, also-empty seating area in the back. The kitchen, he said, had begun to close but he could offer us some premade salads and a last batch of fries. We gratefully accepted.

Our waitress kept disappearing. Nicole could barely keep her eyes open. Tara wanted to talk more about the women we'd just met. Our wine arrived. I noticed that Nicole didn't touch it.

"Are you okay?" I asked again. My mind flashed back to the haunted look I'd seen on her face earlier. I remembered that at one point, she'd left our group and vanished from sight. Where had she gone? I had the sickening feeling that something was terribly wrong.

"No, I'm not," Nicole replied. "Someone started following me on the street on the way to the bar."

I shriveled inside as Nicole told us what had happened. We'd all decided together that Tara and I would rush ahead to the bar, but no matter how I sliced it in my head, Nicole had been left alone on a street in a foreign city. And that hadn't been a good decision.

Limping along with her broken heel while alternately searching for a cab and staring at Google Maps, Nicole suddenly had that prickling sensation you get when someone is way too close. She turned around. The street had been empty moments before, but a man had materialized. When Nicole stopped, so did he. When she started walking again, he did too. Nicole turned to look at him again and felt the first stab of panic. His vibe was way off. She picked up her pace. For a terrible minute she wondered what the hell she was going to do. Was there 911 in France? How did that even work? Then Nicole saw a store whose lights were still on and dashed toward it. A broad-shouldered clerk, who looked to her like a shining angel of mercy, happened to be at the entrance, leaning against the open door while he smoked. The terrifying man fell back. He waited across the street, staring into the shop, walking slowly away only when Nicole's Uber arrived.

Tara's face went white with remorse as she listened to Nicole. I wanted to crawl under the table and disappear. It didn't matter what my intentions had been. I'd chosen being a little less late— for an empty bar!—over my steadfast best friend of almost twenty years. I began to apologize, struggling to find any words that were even remotely right.

But Nicole held up her hand. "Tash, you're not responsible for every potentially rapey guy's creepy-ass behavior. No woman is. It's true, I could have used you back there. And I shouldn't have told you to go. It's fucked up and it's nobody's fault. At least, nobody at this table. I'll feel better after I get some sleep."

"Is that why you disappeared at the bar? I was going to look for you but then you suddenly came back."

"Yeah. I gave in and tried to call Justin but he didn't pick up and then I kind of spiraled. Can we not talk about this anymore? The women who came out for you tonight were spectacular. I'm glad it happened. It was magic. I'm honored I was there to see it. I'm just exhausted. It's late."

Shit. She'd called Justin. That underscored for me how alone Nicole had felt. I'd fucked up big-time, no matter what she said. I reached over and took her hand. "I'm so, so sorry, Nicole. What happened on the street should *never* have happened. Let's get our check and go." I waved at the waitress as she drifted across the other end of the dark restaurant. Her curt nod told me she saw me. This wasn't at all how I'd hoped the evening or the trip would end. Everything had gone dark. But I didn't know how to change that. Our last hours in Paris were rushing away.

Then my phone pinged.

Chloe, the confident, free-spirited artist and daughter of a man born on November 2, 1968, the woman I'd been almost desperate to meet, had at long last agreed to lunch—tomorrow, about two hours *after* our flight left. The timing couldn't have been worse. Part of me wanted to quickly text her back to say it was too late, I was leaving. But what if Chloe's dad, or Chloe herself, was who I was meant to meet? Did I come all this way to *not* find out?

"Nicole . . . I think . . . maybe . . . I know this sounds off right now, but look." I showed her my phone. "I could have another actual date with someone from my list. Should I stay the extra day after all? I don't know when I'll be able to come back. With the way work is going, it could be years."

"Only you can decide, Tash. Tune in. What's your heart telling you to do?"

In an instant, it clicked: I had to stay. It was just one more day, a day that could change my entire life. I had worked for the better part of a year to track down 2 Novembre 1968 matches. Telling Chloe no didn't make sense. It felt too much like giving up, which was the opposite of what I wanted to do, the opposite of what I'd told my dad I'd do. What was it that the coach at the boxing gym said about doubling down in the final round? Fall down seven times, get up eight. Or something like that.

"Okay. I'm doing it. And I'll try to set up a second date. That cute bike-obsessed guy Amir finally surfaced and said he'd be in Paris tomorrow night. I'll tell him I will be too now. This could still work out." The magic and possibility that I'd felt back at the bar began to return. All was not lost. I had another whole day in Paris.

I didn't notice that Tara hadn't said a word as I talked to Nicole about Chloe and Amir and changing my travel plans.

I opened my airline reservation and with a few quick taps adjusted my flight.

"Are you serious?" Tara's voice quavered. "*Now* you decide to stay? Like, less than eight hours before your cab to the airport is supposed to pick you up?"

I looked up at my sister. Her eyes brimmed with tears, but she wasn't sad. She was furious. I still can't believe I didn't immediately see why.

"Yes," I said, confused. "I have to give Chloe and Amir a chance. I told all the women tonight I wouldn't give up on my soulmate search. I think I kind of promised that, remember?"

"No. You promised *Dad* you'd meet him here. You promised *me* we'd do Paris together. Did you forget all that? I've been asking you for weeks to stay an extra day with me, just us sisters. But you couldn't do it. Until now. And all it took was a total stranger—who isn't even one of your matches, her *dad* is, not that he knows that—to ask you."

I opened my mouth and then shut it again. *Damn it*. This night kept going sideways.

Tears streamed down my sister's face. She wiped her eyes. "I don't know what's wrong with me. I want you to stay, of course I do, but maybe spending tomorrow apart is a good idea. You go on your dates. Honestly, I probably need some time for myself. I haven't slept a full night since Dad passed. I see his face in my dreams. He's sick and gasping for breath. I wake up night after night thinking I forgot to do something. Pay an insurance bill. Call the hospice nurse. Find the pills that could save him or at least help his pain. I need a break. This trip was supposed to be that. I didn't realize we'd be running around so much."

Nicole wisely didn't touch Tara this time. But she did start talking. "Lean into your grief, Tara. Allow what's present for you right now to come up. It's seeking release. You don't need to hold it together all the time."

Oh, shit.

"Lean in to grief? Release it? Are you kidding? News flash: There's no spiritual quick fix. It's been almost a year and I'm still barely treading water."

Tara was sobbing now. Nicole and I sat there, frozen. Out of the corner of my eye I saw our waitress approach and then back away.

"Do you even realize how much I'm still doing for Mom, Ta-sha? *Do you?* Dad kept every medical bill and receipt from when we were born until last year. Boxes of files. In every room. I've had to close his business, send death certificates to credit card companies, sell his car, pay taxes . . . it doesn't stop. My family needs me too. You have no clue how hard it was for me to figure out how to come here for six days. And you know what has felt best to me so far on this trip? The plane ride here. When I was alone in that tiny seat and nobody asked me for anything."

Tara had basically moved in with my parents for the six months before Bob died, with responsibilities at all hours. At the time, it made sense. Her schedule was more flexible than the unpredictable real estate life Edna and I lived. I came to Summerland whenever I could, which was often, but when I had my kids, I was stuck. The pressure on all of us was intense. But Tara quietly shouldered more than her share and it had been too much. It still was. Not only had I never seen Tara cry like she did that night at the restaurant, I'd never heard her say she needed a break. Ever.

Here was my *sister.* She needed my help. And here was my *best friend.* She needed me to honor her life the way she did mine. And here I was, growing and changing in ways both beautiful and awful. My soulmate was out there and I was still hell-bent on finding that person, but I needed to get my house in order first. And not my astrological one.

"Dad would be heartbroken if he saw us fighting," I finally said, holding on to the one other thing I knew for sure in that moment, the thing I knew would reach Tara in her distress.

Tara blew her nose. "I know. I know. I'm sorry. I have to get hold of myself. I've loved this trip, honestly, I have, Tash. I don't know why I said that about the plane ride. It was great, yeah, but so was Paris with you. I'm going to go to the bathroom and clean up, splash some cold water on my face, and then we can go. I can't imagine what the poor waitress must think of me. I'm so embarrassed."

Nicole and I paid the bill and were gathering our coats when Tara came back from the bathroom. She held a small white card in her hand. The look on her face was surprise. Shock, even. And . . . a smile.

"Tasha, you haven't been here before, have you?"

"Where? This restaurant? Uh, no."

"I think you'd better look at this. I found it pinned up on the bulletin board by the bathroom."

Tara handed me the card. It was one of mine: *Nous pourrions être des âmes sœurs.* We might be soulmates.

"So? I've passed a *lot* of these out. Like, a *lot*, a lot."

"Turn it over."

On the back of the card, where the birthday and my contact information were, someone had written in English, in black ink: *Anything can happen.*

I was dumbstruck for a moment. The air around me felt charged. In a good way. The card was another coincidence, for sure. Logically, I knew that. Of course I did. Ghosts didn't write on cards, didn't use bulletin boards.

Anything can happen, child. Anything can be. My dad. The picture of me at age six. He'd written that on the back of the photo. And now here were those words again. Inexplicably.

"Oh my God."

"Whoa," Nicole said.

"It's Dad," Tara said.

Smiling, I tucked the card into my jacket pocket. It sounds so corny but it was almost as if stardust went in there with it. I felt different, floaty. It could have been all the wine or the late hour, but I like to think it was Bob.

I hugged my sister. And she let me. I hugged Nicole too. We walked out into the cool darkness, grateful that our hotel was mere feet away. We couldn't have managed anything farther. Back in the little attic suite, I melted into the soft, huge-seeming mattress. A real bed at last.

Tenth House

La Vie en Rose

This house rules public life, reputation, fathers, authority figures, abandonment, loneliness, government, anxiety, burdens, success, and fame.

The Tenth House is the second most powerful house in the chart after the First House. And yet it is very impersonal and all about how we stack up in the eyes of others. We work hard to find success in the eyes of the world only to discover it genuinely is lonely at the top. The Tenth House is a tough teacher. It teaches us that we must live by the rules and then teaches us that the only rules that matter are the ones that bring us personal fulfillment and happiness. No wonder the Tenth House is the house of the tricksters and sarcasm.

This house is also where we experience self-doubt, anxiety, disappointment, and depression. And yet, all the houses are equally important on our inner journey to discover our authentic selves. Once we understand that those things that society holds up as goals are not necessarily the keys to our own satisfaction, we start to identify what does unlock our heart to experience the greatest joys in life. Sometimes the best gift is finding out what you don't want.

My point of destiny, or the North Node, is in my Tenth House. It is in Sagittarius, the sign of truth. And nearby sits Neptune, the spinner of illusion until one finally seeks spiritual understanding.

"GOOD MORNING." MY VOICE WAS THICK WITH SLEEP AS I turned to Nicole, who was also just waking up. She had an early flight to catch. "That was a wild night. My head feels like a French garbage truck hit me in my sleep. I think I might have spiritual or emotional whiplash or something like that. How are you doing? Are you okay?"

"Yeah. I am. You're right, though. Yesterday was a lot. For all of us. But I'm not surprised. We're on a journey together, Tash, and while I don't have a clue what Tara's soul map determined she'd face in Paris, I do know our souls picked nearly identical birth charts and found each other for a reason. Like Stephanie said, we're both Libras with Pisces rising. And, most important, we're both Pluto aliens."

I started laughing. "I love you but it's too early. I'm confused already. We need Penelope back. She's the only one who knows how to work the coffeemaker in this room."

"I'll make it easy for you. Pluto is all about the truth, about kicking bullshit to the curb. That's what's needed here on your last day in Paris."

"How am I going to do that? I don't know where to start. Bull-shit is kind of a big category."

"Maybe thinking about how your soul can be of service to others might bring clarity. That's what centers me. And it's about as no-bullshit as it gets."

Tara came to mind instantly. I knew exactly what I could offer to her. Paris. Just the two of us. *But what about my dates?* Just as I'd hoped he would, Amir had agreed to meet me later that evening. And there was Chloe. I had two dates—*two!*—with potential soul-mates. I asked Nicole what she thought. And apologized for not flying back with her as we'd planned.

"You're *supposed* to be here today with Tara. Your dad wouldn't have it any other way. Plus, I'm going to sleep the whole plane ride home. Honestly, I can't wait. And you're also supposed to meet Chloe and whoever else you can. I'm sure about that. I'm feeling that your sister's and your journey are intertwined. I think you're going to find your big love. I truly do."

"From your mouth to the universe's ears."

"I have a direct line." She winked.

After I helped Nicole with her bags and saw her off, I took my time folding and organizing all the sexy, hopeful clothes I'd brought, ultimately choosing jeans, a comfortable top, and sneakers for the day. My hair, though clean and brushed, was no longer curled and sprayed. Nicole had offered to leave me the curling iron, but without her to do my hair, it was useless. Same with makeup. I'd all but abandoned it. With my coconspirator in chief gone, I was just the little sister again.

The sun slowly burned through the gray sky as the morning wore on. I pushed open the casement window one last time and settled in on its cushioned seat with a cup of coffee I'd grabbed from the lobby. For the first time all week, I wasn't in a rush. Our check-in at the new hotel wasn't until three p.m. and Tara needed sleep. Last night we'd made a plan to wake up slowly, pack, leave our bags with the concierge, and then wander in the Marais. I had lunch with Chloe to look forward to after that, and then I'd meet Amir for a walk. My last two dates of the (at least) sixteen I'd believed I'd have this week. Tara hadn't decided yet what she'd do while I was with Chloe and Amir. Maybe visit another museum? But later, we'd have dinner, just us sisters. It was going to be a good day.

Outside my window, the city was quiet. I let my mind drift. I stopped wondering what Chloe might think of me or what chemistry might flicker with Amir in person. I closed my eyes and felt the fresh morning air on my skin. And then I noticed the faint, brassy notes of a trumpet in the distance. Someone was playing a song. One I knew. I listened harder, finally catching the melody: "La Vie en Rose."

Our song. It didn't matter who sang it—Edith Piaf, Grace Jones, Lady Gaga. It had always been, to my ears, mine and Philippe's. The last time I'd heard it, Piaf's version in French, was at Bob's celebration of life, and I'd fallen into Philippe's waiting arms. We'd found each other again, or so I'd thought.

"Do you remember what the lyrics mean, Natasha?" he'd asked, whispering into my ear.

Of course I remembered. He'd translated it for me many times. The sky-fall into passionate, all-consuming love. The spell of a lover's embrace. Hope after despair. Not exactly easy to forget. Not where Philippe was concerned.

But that morning in Paris I heard the song differently, more like my father had wanted me to hear it whenever we'd watch his all-time favorite movie, the original *Sabrina,* together. "La Vie en Rose" was the film's theme song.

"'Life in Pink,' Natasha. That's what the song's title means," my father would say. Rose-colored glasses, in other words. That's how he wanted his girls to go through life: never having to take them off. There's a lot to be said for seeing the best in others and in the world around you and for faking it until you make it, believing it will all come out okay in the end. But the unvarnished truth has its place too.

See you downstairs in five, I texted Tara.

"Where should we go first? Shopping?" I asked Tara once we were out on the street.

"This is going to sound silly," Tara said, "but could you take a couple pictures of me so I can send them to the kids and to Mom? I realized last night that I don't have a single one of just me in Paris. I have a ton of you and Nicole but . . ."

God, I was an idiot. "Tara, I am so sorry. You should have asked. No, wait. *I* should have offered. Give me your phone."

We floated down the streets, me taking shots of Tara posed in front of big, lacquered doors, perched on bistro chairs, pretending to hail a taxi. I loved seeing my sister dork out like when we were kids. We texted the pictures to Edna, promising we'd FaceTime her together later.

"Are you going to post some of these to Instagram so KC and Heather have proof of life?" I joked.

"I posted something earlier today. To the *twelve* followers I have now, ha-ha-ha. A selfie with you at the opera house. What about you? Shouldn't you let people know what's happening today with Chloe and Amir?"

"Time for a bachelorette confessional," I said as I went live.

"Is he at the café? *Non.* Is he at the butcher? *Non.* Is he in the street? *Non.*" I spun around, filming the street. "It's my last day in Paris! And I have *two* dates. More soon." Back my phone went to the bottom of my bag.

Tara and I were like irrepressible teenagers that morning, swept up in fits of uncontrollable laughter. We bought BONJOUR ASS-HOLE coffee mugs and matching *je t'aime* necklaces and we obsessed over a candy-apple-red rude garden gnome statue in the window of a boutique. Why rude? Well, the gnome's extended middle finger told the universe exactly what he thought. It was the kind of art I could appreciate. Bob would have loved it.

"Take a picture and text Nicole that I've finally found my spirit animal." Tara laughed as she posed in front of the statue with her own middle finger extended to the sky.

Then we went to APC, where Tara had fallen in love with an expensive black handbag the day before. Though it included a shoulder strap, the bag's two shorter curved handles were meant to be worn over the arm, like something Grace Kelly would have owned. It was stylish, sophisticated. An effortlessly cool classic. But a little dressier than the bags Tara usually carried.

"I'm worried it's not me," Tara said. "Will I use it? You know what I usually wear. And don't think I don't know what you think about my cargo pants. So be honest with me. Can I pull this off?"

Okay, so I wasn't a fan of the army-green cargo pants Tara had worn on repeat in the months before Bob died. Or any cargo pants. I hadn't said anything because it wasn't like I didn't have a collection of obnoxious sequined skirts and loud statement tees—the sartorial version of the fuck-off garden gnome—in my own closet. *Vogue* certainly wouldn't be calling me about those anytime soon. I knew all about fashion security blankets, even if I did want to trash and burn my sister's.

"Didn't we bury those pants with Dad?" I joked. "But seriously, Tara. I *love* this bag for you. You don't already have something like it not because you can't pull it off, but because you almost never treat yourself. Get the bag."

I could see my sister debating whether the purchase was justifiable. Practical. She glanced down at her trusty, nondescript crossbody. Her eyes strayed to my red Celine bag, which, I must say, still looked undeniably chic, even after years of use.

"I'm doing it," Tara announced, resolute.

"It's not a midnight run to Don Q's," I teased. "It's a purse."

Tara sneakily gave me the middle finger as she carried the beautiful handbag over to the counter.

While Tara completed her purchase (and asked if it could be waterproofed on the spot), I checked WhatsApp. I wanted to make sure Chloe wasn't canceling. Or Amir. Neither had written, but Fabrice had. It was the first I'd heard from him since he'd let me know about his father's death yesterday.

Thank you, Natasha, for your thoughts, it touches me a lot. You have a beautiful soul and I wish the best for you, with me maybe in your life one day. Our 2 souls coming together for a common love. I hope your stay in Paris was only happiness. And that you come back.

I showed the message to Tara. It was, in true Fabrice fashion, overflowing with emojis. "He's my favorite," she said. "There's something about Fabrice."

"I know. But the timing is just off. I guess I have to accept that."

Tara checked her own phone, where a message from our new hotel waited. Our room was ready early. As we were walking back to retrieve our luggage, I stopped to tape up some flyers on a wall next to a *pâtisserie*. My soulmate could still be anywhere. But Tara quickly tore them down.

"People can see you! You're going to get arrested for vandalism on our last day!"

"Where's the hotel, exactly?" I asked. Tara had given the address to the taxi driver, but the street name meant nothing to me.

"You'll see."

Ten minutes later we pulled up to the five-star Hôtel Regina Louvre in the first arrondissement. Tara pointed out the cab's window to a massive bronze statue of Joan of Arc nearby. Joan wore armor and sat triumphantly on horseback, one arm hoisting a billowing flag high.

"She reminds me of you in a way, Tasha. There's something hopeful about her. Powerful. Strong. Did you know she heard voices in her head too? Ha-ha-ha. I think she's the perfect patron saint for your journey. That's one of the reasons why I wanted to stay here."

I may not have been a scholar of history, but I had heard of Joan of Arc. "So . . . you don't think I'm crazy for staying to see what might happen because of Chloe? Or Amir?"

"No," Tara said, serious now. "I don't. I never have."

A bellman greeted us curbside to collect our bags. The flags of France's allies hung from the hotel's grand exterior, and a huge revolving glass door led inside. A doorman in white gloves escorted us to the lavish reception area. Elaborate crystal chandeliers hung

from high ceilings, and gold sconces lined the cream-colored walls.
Tall windows and checkered green marble floors added to the airy
opulence. Tufted sofas and chairs were arranged in conversational
groupings, and accent tables boasted massive bouquets of white
flowers. There were no tiny lifts, no tiny spiral staircases; there was
no tiny *anything* about this luxurious five-star hotel.

"How did you find this place, Tara?" I asked, awestruck.

She blushed. "I didn't. Erik did. This night is a gift from him.
He saw how hard the past year has been for me. He wanted me
to have an unforgettable final night in Paris." Tara glowed as she
looked around the magnificent lobby.

"Thank you for sharing this with me. You definitely didn't have
to," I said in a quiet voice.

"Bonjour! Welcome." A fresh-faced young woman who looked
more like a Parisian influencer than the uniformed hotel clerk she
was came striding toward us, smiling brightly. "You must be Tara
and Natasha. I have been expecting you."

Huh? How did she know who we were? I looked question-
ingly at Tara, but she'd already turned to follow the clerk, who
quickly checked us in and then insisted on taking us up to our
room herself.

"I have a special surprise for you," the young woman said as she
opened the door to our room, a cozy retreat decorated in shades
of cream and gold with two queen-size beds.

"You found my soulmate?" I blurted out, joking. God, this
woman was going to think I was a weirdo. Or an idiot. Or both.

But she didn't miss a beat. "Almost as good, I promise." She
crossed the room and whisked open the curtains with a flourish.
"*Voilà.* One of the best views in all of Paris. The Eiffel Tower; it
will light up and sparkle like the stars you follow. That is, until the
last show at one a.m."

The view from our window was breathtaking, so much so that
I didn't think to ask how she knew about my stars. We could see

Joan of Arc glinting below us, the Jardin des Tuileries unfurling in its emerald glory, and, rising in the distance up into the bluest of skies, the Eiffel Tower, just as promised.

"This is absolutely stunning," Tara said. "A dream. Is this an upgrade? I only reserved a basic room. I didn't think we'd get a view."

The clerk smiled and nodded. "*Oui,* you are correct. Natasha, when your sister made the reservation, she told us a little about you. Since then I have become captivated by your search. I too am looking for love. You have inspired me to not give up, and I in turn would like to inspire you. With our beautiful city."

I couldn't believe it. Neither could Tara, judging by the look of shock on her face. "Thank you," I said. "Thank you so much for the gift of this insane view. I *am* inspired. By the view, but also by the women I've met in Paris, incredibly open and generous women like you. That's been one of the best things about the whole trip. But I'll have to keep you posted about my search. My soulmate hasn't shown up. Yet."

"I am glad you like it," the clerk said. "And I believe that we will find it. True love."

"I hope you're right," I replied as she left us to settle into our room.

We didn't unpack much. My flight left in less than twenty-four hours and Tara's wasn't long after that.

"Thank God we have two beds," Tara said, choosing the one closest to the bathroom for herself. "Remember when we shared a bed as teenagers? In that tiny apartment Mom and Dad were living in after you got expelled and I came home from college? I remember fighting for leg space and screaming at you for getting blue eyeliner and Aqua Net on my pillow."

"How could I forget? You threw my McDonald's uniform onto the balcony because you claimed you were allergic to the smell of Eternity perfume mixed with stale hamburgers. It was absurd."

"I stand by that allergy."

"Mom and Dad wanted to kill us. For real. We were such a

handful. That was the summer Mom told us we had a sister. Remember her driving up to Vancouver? She was heartbroken. There was a lot going on."

That summer had changed everything and nothing about the way I pictured my immediate family. *We have a sister.* I'd love to be able to say it all had a happily-ever-after ending, that the only reason Catherine hadn't joined us in Paris was that she had a work trip or another obligation, or even that she thought my quest was inane and she didn't feel like watching me make a fool of myself. But anyone whose family has a story like ours knows that a happy ending isn't always possible, no matter how much you might wish for it. What I say to myself now is the same thing I thought that afternoon in Paris: *My heart and my door are open. They always will be.* And: *How lucky I am to have Tara in my life.*

"Tara, if I never said it before, you were a champion big sister then. Buying me stamps so I could write my friends. Sneaking out and getting me a pregnancy test. I was so scared and alone."

"Of course you were. It was awful. You were only fifteen— Margot's age. I promised myself that summer I would never let anything happen to you again. Or to Mom. That's probably why I worry so much. I don't mean to be bossy. I'm just trying to take care of our family. Like Dad did. I told him I would take over when he was gone. That was the last thing I said to him."

I was quiet for a minute. I couldn't remember the last thing I'd said to my father before he died. Tara had been the only family member in the room when it finally happened. In the days and weeks and months that followed Bob's death, Tara spoke of the terrible, indelible beauty of bearing witness to our father's passing. She'd walked with him right to the astonishing edge. And I'd missed it. I knew logically that death can't be perfectly orchestrated or understood, that we're only ever grasping parts of it. That it's messy. Me missing Bob's passing wasn't anyone's fault, but there'd been no logic to my feelings.

"Tasha," Tara continued, "I should've said this a long time ago, but I'm sorry I told you to leave the room and go wake up Mom when Dad was dying. I didn't know what to do. I thought we had more time. And I'd promised Dad I wouldn't leave his side, that I would make sure the nurse helped him be comfortable. But it still wasn't right and I'm sorry."

"I could have ignored you. I think I knew deep down that Dad wanted me to be out of the room with Mom so we wouldn't have to see him go. It would have been too hard for Mom, the way he was then. And too hard for me, even though I don't like to admit that."

"I'm still sorry."

"Thank you. But it's okay now, I promise. Hey, does this go on page two hundred and fifty-six of that death manual we never got?" I cracked a smile. It was time to lighten the mood.

"Are we okay?"

"Always."

Tara began transferring her wallet, phone, map, and lipsticks out of her cross-body and into her new bag. "I guess I'll go to the Louvre and meet up with you after your date? Or maybe I'll FaceTime Spencer and Colin from the Eiffel Tower. What time do you think your date with Chloe will be over? Can you share your location with me in case something happens? Sorry, I know I'm paranoid. Old habits."

It was almost time for me to meet Chloe. But leaving Tara behind no longer felt right. "Would you like to come to lunch? It would be amazing if you did. I would be honored to have you as my copilot. It's what Dad would have wanted."

Tara lit up. "Yes! I'm dying to see how your story ends. Or not. And I love that Chloe wants to meet you for her dad. Of course she has to check you out first. I like her already."

Chloe had suggested we meet at Les Bains, a nightclub turned luxury hotel that had once attracted the likes of Mick Jagger, David Bowie, Kate Moss, and Catherine Deneuve. The scene had been Paris's answer to Studio 54 and Chateau Marmont. Tara and I took in the hotel's dark, edgy interior and decided it was the coolest place we'd been thus far in Paris.

"I'm officially nervous again," I told Tara as we sat ourselves at the bar. "I'm not kidding. Chloe's the match that feels the most like fate. She wasn't looking for anything when her cousin saw my ad. That just feels like destiny, like I'm supposed to meet her."

I started talking to the bartender. "Do you believe in astrology?" I asked after I told him where we were from and what we were doing in Paris.

"*Non*," he immediately replied. "*Très américain*. But I do believe in tequila. One of the only LA trends I understand. I'll keep the tab open."

And then my cell phone rang, surprising me. It hadn't rung for real since I'd been here. People back home WhatsApp'd or Face-Timed when they needed to be in touch. But now someone—an unfamiliar number with the France country code—was calling.

"Bonjour, is this the beautiful Natasha?" A warm, low, French-accented male voice.

"Um . . . yes?" I replied, deciding to go with it and motioning for Tara to lean closer so she could hear. I felt my face flush.

"It's Julien. Remember me? I found your number online. You've been on my mind."

I sure did remember Julien. He was, hands down, the sexiest November 2 I'd come across so far: tall, broody, and ripped. He had slid into my DMs a couple days ago after he'd seen one of the flyers I'd tacked up around the city. (Yes, they worked. Kind of.) But there was one problem with Julien: his birthplace—Luxembourg City.

"I've been waiting all day just to see you, to feel you. *Je veux te baiser*," he said in a low voice, "now."

My sister pulled up Google Translate and her jaw about hit the floor.

I didn't have to ask Tara to show me what Julien had said. His meaning was clear. I blinked, clearing my head.

"I know this makes no logical sense," I forced myself to reply, "and I already regret saying it. My friend Katie would smack me across the face if she were here. But I can't meet you. As weird as it sounds, the birthplace is important to me. I have to stick to the plan."

Tara gave me the Sizlo thumbs-up. But she also put her hand to her heart, because that took willpower. She'd seen his pictures.

"I could make an hour very memorable for you, Natasha. Call if you change your mind." *Damn.*

Just then, Chloe swept into the bar. With her leather jacket, faded jeans, and heeled boots, she looked like one of the rock stars who used to hang out there.

"Hey," she said, kissing each of us on both cheeks, "would you like to sit outside? So we can smoke?"

I paused, wondering how Tara would react, but she readily agreed.

Chloe's dark brown eyes complemented her natural curls, which fell in a wild tumble down her back. Her olive skin glowed, though I couldn't detect any makeup. Certainly none of the highlighter-y gleam that many women in LA favored. A black-and-tan Fendi scarf accented her outfit, but on her, the scarf with its bold *F* pattern seemed practical rather than braggy, like something she'd need for warmth when riding a motorcycle later. She also wore an actual beret. And it looked super-chic. I had tried one on in a shop earlier that morning, and I'd looked like the Purple Pieman from Strawberry Shortcake. If the impossibly cool Chloe just downed her drink and left, I would understand.

But we soon discovered that Chloe was the kind of person who, if she decided to do something, was all in. She was at once raw and utterly secure. She drew on her cigarette, exhaled, and said, "We are all three of us here because of our fathers, yes?"

And so I told her about Bob. And this time, Tara didn't cry or bolt. The story of our father felt different to me too. Less painful, less like a tidal wave I needed to run from. For the first time since he'd died, talking about him was joyful. Which felt strange at first, because the ache of grief hadn't disappeared. I guess I'd thought it would be a while before I could belly-laugh at memories of him again. But Bob would have approved. He would have said I'd found my rose-colored glasses. Chloe listened intently, nodding in places.

"You have faith in your father and in love. I understand that because I do too. My father and I, we are strong people who do not always agree. But I have faith in him."

Chloe's father, a successful businessman born in Paris on November 2, 1968, lived in Dubai most of the time. He and Chloe were close, but they didn't have an easy relationship. When she told him she'd fallen in love with a woman, he'd disapproved at first. But in time, he understood: she'd found her person. The One. Now she wanted him to find love again too. Chloe's parents had divorced long ago.

"I do think you and my father, the two would connect," Chloe said decisively. "Soulmates? I do not know that. He will not like astrology, for one. Or Instagram. But someday, you should meet. I like you for him."

"Here's to your dad. I hope I do get to meet him," I said, raising my glass. "Thank you for meeting me. Honestly, I thought you'd cancel."

"No, no, no." She shook her head like the notion was preposterous.

"I thought you would think, *She's crazy, she's chasing down my father . . .*" (I had sent Chloe sooooo many text messages confirming our meeting, it was a miracle she hadn't blocked me for stalking her.)

"Not at all," she replied, her voice deep and full of confidence. "We have a similarity to us, Natasha. I hope I can explain it. We know love when we find it. We are certain. And we don't apologize. But also, we are the kind of people who are cold if they are not playing with fire in some way. That scares some people. I was immediately drawn to you. Because I am a woman who made a commitment to my partner before I even met her." Chloe pulled up her sleeve to reveal a beautiful tattoo on the underside of her forearm: a swallow in flight and a woman's name in script beneath its wing. "For love. I had my girlfriend's name tattooed across my arm the day before we met. I saw her photo and just knew." Chloe traced the blue ink with her finger and laughed. "She thought I was a madwoman but we've been together ever since. Sometimes doing something crazy is the only way to stay sane."

"We were definitely supposed to meet," I said. "Talk about faith."

"I have faith, also, in you," Chloe said.

It was almost 4:30 p.m. when we left Chloe. I'd asked Amir to meet me at 5:30 on the Pont des Arts, which seemed like the ideal spot to begin a first date with destiny—my last chance at one in Paris. In the final scene of the remake of *Sabrina* (Bob liked that version too), Harrison Ford and Julia Ormond kiss passionately on this bridge as the movie fades to black. I'd seen the film with him so many times, I could easily envision my own Pont des Arts embrace. Fingers crossed.

And then there was the evening itself. Two nights ago, Penelope had taught me the phrase *la nuit tombe,* which means "the night is falling," to describe the enchantment you feel walking along the Seine at dusk as the sun sets and the twinkling lights of the city, like stars, take its place. In fact, the soft yellow glow of the streetlights, the restaurants opening for dinner, the electric sparkle of monuments, and silvery boat lanterns *were* the city's stars, as the actual ones in the sky weren't easily visible because of light pollution. Between Bob's spirit, which would surely be watching over me on the Pont des Arts, the aphrodisiac of Paris at twilight, and whatever stars we could muster between us, I felt I'd engineered the date with Amir perfectly. Another roll of the soulmate dice.

"Aren't you going to go back to the hotel to change into something sexy?" Tara asked.

"No," I said. "Let's just take our time walking to the bridge. It's not far. And I want you to meet him too."

"You do?" Tara asked. "I'd love that. Plus I think the Pont des Arts is the bridge where couples used to hang locks as a symbol of their enduring love." She tapped away at her phone. "Yes. That's the one. I'd like to see it."

I *had* picked a brilliant meeting spot. "Of course you should be there. Who else will save me if he's creepy?" I joked, taking my sister's arm. "I'm glad you had fun with Chloe. Even with all the smoking."

Tara poked me. "I'm not the smoking police."

We arrived at the bridge in plenty of time. And thank goodness, I thought, as I saw the crowd of people there. I'd need to text an exact meeting spot to Amir or he'd never find me. Though the city had banned the hanging of locks on the bridge and had even gone so far as putting up special barriers to further deter lovers, people improvised. They hung locks on lampposts or took selfies together, one person holding a lock and the other—you guessed it—the key. Within minutes, we noticed that none of the couples on the bridge seemed to be French. They all had cameras, fanny packs, and shopping bags full of souvenirs. We heard English, Japanese, Spanish, German. Hmm. Had I accidentally selected one of the most touristy, not-hot spots in all of Paris for my last shot at a wild and sexy date with a potential soulmate? Because absolutely nothing about the scene in front of me said *Let's go make out in the shadows along the river later tonight.* Fuck. (And yes, Tara had said she'd happily duck out if she sensed chemistry between me and Amir.)

I texted Amir. Bonjour, so the Pont des Arts is a little busy. I'll be on the Louvre side of the bridge, 2nd streetlamp in. We don't have to stay, obviously.

It was 5:30. Then 5:35. Then 5:40.

"Let me take a picture of you," Tara said. "The light is awesome. And Mom will want to see this bridge. Even if it's a bit of a tourist trap, it has a connection to Dad."

It was 5:45. Then 5:50. I checked WhatsApp. Amir had read my message, but he hadn't replied.

No problem if you are running late, I added.

He read that message too. And didn't reply. Any butterflies I'd felt disappeared, and my excitement began to curdle into something more like annoyance, but I tried to tamp those feelings down. Maybe Amir was on his way and couldn't type for some reason. Like, he could read texts while biking but couldn't reply to them.

At 6:00 I said, "I don't think he's coming. I think . . . I might be getting stood up. Which is worse than ghosting, right?"

"I don't know," Tara replied carefully. "I guess the question is, do you want to wait for him?"

The day before, when talking with Shayna, I'd been so sure that my answer would be yes. Yes, I would wait. But on the bridge, I didn't know what I felt. "What if he got here, saw the crowds—or even saw *me*—and just left?" I pictured handsome Amir cycling by, getting a glimpse of an American in jeans and sneakers standing in a gaggle of sightseers, craning her neck looking for him (that's what I'd been doing), and then . . . changing his mind. Yikes.

"Hey," said Tara, "I have an idea. Let's give him a few more minutes, or however long you want, and if he doesn't show up, I say we go to the Eiffel Tower, ride up to the top, and fling the rest of your flyers into the air! They'll float down over the city. Who knows? Your soulmate might pick one up."

Was this *my sister* talking? I couldn't believe it. Because that sounded like an excellent way to attract the Eiffel Tower's security guards.

Something about my sister's outrageous (for her) suggestion made me stop in my tracks and consider what I was doing in a different light. What would I have said to Margot if she were waiting for an Amir? Or to Katie?

All this time, I'd been trying to force fate, force destiny, by coming to Paris in search of my soulmate. I told everyone it was what my astrologer had said to do. But Stephanie never told me to go anywhere. She never said to stand on a pillar in public and shout, *"I'm ready!"* Did I seriously think destiny was then going to deliver a hot French guy as if I'd placed a cosmic Postmates order? (Fine. Yes, I did.) Stephanie told me to stop comparing myself to others. To start writing again. To understand that I didn't really need a partner, which was how I could finally become open to The One and know what a true partner is. I definitely didn't understand that aspect of the reading yet (what on earth was wrong with needing your soulmate?), but something else Stephanie said resonated mightily in that moment—she'd said to have fun. And this wasn't fun anymore.

"No Eiffel Tower," I said, meaning it. "You know what? I'm done." I stared up at the sky. "Message received!" I yelled. "Oh, and fuck off, Saturn!" I didn't care if a bunch of random tourists heard me. After all, I was one of them, and that was fine by me. "Let's go get ready for dinner. I'm starving."

"You sure?" Tara asked.

"Yes."

Arm in arm, we walked back to our hotel. On the way, I emptied all the flyers I had in my backpack into a public trash can. I tossed in the last of my soulmate-search business cards too. It felt great.

"Should you be doing that?"

"Yes."

"Okay. As long as you're okay."

"I am. Hey, maybe we can find an open chapel before we go to dinner? We have lots of time now. We could finally light a candle for Dad."

"Tasha, Dad's been with us all day."

*　*　*

"You're not dressing up?" Tara asked, eyeing my lackluster evening ensemble, which was basically what I'd worn all day.

"I'm done, remember?" I said, flopping onto my bed. "Should we just order room service?"

"Noooo, sister! It's our last night in Paris! It's going to be fabulous!"

"Fine. How about my jeans with this green top and these boots?" I laid out the look, thinking it had a polished but decidedly off-duty vibe.

"That's more like it," Tara said, setting her hair in hot rollers. "Should we play some music?"

I synced my phone to the speaker and put on "Hello" by Lionel Richie; it was one of my favorite love songs of all time and yet somehow it wasn't on any of my playlists. I made a mental note to fix that later as my sister and I crooned "'Is it me you're looking fooooor?'" while swooping dramatically around our room. The message of the song was simple: Sometimes the thing you want is right in front of you but you just can't see it. I felt the push and pull of time, the new memories we were making layering themselves gently on top of the old. Tara and I hadn't been alone together for more than an hour or two since the fraught, horrible weeks before Bob died.

"I'm sorry it took me so long to remember why we came here in the first place," I said as we stood together in front of the bathroom mirror, each of us swiping on a final coat of red lipstick before heading out the door. "I love you, big sis. Always and forever. To infinity."

"To the nth degree," Tara replied. "But I'm not so sure I'd tell you to do anything different."

I don't remember who told us we absolutely had to go to the Hôtel Costes for dinner when we were in Paris, but I'm glad whoever it was did. The hotel's restaurant was a warren of dark, cozy candlelit rooms furnished in red velvet and polished wood, a place for the beautiful to see and be seen and where a DJ spun sexy music to further set the mood.

Five days ago, I would have been frantic to blend into the über-cool scene, spot a potential soulmate, and record it all on Instagram. No more. Sitting with my sister at a candlelit table, delighting in our shared laughter, selfies, and toasts to each other and to Bob, was profoundly enough. My phone mostly stayed in my bag, where it belonged at a fancy dinner. We ordered dishes Bob would have loved, including a club sandwich and fries. Not exactly classic French, but it was the perfect last meal in Paris for us. Tara took one of the frites and pretended it was a cigarette. "Bonjour, my name is Natasha, are you my soulmate?" she joked in a mock-French accent, waving her potato-cigarette in the air.

"*Oui, oui,*" I answered.

It was past midnight. We weren't tired at all, but we had to try to get some rest before our flights the next day. Mine was early. As we left the table, Tara said she needed the bathroom. I said I'd wait for her out in front of the hotel. Honestly, I wanted to smoke a last cigarette in private. Like one does on the street in Paris after dinner. Oh, who was I kidding? I had no idea if that was what one did. But I needed to say a final goodbye to the Paris I thought I'd find, to Philippe and all the fun we'd had together, and give a middle finger to my father's battle with lung disease. I walked down the red carpet to the entrance of the hotel and reached for the massive door.

But before I could open it, the door was opened for me—by a man standing just outside. Our eyes met and I found I couldn't look away. Or even speak for a moment. Dimly, in the back of my mind, I registered that *this* was what people meant when they spoke of an instant, electric connection. Was I dreaming? Tall, dark, and devastatingly handsome, here in front of me was surely the most gorgeous man in all of France. His brown eyes were alert and intense. A fine stubble shadowed his strong jaw. He wore a crisp white shirt that was, at this late hour, unbuttoned at the neck and ever so slightly mussed.

"*Merci,*" I finally said, stepping outside and taking the cigarette from my bag. He lit it.

"Bonsoir," he replied, never taking his eyes off mine. His voice— how can I describe it? It was exactly the gravelly half growl you want to hear late at night in Paris. Preferably in bed. Naked.

A light drizzle cooled the air. The streets were empty. We were entirely alone.

"Beautiful hotel. Are you staying here?" I finally asked, break- ing the silence as my heart pounded madly. *What if he doesn't speak English?*

"I am," he replied in an accent I couldn't place. "And you?"

"Oh, no. Just dinner. With my sister." I fiddled with my ciga- rette. Every part of me felt lit up, alive. "So, uh, what brings you to Paris?" I blushed.

"A meeting with my editor to discuss a book on economics I'm writing. Boring, I know. Mostly I write about love and destiny. That's my passion. Tell me, why are you in Paris tonight?"

Love and destiny? Was he for real?

"It's totally ridiculous, but I came here to find my soulmate. It's an astrology thing. You weren't born on November 2, 1968, in Paris, were you?" I couldn't stop myself.

He raised his eyebrows and smiled but didn't laugh. And still, his eyes didn't leave my face.

"November 12, 1968. Not Paris. Does it matter?"

Does being close count in astrology? I thought. I knew it didn't, but I no longer cared. It was like the universe was speaking directly to me.

Fuck it.

I laughed, understanding the absurdity of it all. This man was fire-hot, writing about love and destiny was his passion, and our chemistry was undeniable. I moved closer and so did he.

"Are you cold?" he asked.

God, he even smells good. Like amber and incense and fresh sheets.

Just then, Tara appeared. "Oh, hi," she said, uncertain, sensing that she'd walked into something.

How I wanted to call Tara a taxi, follow this beautiful stranger inside, have a drink, see where the night went, and then meet my sister at our hotel in an hour or, if my intuition was correct, at dawn. But I had made a promise to Tara.

I stepped a little away from him. I didn't want to, but I did. There was an awkward silence. "Well, here's my sister," I said. We hadn't even exchanged names.

Then I put my hand into my coat pocket and found the card that Tara had pulled from the community board at the restaurant last night. *Dad.* It was the only card I had left. I gave it to him, fully aware that it might scare him off the way it probably had all the others. He studied the card, the photo of me holding one of my signs, and flipped it over.

"You're American. This is an LA number," he said, staring at the card and then at me.

"Good night" was all I could manage before tugging on Tara's arm and walking into the quiet street. I looked over my shoulder and saw him watching me go. He didn't look away.

"What the hell was that?" Tara said urgently as we rounded the corner. She stopped and turned to me.

"I don't know," I replied, lust-struck. I explained as best I could about the encounter I'd had outside the hotel. *Did I really just meet a beautiful, living, breathing man who not only believes in love and destiny but talks about it out loud?*

"Oh my God, could he be The One?" Tara asked. "Holy shit, Tasha, you have to go back. Right now! Before he disappears."

"But is that weird? I mean, he's probably gone inside the hotel by now. How would I find him? He could be in the bar or on his way to his room. What am I going to do, knock on every door? I don't even know his name."

"Yes! That is exactly what you should do. After what we've

been through in Paris, not to mention this past year, you running through the streets after the hottest guy in all of Europe is literally the most *not* weird thing. He said it himself—you just had a brush with destiny. Does a crystal ball have to fall from the sky and hit you on the head? It's meant to be. This guy might be your soulmate." Tara sighed. "Isn't this what you came here for?"

It was an unusual moment for us. Another role reversal I hadn't seen coming. My whole life, Tara had reminded me of my own gravity, calling me down to Earth when I was floating out to space, rescuing me from the deep end. But not today, not tonight. Tonight I was reeling Tara in. "I'm not dreaming, am I?"

"No. It's late, but you're not dreaming. I was there too. There's something about him. He's different from the others."

Even though I felt a strong urge to turn back and go after the man I'd just met, to continue the strangely electric conversation we'd started, I knew in my heart I couldn't do it. And not because he had the wrong birthday.

"I'm not leaving you," I said. "It's true I made a promise to Dad to always believe in magic and never give up on love. I'm keeping that promise, don't worry. But it's the promise to you I'm thinking about right now. Today was for us and tonight is too. If that was my soulmate and we were meant to be together, love will find a way. I believe that. Also, he has my business card."

"Okay. You're in charge. Though let the cosmic record show, I still think you should go after him. And I wouldn't exactly call that a business card."

"Duly noted."

We walked through the night exactly like we had walked through our days as children, arm in arm, heads close together, talking the whole time. The world fell away, except for the Eiffel Tower twinkling brightly against the deep black sky in the distance behind us.

Eleventh House

Au Revoir

The Eleventh House rules air travel, networking, socializing, the media, friends, lighting, charity, benevolence, wake-up calls, breakthroughs, divine intervention, the sky, genius, the future, politics, rebellion, towers, astrology, and all things weird and bizarre.

If the planet that rules your Fifth House of love, Seventh House of marriage, or Eighth House of soulmates is in your Eleventh House, there is a strong likelihood that you could meet that perfect stranger on a flight or while waiting in the airport. The house ruler is determined by the planet that rules the sign on the cusp of that house.

I have the sign of Capricorn occupying my Eleventh House. Capricorn in its own strange way is about destiny and what your soul has planned for you before incarnating into this life. In the Eleventh House, Capricorn feels compelled to believe in hopes and wishes being fulfilled.

IT HAD TO HAVE BEEN A DREAM, RIGHT?

That was my first thought upon waking up to my blaring alarm far too early the next morning. The handsome stranger outside Hôtel Costes after dinner. Our instant, electric connection. His eyes. Love and destiny. It must have been a midnight fantasy. He couldn't possibly have been *that* hot.

"Tara. Tara? We have to wake up," I said groggily.

My sister groaned. "Noooooooo."

I could have closed my eyes and gone immediately back to sleep. But I had a cab coming at 9:45 a.m. and then an extraordinarily long day of travel in front of me. Tara's direct flight didn't depart Paris until late afternoon. She would have one last walk through the city, one more lovely Parisian lunch. But I needed to dress, pack, and get downstairs, with hopefully enough time for a coffee.

The hot shower cleared my head. And it wasn't a dream I saw more clearly, but a truth: I missed my kids and knew I had to return to work and real life, but there was a part of me that didn't want to go home. Remember all those fucks I didn't give anymore? Turns out they were right there all along. Because soon I'd have to talk about something not fun, something potentially humiliating: How I *didn't* find my soulmate in Paris. How my happiness wasn't written in the stars after all. It was probably going to be hugely embarrassing. That was something I should be used to by now, except I didn't think I'd ever be able to truly stop caring what people thought. Stephanie had said that would happen for me this year, but, like my soulmate, it didn't seem to be in the cards.

At least I'd made some real friends, I told myself: Mercedes. François. Ashley. Some of my 2 Novembre 1968 matches. I knew I'd stay in touch with Fabrice for sure. That was just my way; whenever I tried and then failed at something—and there'd been plenty of somethings over the years—I always came away with new friends. And I kept them.

Which gave me an idea about how Billy and I might, just might, recover our eight-figure sale. I knew a *lot* of people from different worlds. People in fashion and retail, in magazines, on production sets, on the boards of nonprofits serving women and children, in higher education, and so on. When I started in luxury real estate, I did what Billy and Penelope taught me: I created a big database of all those contacts, no matter what kind of house they might be able to afford one day. At the Agency, we put a lot of effort into creating editorial-spread-worthy e-blasts for our listings. Even people who are not in the market for a new home enjoy getting a peek inside some of LA's most fabulous properties—that's why *Million Dollar Listing Los Angeles* does so well. An agent never knows where a buyer or seller will come from. Maybe someone's sweet makeup artist or barista mentions me or one of my listings. That's happened! But there was something I hadn't done over the past year: I hadn't fully integrated my November 2, 1968, world with my Agency one. None of the people I'd met online were on my e-mail list. I'd been uncertain about merging my two worlds. Real estate agents were supposed to be serious, whatever that meant. This was big business. But the new people in my life had their own kind of power. And that was serious too. I'd felt it, lived it, followed it all the way to Paris. It was time for my two supposedly disparate universes to meet. The pop star's house was special. I still believed that a quick sale was possible. With two plane rides and a layover ahead, I'd have plenty of time to put together a new off-market listing e-blast for my about-to-be-expanded contact list. I'd schedule it to be sent as soon as it was a decent hour in LA and let fate take its course.

"Tasha, out!" My sister banged on the bathroom door. I smiled to myself as I dried off from the shower. Some things between sisters never change.

I threw on the hotel's fluffy white robe and matching slippers, packed up the last of my things, and thought about what to wear for the trek home. Just one travel-appropriate outfit remained clean and unworn: a snakeskin-print jumpsuit. Subtle? Not exactly. But it was unbelievably soft, as I'd discovered when I'd tried it on back home. It looked and felt more like onesie pajamas than anything else, and as I intended to sleep on the plane as much as possible, it was the perfect choice. I hung the jumpsuit in the closet while I tidied my suitcases. Rearranging toiletries, sweaters, and a few stray souvenirs, I came across the floor-length silk-velvet gown my designer friend Tony had generously lent me to wear for when I found true love. I pulled it out and studied it. High neck. Dramatic batwing sleeves. The deepest shade of midnight blue. Chic. French. Perfect. Tony had been so excited to lend it to me, so sure I'd need it. The dress was one of a kind. And I'd never had an opportunity to wear it.

"Did you bring an actual gown to Paris?" Tara asked in astonishment as she came out of the bathroom. "Your suitcase is like a couture clown car. How do you keep pulling out more outfits?"

"I have to give it back." I sighed. "I was supposed to wear this when I found true love." I explained about Tony.

"It's beautiful. It totally deserves a Paris debut, guy or no guy. Put it on and I'll take a picture."

I shrugged off the robe and stepped into the fairy-tale gown. Tara zipped up the back and I spun around.

"Wow," she said. "I don't think a dress has ever suited you more. It's gorgeous. Maybe Tony will let you borrow it again when you do find your soulmate."

"I'd be too embarrassed to ask," I replied. "Let's just get some pictures so Tony can see how perfect this dress is for Paris."

I moved over to the window. The view would be a spectacular backdrop.

Tara pointed her phone at me. I smiled but didn't ask her to make some cheesy video like I might have only the day before. If I posted this image at all, it would be for Tony, to show him how perfect his dress was for Paris. It was time to leave. This was my goodbye.

My phone, which I'd left on the dresser, pinged. But I didn't look at it right away because I needed to get out of the gown, put on my traveling clothes, and get downstairs.

Tara sat on the edge of her bed, watching me tuck the last few items into my suitcase.

"Are those the hotel slippers in your bag? You're taking them?"

"Of course. Aren't they cute? I want something to remember this place by."

"Wait a sec. Is that legal?" Tara raised an eyebrow.

"Tara. For real? You can't be serious. These are disposable slippers. Do you think this five-star hotel washes them each time and then gives guests *used* slippers? No. They are ours. To take. Back to Los Angeles."

"Oh . . . I'm not so sure about that." Tara grabbed one of the white slippers from my bag and examined it closely. REGINA PARIS was embroidered in gold across the fluffy toe box.

"Even if I'm wrong, what's the worst that can happen? They charge you for slippers? Okay! Worth it! I'll Venmo you. And I'll pay for yours too. Here," I said, tossing her the other pair from the closet. "Sometimes it feels good to break some rules. Trust me."

I could see Tara having an internal debate. Then we both started laughing: How different we were. And how the same. Tara picked up the second pair of slippers and placed them (reluctantly) on her suitcase. And then I remembered.

"Wait! I have something for you! And I promise I didn't steal it or break any slipper laws to get it."

I crossed the room, dug deep in my purse, and found the candle from the Musée d'Orsay's gift shop. It was wrapped in tissue. I handed it to her. "Here. So you can light a candle whenever you want to."

Tara carefully unwound the tissue and then went quiet for what felt like a little too long. Maybe reminding her that we hadn't ever made it to a chapel wasn't my best idea. *Shit.*

"If it might bother your asthma, I'll keep it. I just thought—"

"Tasha, this candle is inspired by *Swan Lake*. That's what the little drawing of the swan wearing a tiara is all about. Did you know that's my favorite ballet? And Dad's too?"

Honestly, I didn't know that. My sister had danced with the Santa Barbara Ballet Company for years, and Bob had elbowed his way to the front row for dress rehearsals and performances, but to me all the ballets seemed mind-numbingly similar. As a kid, I'd preferred Madonna to Tchaikovsky.

"I guess I got lucky in the gift shop," I said.

"I don't think so," Tara said softly. "I think it's Dad. Thank you. I love it and I love you."

"I love you too, sis. Thank you for letting me stay with you in this swanky hotel. After I turn into a real estate mogul, we'll come back. My treat."

"Definitely."

I took one last look around the room and spotted my phone on the dresser. I grabbed it and read the message that had come in earlier. It was from an unknown European number. But this time, it wasn't Julien making another case for Luxembourg.

It was so nice meeting you in Paris at the Costes Hotel. Hope to meet you again. Cheers, A.

"Tara! It's him. It's the guy from last night. What was his name? Oh my God! I can't believe he texted me!" Suddenly, I was wide awake.

I showed Tara my phone and her face broke out in the biggest grin.

"You have to text back. What will you say?"

"I don't know. I don't know what to say! Wait, do I care that he doesn't have the right birthday?" I said as I saved his number under COULD THIS BE THE ONE?!

"*No,*" Tara replied, emphatic.

And then I knew. Do you believe in fate? For real? I typed.

He replied immediately.

YES.

Three dots appeared as he wrote more. Then: Can I see you? Today?

I wish. But I'm flying home today.

Will you come back?

I don't have plans to.

When are you leaving for the airport?

In 45 minutes. I'm a few blocks from your hotel at the Regina Louvre if you want to see me off. I'm heading to the breakfast room now.

On my way.

Oh. My. God. What did I just do? Shaking, I passed my phone to Tara so she could read the exchange.

"Go down there, Tasha. Right now. And I'm not coming with you this time. I'll get my coffee later. But you better let me know what happens. The first second you can."

"I promise. Okay, I'm going. Right now." But I didn't move. I couldn't decide if I should check my hair one last time or just run for the elevators.

"Go."

I left my bags with the bellman and went to the breakfast room, where I ordered a quick coffee and croissant, along with the check, practically in a blind panic. The waiter dropped off all three and when I looked up from signing the bill, there he was, COULD THIS BE THE ONE?!, standing right before me.

His warm brown eyes met mine. He smiled. I smiled. I stood.

"It's you" was all he said. In that voice.

He leaned in for *la bise*. By now I had perfected the fine art of cheek-kissing like a real French person. I knew the drill. And I also knew that this kiss was . . . something more. It was not a fleeting, casual cheek-to-cheek touch. There was no air-kiss noise. His soft lips landed directly on my cheek. And they stayed there for the sweetest second. I felt my pulse quicken, my face grow warm. What would happen next? I had no script.

He sat down across from me and introduced himself as if we had all the time in the world. His name was Anton. We chatted about what he was doing in Paris, who he was, who I was. An accomplished journalist, Anton covered economics, but for pleasure he wrote about the history of love. And destiny. He was a romantic just like me. The tension between us crackled. We were in a bright breakfast room, but it might as well have been a private nook in a cozy bistro.

Anton's face was different in the light of day. He was still hand-some in a knee-weakening Greek god sort of way, there was no denying that. And tall, at least six inches taller than me. Lean. And yet his expression was somehow more approachable, more open. I liked it. A lot. Perhaps he saved his dark-eyed intensity for night-time, a thought that made me blush even harder than I already was. He wore a black collared shirt and a well-cut blazer, also black. I noticed the hint of a tattoo peeking out from his sleeve. *Oh my God, could he be any sexier?* I could smell his cologne, those heady notes of amber and incense again. His appearance was flaw-less except for one thing—a small nick on his chin where he had cut himself shaving. The cut still bled the tiniest bit and must have happened only minutes earlier. Had he rushed to jump in the shower and shave before meeting me here? Was he freaking out a little too? Anton was French, from Alsace, his voice low and his accent slight. He listened when I spoke about November 2, 1968, and how that date had led me to Paris. To this table, with him. I didn't tell him much, just enough. We didn't have time. He had his own flight to catch later that evening.

"It's strange, coming here to see you off like this," he said. "Tell me, did you truly fly all the way to Paris just to find love?"

"I came to Paris to find someone. But nothing turned out as I expected. Nothing." I laughed nervously, my eyes straying to the clock on the wall. I couldn't miss my taxi.

"Are you sure you're not returning to Paris soon?" Anton asked.

"I want to, but the soonest I could come back is not soon at all. At least a few months. I have work. And two kids," I answered honestly. "This is goodbye for now. I should go get my bags. My taxi will be here soon."

We walked out of the breakfast room and into the bustling lobby: People checking out. People checking in. A couple con-sulting the concierge, who dutifully circled locations on a map. A small child pleading for a sweet. A woman on her way to the ele-vators carrying a large box from Hermès. The gray Paris morning shimmered just outside, visible through the windows, while the chandeliers sparkled overhead. Maybe this is where I should tell you that the Hôtel Regina Louvre's lobby—the majestic grande dame of Parisian hotel lobbies—was the backdrop for dozens of films, like *La Femme Nikita* and *The Bourne Identity*. There was something about the sublime space that made visitors feel as if anything could happen, that all was never lost. Behind the reception desk, the young clerk who had escorted Tara and me to our room the day before met my eyes. She registered Anton at my side and smiled approvingly, her lips curving with open delight. Had she been American, she might have given me a big thumbs-up.

Anton and I stood smack-dab in the middle of the commotion. I'd all but forgotten about my bags and the taxi as I looked up into his eyes and he gazed down into mine. There were no candlelit corners to hide in. No girlfriends or sister cheering me on. No iPhone cameras pointed at me. No sea of drinks to quell my anxiety or soften reality. It was just the two of us, very much in the actual moment.

"So, uh, remind me, what's your birthday again?" I blurted out.

Anton gently tipped my chin up. "May I kiss you?" he asked.

Before I could answer beyond a nod yes (because *yes!*), his lips were brushing mine. Softly at first. One hand moved from my shoulder to the small of my back and the other cupped my cheek. He kissed me again, feather-light, and I kissed him back. There was still time to stop, to rewind ever so slightly, to say "Till we meet again" with some semblance of mannered grace. Then he drew me closer, and his kisses grew deeper, harder. In an instant, we were like besotted teenagers, fully making out. He held me tightly, his body adjusting to the shape of mine. I softened in his arms. His mouth moved to my neck, nipped lightly at my ear. Then his hand was in my hair. I could hear his breath quicken. His weight against my body made me feel alive. The sunlight streaming in through the windows warmed my face, and I dimly heard the world moving all around us. I'm pretty sure we were in everyone's way. And yes, I had on the head-to-toe snakeskin-print jumpsuit/onesie. Not a drop-dead gown or even a cute dress. But I didn't care. I was on fire, the best kind of fire, the kind you read about in delicious, beach-bag-worthy romances. I thought I might dissolve into a pile of pure bliss right there. If I'd had my own room, I would have led Anton right up to it and changed my flight yet again, even if it meant a layover in Iceland and a twenty-six-hour journey home.

Was it five minutes or twenty hours or thirty seconds? I don't know. It felt like forever and also nowhere close to long enough.

A little second of eternity.

I'd listened to Colette's translation of Jacques Prévert's poem so many times that it had embedded itself in my brain, much like song lyrics do. Snippets would surface and then sink down deep again at the oddest of times. I'd hear a line or two while waiting at Starbucks. Or folding the laundry. Or hiking Temescal Canyon. I almost never knew what signaled my brain to send up a poetry flare. But in the lobby of the Hôtel Regina Louvre I had no question.

The little second of eternity
When you kissed me
When I kissed you
One morning by the light of winter

Slowly, Anton pulled away. And reality rushed back in. My cab would arrive any minute.

"You'll miss your flight," he said, brushing his lips across my forehead one last time.

I don't remember saying goodbye. I don't remember anything about the moment he left. But I must have said goodbye and watched him leave because I have a photo I took of him exiting the lobby through the revolving wooden door. Proof that *this had happened*. Though the photo didn't exactly come out. In it, Anton is a blur, a tall dark figure disappearing through a door in motion.

Then I was in a taxi with all my bags. I sent a quick text to Tara almost before my butt hit the seat just so she'd know I hadn't been abducted.

WE TOTALLY

MADE OUT

IN THE LOBBY

AND IT WAS

🔥 🔥 🔥

Tara instantly texted back.

TELL ME EVERYTHING!!!!

I glanced out the window at the hotel. At the Eiffel Tower in the distance. At Joan of Arc. The magic of Paris. And then I saw Anton on the sidewalk. He was staring at me, waiting for my taxi to leave. I lifted my hand and waved as we drove off. Then we turned a corner and I could no longer see him or the Eiffel Tower or Joan of Arc or any of it . . .

I remember looking out the window of the taxi the whole ride, trying to make sense of what had just happened and imagine what might come next. I was both thoroughly exhausted and exquisitely alive. It was the strangest, most beautiful feeling. The city of Paris rushed by until it slowly blurred from urban magic into the more humble outskirts of the city, the changing colors and landscape of the ride to the airport.

Ping. Tara again.

She'd texted a string of images. Her and me in front of the Arc du Carrousel, me clutching my flyers, of course. Nicole, Penelope, and me at dinner with François. Me standing outside Little Red Door, terror and anticipation on my face. Me with Andy, beaming at the opera house.

And then me with Bob.

Hi, Dad.

I almost missed my flight. I was the last person to board and they had to hold the plane for me. As I settled into my seat, apologizing to my neighbors, my phone pinged again. Another text. I couldn't wait to see more pictures from Tara. I didn't want Paris to be over.

But the text was from COULD THIS BE THE ONE?!

You know the expression "coup de foudre"? I got a good idea of it in our encounter.

"Please turn off all electronic devices, including your phone, as we prepare for takeoff." The voice over the loudspeaker was no-nonsense and I saw the flight attendant at the head of the plane quickly checking each row with practiced precision. But I was way in the back. I still had at least thirty seconds.

I opened the Google Translate app and typed in *coup de foudre,* because I didn't know that expression. On my phone, the translation appeared:

Love at first sight.

Twelfth House

A Skyful of Stars

The Twelfth, and final, House rules endings. This house covers the final stages of a project, tying up loose ends, completions, the afterlife, and surrender. The purpose of your Twelfth House is to help you evolve and grow into your more complete and fulfilled self.

Aquarius engulfs my Twelfth House. Everywhere I go in the world I find friends. They may be friends for a short journey or friends for a lifetime, but none of them are new. Stephanie says we've all met before when we were in different roles, maybe different genders, in all kinds of places in our past lives.

The planet Uranus rules the sign of Aquarius so Uranus rules my Twelfth House. I was born with Uranus in Libra, which is about companionship. Though Uranus rules my Twelfth House because of Aquarius, it's important to know that on the day I was born, the planet Uranus was in my Eighth House of reincarnation of the soulmate. The Eighth House is also about wanting to control circumstances, but Uranus defies control. It needs freedom to breathe. From this vantage point, Paris had to happen the way it did.

✳ ✳ ✳

AT FIRST, IT FELT GOOD TO BE HOME IN LOS ANGELES AND back in my little yellow house. Though I'd been gone for less than a week, I'd missed everything about it: The butterflies and flowers in the yard, my ancient but oh-so-comfy mattress, my kitchen where I knew how to work the coffeemaker. The warm sun. And, most of all, Margot and Dash.

Dash greeted me with hugs and a hundred questions about the food in Paris. Had I eaten French onion soup? Steak tartare? Was it true that French people didn't snack? Were there vending machines with baguettes in them instead of candy?

"Oh. Hey, Mom. How was Paris?" Margot said in passing. "Did you find your soulmate? Looked like fun."

And off she went before I could answer but not before she told me she'd auditioned for—and won—the part of Pali High's school mascot. The Dewey Dolphin? *Margot?*

I had to go back to the office. But I did *not* want to do that. Not because I didn't love my work and colleagues—I totally did, of course. And let's face it, I needed money, immediately. But I didn't want to see my coworkers and clients because I felt just as embarrassed as I'd feared I would. Who could blame me? Beyond a ridiculous (but hot) public make-out session with a wrong-birthday guy, I'd failed in Paris, and a lot of people knew it. It wasn't hard to imagine the *Bummers* and *Well, that must have been awkwards* waiting for me at the reception desk and copy machines. I'd have to take down all the posters in my office too. How mortifying. Was it any wonder I put off going in for as long as I could? Which turned out to be not long at all.

Just days after my return home, I was offered a free spot in an exclusive Ninja Coaching workshop for the Agency's top performers. This high-level, weeklong sales-training course would normally have cost a small fortune. And even if I'd had the spare cash, I didn't belong there. The heavy hitters responsible for selling hundreds of millions of dollars of real estate—that's who goes to Ninja training. But someone dropped out at the last minute and someone else thought of me. Before I could think too much about it, I accepted. Because if Ninja Coaching was good enough for Billy and Mauricio, who was I to turn it down?

The training began at 8:00 a.m. at the Viceroy L'Ermitage Hotel in Beverly Hills. *That sounds like a big-room kind of thing,* I thought to myself as I drove there. *Nobody will notice me or the fact that I'm a little late. I'll just slip in the back and take notes on my phone.*

Wrong. The workshop was intimate and held in a small conference room. Worse, everyone else had arrived on time. And so all eyes were on me as I cracked open the door and tried to sneak in.

"Bonjour!" Mauricio called out, his inimitable voice booming across the room. "She's back!"

"Did you find your soulmate?" someone else said.

"Welcome home!"

"Yay, Natasha! You did it!"

"How was Paris?"

My colleagues applauded me as I found a seat. I didn't know what to do. I thought I'd be hiding my head in shame, stumbling over my words as I deflected humiliating questions and admitted that my plan had failed. But not one person acted like I was a delusional loser who'd been served up a platter of cold reality. Instead, they offered their congratulations.

"Uh, thanks, but . . . why are you congratulating me?" I asked, trying to laugh and keep it light while I was waiting for the trapdoor to open.

"You got on a fucking plane to Paris to track down your soulmate. So maybe you didn't find him this time, but my money's on you, kid," said one of the agents, someone who, honestly, I didn't think even knew I existed. Why would he? My business was a Popsicle stand compared to his empire.

"What happened with that last guy? Dying to know!" Monique whispered as our instructor told us to settle down and turn our attention to her.

"Let's do a warm-up," the instructor said brightly. "A lot of people are scared of talking on the phone these days. Cold-calling especially. This is an exercise that helps build confidence. Everyone here is going to call someone right now. It could be an old client. A new client. A colleague. A friend. Your mother. Your sister. It doesn't matter who just as long as you call them, they answer, and you have a conversation. And if you're unsure of who to call, I want you to play a little Russian roulette with your phone. That's where you close your eyes, scroll through your contacts, and dial whoever your finger lands on."

Cell phone roulette felt like the obvious choice. I didn't want to get on the phone with my friends yet. There would be wayyyy too many questions. I stepped outside, found a quiet spot, closed my eyes, and spun my contacts. When I opened my eyes, I couldn't believe where my finger had landed: 97.1 FM RADIO.

You've got to be kidding me. I considered spinning the wheel of contacts/fate again, but I continued with the exercise and pressed Call. The screener who answered was the same person I had spoken with months ago. *Might as well just rip the Band-Aid right off in a big way,* I decided on the spot.

"Remember me? The woman who was chasing down her soulmate in Paris? Hi. I just got back," I began, then explained about Ninja Coaching and why I was calling.

"A sales training? Ninja? *Right now?* Oh, the DJs are gonna want to talk to you," the screener replied.

The DJs had a good laugh over me in my sales training and welcomed me back from Paris, reminding their listeners of why I'd gone in the first place. Then they asked what I wanted to say now that I had their attention and was on live radio.

I hadn't thought about that. I'd simply been going along with the training exercise. And Mauricio had just walked up to me and was listening to the whole thing.

"Are you . . . on *the radio*?" he asked, incredulous.

I gave him a thumbs-up and a tentative smile. Then suddenly I knew what to say, what I'd felt from the moment I saw that my colleagues *weren't* going to hold me up as a cosmic "Don't" that week at training. Or anywhere else.

"What I most want to say is how grateful I am for so many of the people in my life. Even for this radio station. Every morning on the way to school, my son and I listen to your show. I didn't realize it at the time, but your show was one of the things that lifted me up when I needed it most this past year. It reminded me to get myself *up* each day. So, um, thanks for being you."

I know I babbled on and probably sounded painfully saccharine. But I was sure of one thing: the swell of deep gratitude I felt for the people in my life who were supporting me, cheering me on, as I tried for a second (okay, maybe third or fourth) chance at a happily-ever-after.

Just before I hung up I added: "If anyone out there is looking for a house to buy or has one to sell, hit me up."

"You went on a live morning show? Well, that's a first in all my years of doing this," the Ninja coach said, surprised. We'd all had to go around the room and share.

I made it through only two half-days of Ninja training. The instructor wanted us to put away our phones and laptops and focus from eight a.m. to six p.m., and ADD me couldn't handle that. But I did learn something invaluable: People I respected were seeing me for who I was at heart—messy, hopeful, impulsive, hardworking, hell-bent on succeeding—and they liked me for it. They even seemed to respect me right back. Oh, and I also learned that the sale of the pop star's house was likely back on, though not with the same buyer. The e-blast I'd sent out to my all-corners-of-my-new-universes contacts list had, miraculously, yielded a motivated buyer looking for a house exactly like the pop star's. Billy pulled me aside on one of the breaks the first day of the training to give me the good news.

"I received a call this morning from someone who saw your e-blast. Coincidentally, I represented her a lifetime ago when I was an entertainment lawyer. She's awesome—and expecting her third and fourth children. Twins, how about that? She needs a bigger house yesterday. She's all-cash, will write an incredibly clean offer, and is looking to close fast. There's a good chance we'll open escrow this week. And she doesn't care about the little gathering our seller just had."

I had always felt that the pop star's house was meant for a family. Houses, like people, have energy. I had a good feeling about this.

"If I ever get married again I'm doing it in a white version of this dress," I said to Tony as I handed him back the velvet gown he'd designed and lent to me to wear in Paris with my soulmate. "Thank you for trusting me with it." We were in his studio.

"Are you celebrating today?" Tony asked.

"No. Why would I be?" I replied, confused.

"The date! *Chérie,* today it is *le deux Novembre*! You must make a toast or celebrate somehow. November second is at last here."

Tony obviously didn't know how bad I was with dates. But he did have a point. Back home, I sat on my couch with a glass of sparkling water (bubbles were called for, after all) and texted birthday wishes to all sixteen of my potential soulmates. Even Scar Guy. Even Amir, who had stood me up on the bridge.

One by one, many of the guys wrote back. Chloe did too.

Maaz: Merci!

Antoine: Hey.

Chloe: I think about you a lot! You and your sister.

Alcide: I hope we see each other in 2020. (This from a man who'd never replied to any of my messages in Paris—not one!)

Amir: Thank you very much! How are you? I thought you forgot about me. And when are you coming for our love? (Um, what?)

Thierry: Hello a bird from Paris With a smile and a kiss (What the hell did that even mean?)

Some of these guys obviously liked me better now that I was back in LA.

Fabrice: Thank you for the birthday Natasha 😿★,it touches me a lot, the party was minimal because the disappearance of my father, does not give too much taste to party without him for the moment. My mother she is now resting at home with us around her. What sadness you must have had, too. You are adorable thank you for your words. I kiss you.

And then I texted Philippe.

Happy Birthday, P. I've met a lot of men born in Paris on 2 Novembre 1968. No one quite like you. All my love. xx

But Philippe didn't answer, not that day or the next. Weeks went by before I heard from him.

November 2 wasn't the only date I should have been paying attention to as 2019 came to a close. Tara and I were talking in my kitchen one afternoon when she spotted the tiny Pyrex bowl that I'd overturned to cover and preserve about a teaspoon's worth of chunky gray ash on my special-things shelf. A pink Post-it note affixed to the dish read DO NOT TOUCH! POSSIBLY BOB!

"*What's this?*" Tara asked. I could tell from her tone that she knew exactly what it was.

"Well, that's . . . it's . . . there should be a childproof lock or something on that memorial wand I got for Dad's ashes. It kind of just opens up when I least expect it, and what's inside spills out if I'm not careful."

"*What's inside* spills out? You mean *Dad*? Tasha, it's time to deal with this. Properly. The one-year anniversary of Dad's passing is coming up. December tenth. We need to lay all of him to rest. No more wand. It's what Dad would want."

My gut told me she was right. Before I left for Paris, I'd consulted a psychic named Teresa about my soulmate search, just one of the many alternative avenues I embraced in my all-out effort to find The One. Teresa didn't have a lot to say about my romantic prospects, but she did seem to have a line to Bob. And to my uncle on my mom's side. I know, I know. I called her again after I got home from Paris. I missed my dad. And she, or rather he, she said, had a message for me. He loved me, he was proud of me, but according to Teresa, Bob kept mentioning a photo of him that I had. He wanted me to find this photo and put it, respectfully, in a frame. I knew exactly which photo my dad meant. The one of him as a young man at MIT. After hanging up with Teresa, I went immediately to the shelf in my kitchen and found the photo lying faceup, sprinkled with ash. Oh no. The wand. When I wasn't carrying it around town in my red bag, it rested in that exact spot next to his photo. And, apparently, it had malfunctioned. I wasn't sure what to do. Did I just scoop the ashes back into the wand and wipe up the rest that had drifted onto the shelf? Wiping up my dad's remains with a squirt of Windex and a paper towel didn't feel right. Plus, did my dad even want to be on my special-things shelf? What if he wanted to be somewhere else? An upside-down Pyrex bowl seemed like a good placeholder while I figured it all out. But now, I thought, maybe Bob wanted more than just the photo framed or being (partially) the patron saint of my kitchen. Maybe that's what the psychic had meant. I told Tara what Teresa had said.

"Yeah, that sounds exactly like what a psychic *would* say. I'm glad you framed the photo. It's one of Mom's favorites. And that wand of yours? I'm giving it a one-star rating," my sister said with a sigh.

In the end, we decided to scatter the remainder of Bob's ashes at sea. Bob loved the ocean. Even his burial plot had a great view of the coast. We chartered a small boat, one that would take us out in the water right below the cemetery in Santa Barbara. It would be just the three of us: me, Tara, and our mom. Plus the crew. Oh, and Bob.

"You okay, Mom? Can I get you anything?" I said, rummaging through Tara's Pinterest-worthy picnic basket as our captain pulled the twenty-seven-foot sailboat out of the slip and into the Pacific Ocean. "Kleenex? Visine? Fennel and black-pepper salami? What is this, a burial-at-sea charcuterie?" I asked my sister.

Tara handed me a yellow-label bottle of Veuve Clicquot, a full-size version of the kind we'd had in Paris in our hotel minibar. "Just make sure you check the wind direction before you open that magic wand of yours. I'm serious. I've done a lot of research on ash scatterings and I don't want to get *Big Lebowski*'d by you."

"You worry too much," I said, popping the champagne. "Relax! How complicated can scattering ashes be?"

"Bob would have loved this," Edna said with a genuine smile as I filled her plastic flute with bubbly and synced the Joe Cool playlist to the boat's sound system. Natalie Cole's "This Will Be (an Everlasting Love)" spilled from the speakers and out onto the open waves. It was wonderful to see Mom happy.

Once we were three nautical miles from shore—the legal requirement for the disposal of cremated remains—our captain gently announced it was time to say goodbye and proceed with the scattering of the ashes.

"Right." I swallowed hard, recognizing my cue. But I wasn't sure how to do this. I looked at my sister and mother, both of whom watched me expectantly from behind their oversize sunglasses. Where was that fucking manual on death again? How did Bob's burial at sea become my job? How come I wasn't on Costco-party-platter duty like my sister? Or chatting it up with our cute captain like my mom? My head hurt; my heart hurt.

Be cool, a soft voice whispered. *Be Joe Cool.*

Hi, Dad.

"To the Great Bob Sizlo." I raised my glass. "Thanks for sticking around, Dad. We love you."

I carefully removed the cap from the gold wand and began sprinkling the coarse gray ashes into the sea. *This isn't so bad,* I thought. *It's kind of beautiful, actually. The circle of life. Returning my father's physical body to the earth (or, well, ocean). Ashes to ashes, dust to dust.* The heavier remains of the sand-like ashes sank into the dark water, and a thin film of dusty gray ash floated gently on the surface into the sunset. I tossed a handful of white rose petals in and watched as they swirled and blended with my father's ashes. My mom was quiet. I could hear Tara sniffling. And yet we were all a happy kind of sad. It was time to let go. But somehow this letting go on the boat wasn't letting go at all. It was letting in. We weren't fighting Bob's death or running from it. We were simply being with the fact of it and with him. We rode the waves of grief and love and memory, letting them wash over us. It was perfect.

Perfect, that is, until the last of Bob's ashes got stuck in the wand.

I gently tapped the vial on the side of the boat, trying to loosen the cremains. But nothing came out. I tapped a little harder. Still nothing.

"Is this supposed to be happening?" Tara whispered through clenched teeth.

As I repeatedly banged the vial of my dead father on the side of the boat, I felt the wind kick up.

"Keep your mouth closed," I said to my sister, who looked terrified.

Boy, those ashes were stuck.

Bang-bang-bang.

I continued to thunk the wand against the side of the boat harder and harder, encouraging Bob to loosen up and cooperate with the day's plans, but even dead and reduced to ash, he was a stubborn man. As the boat drifted on the waves, we found ourselves suddenly downwind; the breeze kicked up and gusted unexpectedly in our faces.

"Whoa!" I exclaimed as the ashes gave way and floated dangerously close to both of us. "I guess you were right to worry!"

Tara and I locked eyes for a few seconds, the tiniest of smiles creeping across our lips. I knew this feeling too well: sitting beside my big sister, fighting off a childhood fit of giggles at the most inappropriate of times. I willed myself to keep it together, took a deep breath, and waited for the attack to pass. I could see Tara fighting the same feeling. Tears mixed with laughter. The look in her eye like when she was a kid.

"Not funny, Dad" was all Tara could say before falling over in a fit of laughter.

And then it was time for a sisters' toast. Tara and I moved to the bow of the boat, away from our mother, and raised two bottles of Modelo, Bob's favorite beer, to the sky.

"We love you! We love you, Dad!" we both called out before pouring the amber beer into the glassy dark blue water.

I leaned over the side of the boat, closed my eyes, and spoke directly to my dad. I thanked him for being a great father, grandfather, husband, and friend. I thanked him for teaching me that anything is possible, always. I thanked him for promising to meet Tara and me in Paris on his deathbed. And for showing up in the City of Light one year later, his spirit soaring down the cobblestone streets, giving me strength to live and love again. I thanked him for teaching me to believe, to have faith, to get up. I thanked him for asking me to always believe in magic and never give up on love. For reminding me to *be cool,* no matter what.

The water was still. The sun had set, and the sky glowed with the colors of magic and fire. The huge, almost full moon reflected off the ocean. White rose petals bobbed on the horizon. Tara and I sat next to each other in silence. Then she pulled out her phone and hit Record.

"Our captain's cute," she said confidentially to the camera, shooting me a look and raising an eyebrow. She nodded to the stern of the boat, where Mom was pouring herself another glass of champagne and chatting with our handsome young captain, Johnny.

"Maybe I should ask him for his birthday." I raised my eyebrows back at Tara. "He *does* like Mom."

But Edna was ahead of us. "He was born in 1986 in Miami," my mother proudly announced, hugging our captain tight as we pulled into the harbor. "He's not The One, but aye, he's a braw fella."

"How did we survive our childhood, again?" I whispered to Tara.
"I don't know . . . did we?"

Later that day I shared a few pictures from the boat on Instagram. I'd been mostly offline since I got home from Paris, back to my old pre–2 Novembre 1968 social-media self. It was a relief to just be in the world without any care for how it might look. But I also couldn't stop thinking about the many, many people who had reached out to me over the past year, not about finding The One but about the crushing, unpredictable grief that they too had felt when someone they loved died. I'd been baldly honest about how brutal coming to terms with my dad's death had been. There was no need to pretend with me that everything was fine because I'd already told every person I knew and then some that *it wasn't*. My dad dying was not fine. It *isn't* fine. But it did happen. And that day on the boat, I realized that Tara and my mom and I had finally found our way to the other side of grief. No, we weren't in the land of eternal candy, roses, and butterflies. We were someplace else. Someplace still fucked up at times but also somehow okay. I wanted to say hello to my fellow travelers. *We're here! We're alive. Hello.*

In mid-December I finally heard from Philippe.

Philippe: Hi. I didn't mean not to answer you on my birthday. Didn't know how. I miss you. Should we get coffee?

Me: Probably.

P: Love the enthusiasm.

Me: PROBABLY.

Of course coffee was a glass of rosé. Okay, two.

Philippe and I met at Casa del Mar, and I sat in the exact spot at the bar I had sat in a year ago, hoping to find hot displaced dads after the fires in Malibu. The exact spot I had texted Nicole He can't be The One!!! before deciding I would search the world for every other man born on Philippe's birthday.

What a year.

"So, how *was* everybody with my birthday?" Philippe smiled as he greeted me at the bar.

I could feel my face turn hot and red. "I'm so embarrassed. I don't want to talk about it," I said.

Philippe still looked good. He was wearing his white shirt. Damn him.

"Oh, sorry. I didn't realize that was on the list of things we're not allowed to talk about. How about this topic—do you want to know what it's like being that guy born on November second?" he asked. "Can we talk about that? I had people calling me. People are *still* calling me, I should say. About my birthday and your insane adventure. My mom was so confused."

"Ah, sorry about that."

Philippe just looked at me and shook his head. "It's nice to see you, Natasha."

"Thank you, Philippe. It's nice to be seen."

We sipped our rosé in silence.

"I wanted to tell you how sorry I am," Philippe said. "What we had was . . ." He paused.

"So perfect until it wasn't?" I said softly. "I know. We were messed up. Out of control. The drinking. The late nights. The way we ended. That was hard for me. It still is in some ways. I can't help wondering if it's hard for you too? I know that's probably not fair to ask, but I have to. I've thought about it so much." It was a question I'd never thought I'd be brave enough to voice.

"Of course it was hard for me," Philippe said. "Maybe it still is. I don't know."

And then he stopped talking, like he used to do back when we were still trying, stupidly, to hold things together at the terrible end. We were silent for a minute.

"I interrupted you," I said at last. "You were going to apologize to me. But for what?"

"You asked me to marry you and I didn't ever give you an answer."

"Oh. That was on purpose?"

"You didn't want *me*, Natasha. You wanted someone to save you, to put you back together. And then you left for Paris."

I wouldn't have put it *quite* that way. But I knew it had taken a lot for him to say any of that. And that there was far more truth to his observation than not.

"I'm the one who's sorry, Philippe. I did want someone to rescue me. I wanted that for a long time after my divorce and Bob's death. But you know what? In a way you kind of did. And I'm grateful to you. I always will be."

Were we finally saying all the things we'd never said? Face-to-face? While *not* drunk and not at three a.m.? Yes, we were. It was difficult but also good. Philippe had, once upon a time, been my rock, as had my dad. But I was beginning to see Philippe in a different way. Beginning to understand how he could be aligned with my point of destiny like Stephanie said and also how I didn't necessarily need to be *with* him. Just because something ends doesn't mean it wasn't meant to be. There was room for me to honor and love the very human, beautifully vulnerable flesh-and-blood man Philippe was and still move forward.

I didn't fall apart at the bar that night or fall into Philippe's arms like I might have done on another night, before Paris, before Bob died. And, let's be honest, even after Bob died. Instead, I asked Philippe about the woman he'd been dating. I told him I hoped it was going well. And I meant it.

"It is, you know. Going well. I think I've learned a thing or two, Natasha," Philippe said.

"Funny how that happens."

Soon after that Philippe left to meet up with a close childhood friend of his, Giles, who was in town for just one night. Poor Giles had just embarked on a difficult divorce of his own and Philippe hoped to take his mind off it and lend support.

The old me might have stayed at the bar. Called a girlfriend to come meet me. Had a few more drinks. Hoped for a hot dad displaced if not by fire then by something else that would land him on the stool next to mine. But I went home. Made a cup of tea. Opened my laptop. And started writing and thinking about it all. About my dad. And love. And Philippe. Was our story finished? It felt like it was in one way, but a little voice in my head whispered it had been too easy. *Easy?* I wanted to shout back at that little voice. *What part of this was easy?*

I picked up my phone and sent Philippe a text.

Me: Was that closure?

P: Does it feel like closure to you?

Me: Something like that.

P: Then "something like that" it is.

Me: Did we just have the craziest breakup in the history of breakups?

P: No comment.

Then he sent a selfie of himself and Giles. Two grown men squishing their heads together making kissy faces for the camera. Just like something Katie and I would do. Giles and Philippe had been friends almost their whole lives. And they were at exactly the kind of place Katie and I always did stuff like that, Élephante, a trendy hot spot for finding love, or LA's version of it. *We're all doing the same thing*, I thought and smiled.

Me: Now, that's a love story.

P: 34 years.

Me: Please send Giles my love. And tell him good luck with the hotties at Élephante.

And that was it. I knew I wouldn't be texting Philippe the next day or the next week. But it wasn't like I wouldn't ever talk to him again. I didn't need to erase Philippe. He'd been the right man at a time in my life that was so wrong. Besides, I wasn't looking to let go or move on from love anymore. I was looking to let love in, in whatever form it might take.

As I drove home from Santa Barbara along the Pacific Coast Highway late afternoon on New Year's Day of 2020, I thought about
the night I'd just had and the year to come. What would Stephanie say about 2020? Astrologers must be frantically busy on the
birth of a new year, let alone a new decade. I imagined Stephanie
and her assistant, Sheri, poring over charts and celestial maps for
weeks and then preparing their findings. I said a little prayer to the
heavens for a good year. For my kids. My sister. Nicole. My mom.
Especially my mom. That's whose house I was driving home from.

Margot and Dash had been with Michael and Anna for New
Year's Eve, and Tara was with her family, so Katie and I had taken
Edna out for an early glass of champagne at a fancy hotel and then
we went back to the house and had a quiet dinner, just the three
of us. Plus Friday. My little waggly love-ball of a rescue pup had
moved in with Edna. They had a mutual-adoration society of two,
and the company was good for my mom, though the kids and I
missed Friday a lot. On the whole, and maybe a little bit to my
surprise, the night was sweet. Fun, even. But if you'd asked me six
months ago if I thought Katie and I would be ringing in 2020 with
Edna and a Chihuahua, I would have said: *Are you fucking kidding
me? I'll be making out with my soulmate in Manhattan as the ball drops*
(since New York is halfway between Paris and LA). I don't want to
know what Katie would have said.

The next day, after Katie left, I helped Edna think about her real
estate business. I loved talking shop with my mom, because Edna
was damn good at real estate. I'd learned a lot from her. And sometimes we found ways of partnering on a deal. Edna was up for a
nine-million-dollar listing in Montecito, a one-of-a-kind estate
that we both agreed would shine even brighter with the Agency's
mega-marketing team behind it, so we decided to go after it together. As we sat at the kitchen table discussing her past deals and
future prospects, I saw for the first time how much my mom had
taken care of my dad through the years. I'd always seen it as the

other way around, but they'd been equal partners all along. Bob might have been brilliant but he'd also had his share of career setbacks, and his poor health had forced him into early retirement. In those scary moments, Edna had stepped in and worked tirelessly to bring in commissions that supported our family. More than I'd ever realized before.

Turns out my mom was the Great Edna Sizlo.

My mom had taken care of all of us. To infinity.

The sun glowed like a new copper penny in the late-afternoon sky over the endless blue ocean as I drove. *What a stunning drive,* I thought for the zillionth time. And: *Does it have to end so soon?* The ocean called to me, as it often did. But this time, I wasn't rushing anywhere. So I pulled my car to the side of the road, not by the open sandy beaches of Zuma but by the little rocky cliffs that are nearly impossible to sit on and where almost nobody pulls over. The road was empty as far as the eye could see in either direction. But it was okay. In fact, it was better that way. There were no freak-outs about being alone or anything like that on the horizon for me. Only the sunset.

Ping! A text from Nicole.

Happy New Year, my beautiful friend! I can't thank you enough for bringing me along on your incredible journey. Wishing you a year of dreams fulfilled.

She'd attached a photo of herself in fuzzy sweats and a T-shirt, holding a trash bag. Her two teenage girls had hosted a party the night before and now the whole family was cleaning up. Justin stood by Nicole's side with his arm around her, smiling. They looked relaxed. Happy. And yes, they'd gotten back together after we returned from Paris. As Nicole put it, they'd decided to simply enjoy the perfect impermanence of it all. When she'd told me that, I realized it made beautiful sense, the way many of the supposedly woo-woo things Nicole says do upon closer examination.

Another photo followed: the red staircase at the Shakespeare and Company bookstore in Paris. There was writing on the stairs' risers that I hadn't noticed before. Big letters. How had I missed that? What did the words say? I zoomed in.

I WISH
I COULD SHOW YOU
WHEN YOU ARE
LONELY OR
IN DARKNESS
THE ASTONISHING
LIGHT
OF YOUR OWN
BEING.
    —HAFIZ

Love you, Tash, Nicole added.

Love uuuuuuuuuu, I messaged back, smiling as my heart filled. Of course I'd totally missed seeing that poem back in Paris. I hadn't been ready to read it then. The astonishing light of the setting sun filled my vision and my car. It was part of me and I was part of it. *This* is what Stephanie meant by *spiritual*, I decided. I read the poem again. I'd share it with Margot and Dash as soon as they got back from their trip with their dad. Hell, maybe I'd even share it with Michael.

It was time to drive home.

Then I noticed something in the passenger seat's drink holder: the blue glass jar full to the brim with my soulmate wishes. I'd stashed it there when we were evacuated because of a fire in the Palisades and then forgotten about it.

Immediately, I knew exactly why I was called to the beach that evening. The wish papers needed to be lit on fire, one by one, in order for my wishes to have a chance at coming true. According to the original package, anyway. Sadly, I never seemed to be able to find a safe place to do that. Actual fire was no joke in LA. But on a beach? By more water than I could ever need in case of emergency? That would work. What better way to start a new year than with wishes?

I carefully climbed down the rocks to the beach and found a place to sit. Surprisingly, the beach wasn't deserted. People *did* come down these cliffs; I'd just never been one of them. A small group of teenagers were gathered to my left, joking and skipping rocks, and an older woman walked her dog along the water's edge. I pulled the first wish from the blue jar and read it silently to myself.

Jenga partner for life!!

Good one, I thought as I lit the wish paper. I watched it float up into the air and burn itself out in a fluttering swirl of flame and ash just as advertised. I took a second wish from the jar.

Someone who's romantic

I didn't burn that one right away. Instead, I read another wish. and then another, until the jar was empty. I'd never reread any of the wishes before that night. In fact, once I'd written a wish down on paper, I just folded it up, tossed it in the jar, and forgot about it. Reading all of my wishes in one sitting made me realize something, because this was different from reading my journal or scrolling back through old posts on Instagram. The wishes were a simple record of one thing only: what I had urgently wanted in my secret heart of hearts over the past twelve months. But those wishes hadn't been dormant or forgotten. They had been seeds planted by me in the rich soil of my own life. Every single one of the wishes had taken root, sprouted, and blossomed in some way. Maybe not in exactly the way I'd intended when I scribbled each wish and tossed it into the jar, at times hopeful, angry, sad, frustrated, or impatient. But they had bloomed. Undeniably.

It had taken me forty-five years to ask out loud for what I,

Natasha Sizlo, really and truly wanted. And one year for the universe to answer me back.

Almost all of the wishes in the jar had been fulfilled by someone in my life as I went about this unconventional journey to find my soulmate:

Has a huge heart: Dashiell
Someone who wants to make the world better: Margot
Emotionally available: Fabrice
Someone who isn't afraid to take charge: François
Someone who will dance with me when there is no music: My sister
AMAZING SEX: Dev
Loves pizzzzzza!!!: Also Dev
Someone who inspires me: Chloe
Someone who doesn't give up on people: My mom
Someone who knows and values the importance of friendship: Penelope
Someone who is patient with me as I grow, learn, change, love deeper, make mistakes, be the best I can be: Nicole
Has an actual job: Hope
Someone supportive (of my career, dreams): Billy
Someone who loves my kids or who could: Anna
Someone who's up for anything: Katie
Someone my dad would have loved: Andy
Someone who will make me a better person: Philippe

And, can you believe it, I also had this wish in the jar:

Someone who believes in love at first sight

Just one wish remained unfulfilled:

Someone who agrees that Lionel Richie is music's greatest unsung hero and should be inducted into the Rock and Roll Hall of Fame.

One by one, I burned the wishes and said not goodbye but hello. Hello to love. I had a lot of it in my life. In fact, when I thought about it, I had almost all the love that I'd been so frantically searching for. Might I be getting closer to what Stephanie said about discovering over the course of my quest that I didn't need a partner, that this experience would be about becoming open to one? At the time, I'd hated hearing that because I'd thought it was glaringly obvious that I absolutely did need a partner. And I wanted one too. But as I sat on the beach thinking about all my wishes and the people in my life who had so lovingly fulfilled them, I realized that I could take care of myself. And my kids. I'd been doing it all along, with the help of my incredible family and friends.

The *need* part of my quest had fallen away.

And now that I didn't need my soulmate, did that mean I was finally, *finally* ready for that person to enter my life? And that they might be appearing soon?

Honestly, I wasn't sure about that. It sounded a lot like the tired advice single people get all the time: *Honey, if you stop looking, that's when you'll find him.* If that were true, Tinder would be bankrupt and nobody would put on lip gloss to buy cauliflower at Erewhon. But, all kidding aside, I believed there was something to Stephanie's astrological guidance. Everything she's said to me then and since has resonated mightily, whether I understood it the first time around or not. She's been right about so much.

The next morning, over a croissant and hot coffee, I opened my e-mail. Dash and Margot were sleeping, the sun was shining, and I was ready to sell some houses. But just as I was about to send a new listing agreement through DocuSign (real estate in LA picks up after the holidays), I saw that Stephanie had answered me. I'd e-mailed her a few weeks ago, right after Philippe and I had our

grown-up, something-like-closure ~~coffee~~ wine. Because it had occurred to me: November 2, 1968, can't be the *only* date, can it?

To: Natasha Sizlo
From: Stephanie Jourdan
January 2, 2020
RE: In Search of Soulmate—Part Deux

Hi Natasha,

   In astrology there can be many soulmates, many individuals
we can be happily married to. It won't surprise you to learn
that most people don't want to hear this. They would like to
think they found the one. We have many spouses from past
lives that we bump into in this life and we feel like they are
soulmates. In astrology, contrary to the popular opinion of
our culture, the older you get, the better your options. The
natal chart gives you the description of your partner or type of
person and many people can fill that description.

   So here we go! Drumroll, please . . . look for a person born
on 8/28/1979 or 8/29/1979 in either the westernmost part
of Italy, Corsica, Sardinia, Switzerland, the easternmost part
of France, the western portion of Germany, the easternmost
part of the Netherlands, or the westernmost part of Denmark.
They were probably born between 9:44 p.m. and 2:00 a.m.
So 9:44 p.m. to midnight on 8/28/1979 or midnight to 2:00
a.m. on 8/29/1979.

   Sun in Virgo

   Moon in Scorpio

   Most likely Gemini or Cancer rising

   Sixty-seven minutes, which comes to $469. Let me know
how you would like to pay.

—Stephanie

That's more than Gwyneth Paltrow's therapist, I thought, sending Stephanie a Venmo. And: *Am I seriously going to do this again? Well, Nicole does love Giuseppe Zanotti heels, and Katie and I could learn to ski.* (Katie had recently become convinced that ski lifts were a great place to meet hot guys. Captive audience and all. Maybe she was right.)

The universe must have had me in mind that day, because just as I was thinking through the merits of schnitzel versus carbonara, my phone pinged. A text.

It was from Anton.

Yes, COULD THIS BE THE ONE?! We'd been texting occasionally since my return home. Was he my soulmate? I had no idea. I hadn't asked Stephanie about him and I didn't plan to. I didn't need the stars to tell me how I'd felt standing next to Anton. Plus I'd taken Penelope's wise words to heart: sometimes a little mystery is a good thing.

Anton: Hi.

Me: Hi back. I sent him a picture of my croissant.

Anton: Nice but I think that would taste better in Paris.

Me: Ha-ha-ha. Me too.

Anton: So, what do you think?

Me: About what?

Anton: Meeting me in Paris. Say yes, Natasha.

I didn't reply to Anton right away. Instead, I poured myself more coffee and told Alexa to shuffle the playlist Part Deux. I danced around my kitchen, shaking my head at the timing of it all. My serial-killer wall of Tinder profiles and maps of Paris, all of it now mostly papered over with photos of friends and family and mementos from the past year, caught my eye. I smiled to myself. So maybe it wasn't what most people would consider kitchen decor or any kind of a rational plan. So what?

I sat down at my desk, opened my computer, and clicked on a new Google Doc. As I rested my fingertips on the keyboard, a blank page filled the screen.

What next, Natasha? a voice asked.

Hmm. I like that question.

I took a deep breath. The cursor blinked at me, expectant.

Your point of destiny is to tell a story. Stephanie's calming voice rang in my ears.

And then I did know what to do next. I started typing, faster than I ever had before.

THE AMAZING AND INCREDIBLE TALE OF
HOW NATASHA FOUND HER SOULMATE

Acknowledgments

This book owes a lot to a lot of people.

A *huge* thank-you to my agent, Jen Marshall. (Gemini: Multitalented, fierce intellect, loyal partner and friend. The Mercury-ruled signs of Gemini and Virgo rule literary agents, and Jen is a Gemini with Virgo rising, so she's in the right field.) I'm beyond grateful that fate brought us together. Thank you for believing in my story and for taking a chance on me. I can't wait to see where our collective points of destiny lead.

To the rest of my phenomenal team at Aevitas Creative Management. To Allison Warren (Libra: Diplomatic, charismatic, clever) and Shenel Ekici-Moling in the film and TV department. To David Kuhn—*thank you* for being in the right place at the right time (aka a bar in Los Angeles on a Saturday night in late October 2019), for hearing my story and calling Jen right away. Talk about stars aligning! Drinks on me for life!

To Sarah Pelz (Virgo: Gentle, hardworking, a total badass. Gemini and Virgo also rule editors, so here's another book person in exactly the right place!): Sarah is the most supportive and insightful editor a writer could wish for. This book is better because of her wisdom and kindness in so many ways. Thank you, Sarah, for giving me the green light to write about it *all*. To Emma Peters, Taryn Roeder, Katie Tull, Deb Brody, Abigail Nover,

Emily Snyder, Lisa Glover, and Tracy Roe. The team at Mariner Books and HarperCollins is world-class and I couldn't be luckier. Thank you for championing this book, for believing in me, and for bringing my words and my world to life. You blow me away with your creative vision, thoughtful ideas, and stellar execution. To Mark Robinson, I could not imagine a more breathtaking cover. To everyone who has worked on this publication, distribution, or sale of this book, my most heartfelt thanks.

To Michael Sugar (Cancer: Intuitive, tenacious, protective of loved ones. Cancer initiates through the awareness of feelings from the soul. They are extremely intuitive and often get brilliant hunches): It makes soooo much sense to me now that I know you are a quadruple alien! Thank you for *going all in* and for believing in me. Thank you to Lauren Wall Sugar (Aries: Buzzing with the force of life) for all of your support. To Angela Ledgerwood (Scorpio: Passionate, ambitious, honest): I love uuuuu, Angie!! And to the entire rock-star team at Sugar23—Jillian Kay, Ashley Zalta: *I am so grateful* for all of you.

To my children Margot (Virgo: Hardworking, creative, kind. Virgo children seem wise beyond their years) and Dashiell (Leo: Generous, warmhearted, loving. Leo children remind us that joy is the goal). Thank you for your support and encouragement while I was writing this during the pandemic. And while I was living it before that. You are *my universe, the brightest stars in my sky,* and *I am so inspired and proud of you both.* Always remember, *anything is possible.* You are more than acknowledged. You are *loved to infinity.*

To my sister, Tara (Leo: Strong, loyal, generous—and bossy, ha-ha. The fire sign of Leo rules the heart. If you are fortunate enough to have a Leo family member or friend, seek their counsel, as it will mirror that of your own heart): I would be sooooo fucked without you. There is so much to thank you for, it seems silly to even try. It has been said, a certain darkness is needed to see the stars, and so I consider myself grateful for all of our days, even the hard ones. Thank you for choosing me as your sister. For saving me when I wasn't ready to swim. And for letting me soar when it was time to fly. I love you to my core.

To the sister I've never met: I love you.

Thank you to my mom, Edna Margaret Henretty Sizlo (Virgo: Honest, humble, hardworking. A Virgo mom can be surprisingly sensitive and compassionate given her no-nonsense exterior): For your Scottish braw, kindness, and determination. For your *huge heart*. For your *faith* in me. For being the most incredible role model. *For everything. I love you.*

To Nicole Cannon, my ride-or-die soul sister (Libra: Artistic, caring, strong. The air sign of Libra rules our alter egos, our disowned selves. If you have a Libra friend, you have an accessible reminder of your greatest potential that is yet to be unleashed within you): Thank you for giving me the most incredible gift that led to this adventure of a lifetime. And for teaching me that the world is made up of so much more than what we can see. I am so grateful to go through this incredible life journey with you. Love you forever.

To Penelope Alexitch (Taurus: Romantic, calm, loyal. The earth sign of Taurus rules what we value, including appreciating life through our senses. Pausing to inhale the scent of your lover, to gaze upon birds in flight, to listen to the wind, to feel the sand beneath your feet, and to savor every bite of chocolate soufflé; this is what our Taurus friends remind us to do): *I love you, P.!* I do believe it's time for another adventure!

To Katie Viera (Gemini: Adventurous, talkative, caring. Everyone needs a Gemini companion for lighthearted conversation that turns out to be incredibly meaningful and symbolic): *My plus-one for life.* Who's ready for some après-ski?

To Stephanie Jourdan, PhD (Virgo; of course you have the same badass sun sign as my mother and daughter! Our charts are connected through the sun and Uranus, which show up as a past life history together): *The best astrologer that ever was, is, or will ever be.*

Love you!!! Thank you for your celestial guidance and for your help with this book. You are a magical creature. I am infinitely grateful and look forward to many more lives together.

To Philippe (Scorpio: Passionate, magnetic, loyal. The water sign of Scorpio runs deep, enticing us to look more and more deeply into the unknown so that our own light makes the unknown conscious. It is almost always advisable to get entangled with a Scorpio . . . it's like ten years of therapy in one): Thank you for understanding me. Even when you don't. *I love you forever.* Life is long with you, I hope.

To Michael Barrett (Gemini: Smart, adaptable, creative. A Gemini partner or husband helps us to know what we do want and what we don't want . . . a true gift): *Thank you* for being an incredible ex-husband and father. To Anna Faris (Sagittarius: Adventurous, philosophical, great sense of humor): Thank you for being the coolest evil stepmother *ever.* Turns out you're not so evil at all. I'm eternally grateful for your kindness and love. Our little modern family is a beautiful gift.

I owe a great deal of gratitude to Billy Rose (Gemini: Intelligent, honest, innovative. Gemini shows us how we attract what we think about, even if it is the opposite of what we want, reminding us that we are all part of the great and beautiful spiritual universe). Thank you for teaching me, inspiring me, supporting me while I wrote this book and always. To Mauricio Umansky (Cancer: Loving, protective, intuitive) and all my colleagues at the Agency. Deedee Howard, Farrah Brittany, Allie Lutz, Keri White, Gloria Castellanos, Marci Kays, Monique Navarro, Kate Schillace, Alejandra Sorensen, Kathrin Nicholson, Courtney Lingle, Eric Haskell, Sean O'Neill, Alex Brunkhorst, James Harris, David Parnes, Santiago Arana, Makenzie Green, Paul Lester, Michael Grady, Stefan Pommepuy, Mike Leipart, Doug Sandler, to name just a few. *Everyone* at the Agency. Thank you for this company that encourages taking risks, breaking rules, and making noise. You are my chosen family.

COULD THIS BE THE ONE?!: COVID-19 may have put our love story on hold, but Paris will always be there for us. Thank you for keeping the faith and checking in on me during the pandemic, and I look forward to seeing you soon.

To all the stars in my midnight sky, or, as I prefer to call you, my "Star Band." Thank you for lighting up my world and showing me the way. In no particular order: Allison Oleskey, Lucy Lee, Sharon Ainsberg, and all the women of Fists-n-Ropes; Taryn Weitzman, Kristina Grish, Dawn Davis, Jenny Minton Quigley, Jennifer Gates, Laura Nolan, Ellen Kinney, Decia Lazarian, KC Ryan-Foster, Heather Irving, Varun Soni, Anne Thomopoulous, Charles Alazet, Mitch Smelkinson, Shayna Klee, Clara Fantasin, Anita Pocsik, Sheri Buron, the McVey Family, Cynthia Vincent. All my wonderful clients, Caroline Pinal, Dancing Girl, Anne Burkin, Sarah Conner, Remy Rosen, Rhonda Byrne, Laurie Fortier, Teresa Symes, Dallas, Evelyn Hall, Friday, Bruce Lang, Hope Leigh, Tony Hamdan Djendeli, Felicia Alexander, Kate Walsh, Ashley Park, Lucas Bravo, Darren Star, Andy Fleming, Busy Philipps, Ellen Pompeo, Carrie Byalick, Rob Long, Mercedes Eraso Zamora, Marsha and Ivan Barrett, Shachar Scott, Rhiannon Dourado, Kristiana Tarnuzzer, and all the Avocado Toasts. The Sizlo, Henretty, and Kraber clan. To Erik, Colin, and Spencer—thank you for putting up with weird Auntie Natasha. To my fellow Thacher TOADS—thanks for joining me in protest by wearing all black to Formal Dinner in 1990 and for trying to (sorta) pull the car out of the ditch twenty years later. To the women of Paris who showed up for me when I needed you most—*thank you*. To all my matches on Tinder and Bumble and Facebook and IG, I wish you love and magic and all the things. To everyone I met born in Paris on 2 Novembre 1968, *je t'aime*. To the wonderful caring Carpinteria-Summerland Fire Department, Santa Barbara VNA, and hospice staff—thank you for your tireless work. To all the artists on my Joe Cool, Get Up, Get It, and Part Deux playlists (especially Lionel Richie)—*thank you*! To all the spirits in the little yellow house (and in my head): *Thank you* for helping me and for supporting my highest and best. I could not have done this without you. To all the psychics, tarot readers, astrologers, healers, and totally out-there crystal collectors that crossed my path and to everyone who wished me *bon chance* along the way: Nothing I have done, particularly this book, was done alone. I love you all. To the nth degree.

A very special thank-you to all the organizations that work so hard on behalf of people's right to live, love, and die on their own terms.

To anyone grieving in any way: This book was written for you. You are not alone.

To anyone born in Paris on November 2, 1968, or on August 28 or 29, 1979, in the westernmost part of Italy, Corsica, Sardinia, Switzerland, the easternmost part of France, the western portion of Germany, the easternmost part of the Netherlands, or the westernmost part of Denmark between 9:44 p.m. and 2:00 a.m.: Come find me; it's our destiny.

To anyone looking to buy or sell a house: I got you! Call me!

Finally, to my dad, Robert Joseph Sizlo. Bob. Joe Cool (Aries: Adventurous, courageous, full of love. The fire sign of Aries is aware that there is always more to do, see, experience, and be. Even though it is the most yang of all the signs, Aries people are surprisingly great role models for their daughters, teaching them independence, confidence, and leadership): Thank you for everything. *everything*. None of this would have happened without your guidance and love while you were here beside me and especially when you weren't. You taught me about *magic, love,* and the power of *believing*. I know you had everything to do with this wild ride. I feel you beside me in the little yellow house, in the trees, in the clouds, and I love you to the nth degree. Everything's cool, Dad. Everything's cool.

Reading Group Guide

1. Throughout Natasha's journey, some people—her kids, her ex-boyfriend Philippe, even Natasha herself at times—are skeptical of her mission to find her point of destiny: someone born on November 2, 1968, in Paris. How does Natasha overcome this doubt?

2. At the start of the book, Natasha tells the reader, "I no longer knew for sure what kind of person I was. Or who I would become" (6). Natasha is in an in-between place in her life that feels terrifying and lonely to her. How does she try to cope with her fear?

3. As her father is dying, Natasha stumbles upon a childhood photograph with an inscription on the back, a line from Shel Silverstein: "Anything can happen, child, anything can be" (21). How does this moment shift her perspective? What does this verse mean to you?

4. A few months after her father's passing, Natasha decides to make a dramatic change and dyes her hair blonde. Are there other transformational moments in *All Signs Point to Paris*? Consider physical, emotional, and spiritual transformations.

5. Tara plays an integral role in this story, encouraging her sister ("Paris or bust!") and even accompanying her all the way to Europe. In what ways are the sisters different? How are they alike?

Discuss the ways these similarities and differences affect their travels.

6. Natasha promises her dad that she will always believe in magic. Discuss the different times she encounters "magic"—both in Paris and at home in the States. What does "believing in magic" mean to you? Do you think Bob really believed in magic?

7. To generate Instagram content in Paris, Natasha asks her crew what their definition of a soulmate is. Nicole says, "Someone who can meet me on all four levels of my being: the physical level, the emotional level, the intellectual level, and the spiritual level." Tara answers "Puzzle pieces. Click" (127). Do you agree with either definition? If so, why? How would you describe a soulmate?

8. Were there any suitors in *All Signs Point to Paris* that you particularly admired? Which dates resonated the most with you personally, and why?

9. At the beginning of her journey, Natasha insists she doesn't believe in astrology. What were your preconceived notions about the practice? Have your opinions changed after reading this book?

10. Is *All Signs Point to Paris* a love story? Discuss the different ways Natasha encounters love during her travels—consider her travel companions as well as the people she meets in Paris. Do you recognize any of these types of love in your own life?

11. The book touches upon the ways in which societal and personal expectations of romantic partnerships have and have not changed from Bob and Edna's generation to Natasha's children's generation. Do you think Bob and Edna had it easier, or was it just different?